OFFICIAL REPORT

OF THE

TWENTY - FOURTH INTERNATIONAL

CHRISTIAN ENDEAVOR CONVENTION

HELD IN

THE AUDITORIUM, THE ARMORY, AND

MANY CHURCHES

ST. PAUL, MINN., JULY 7-12, 1909.

First Fruits Press
Wilmore, Kentucky
c2015

First Fruits Press
The Academic Open Press of Asbury Theological Seminary
204 N. Lexington Ave., Wilmore, KY 40390
859-858-2236
first.fruits@asburyseminary.edu
asbury.to/firstfruits

Frank G. Lester   Deane Edwards   Ira C. Oehler   John K. Robinson   Rev. Harry S. Wilson   Prof. H. E. Phillips
Oliver H. Stephenson   B. H. Scurber   Harold G. Lams   G. Winthrop Lewis   Rev. M. D. Edwards   Rev. Charles A. Arnold

George N. Brack   Willard B. Clow   J. Powell Moose   Walter D. Howell   John F. Frisby   Henry C. Capser
                                               Chairman
                                    THE ST. PAUL CONVENTION COMMITTEE

THE STORY

OF THE

ST. PAUL CONVENTION

THE OFFICIAL REPORT

OF

THE TWENTY-FOURTH
INTERNATIONAL . . . .

Christian Endeavor
Convention

HELD IN

THE AUDITORIUM, THE ARMORY,
AND MANY CHURCHES

ST. PAUL, MINN., JULY 7 to 12, 1909

UNITED SOCIETY OF CHRISTIAN ENDEAVOR
BOSTON, MASS.

Machine Composition by SCOTT LINOTYPING COMPANY
Presswork by REMINGTON-ZIEGLER PRESS
BOSTON, MASS.

1

CONTENTS.

3

LIST OF ILLUSTRATIONS.

OFFICERS OF THE UNITED SOCIETY OF CHRISTIAN ENDEAVOR.

Office:
TREMONT TEMPLE, BOSTON, MASS., U. S. A.

President:
REV. FRANCIS E. CLARK, D. D., LL.D.

General Secretary:
MR. WILLIAM SHAW.

Treasurer:
MR. H. N. LATHROP.

Editorial Secretary:
PROF. AMOS R. WELLS.

Publication Manager:
MR. GEORGE B. GRAFF.

Superintendent of the Patriots' League:
MR. GEORGE W. COLEMAN.

Superintendent of the Builders' Union:
REV. R. P. ANDERSON.

DENOMINATIONAL TRUSTEES.

REV. THOMAS ASHBURN, Knoxville, Tenn.
PRESIDENT JOHN WILLIS BAER, LL.D., Pasadena, Cal.
REV. W. C. BITTING, D. D., St. Louis, Mo.
PRES. C. I. BROWN, D. D., Findlay, Ohio.
REV. DAVID JAMES BURRELL, D. D., New York, N. Y.
REV. J. C. CALDWELL, Nashville, Tenn.
HON. S. B. CAPEN, LL.D., Boston, Mass.
REV. J. WILBUR CHAPMAN, D. D., New York, N. Y.
REV. FRANCIS E. CLARK, D. D., LL.D., Boston, Mass.

REV. A. C. CREWS, Toronto, Ont.
REV. W. J. DARBY, D. D., Evansville, Ind.
REV. H. A. DENTON, Cincinnati, Ohio.
BISHOP SAMUEL FALLOWS, D. D. LL.D., Chicago, Ill.
REV. J. H. GARRISON, D. D., LL.D., St. Louis, Mo.
REV. ALEXANDER GILRAY, Toronto, Ont.
REV. HOWARD B. GROSE, D. D., New York, N. Y.
REV. N. B. GRUBB, D. D., Philadelphia, Pa.
MR. WILLIAM PHILLIPS HALL, New York, N. Y.

5

THE ST. PAUL CONVENTION COMMITTEE.

J. POWELL MOORE, *Chairman*,
WALTER D. HOWELL, *Secretary*,
WILLARD B. CLOW, *Treasurer*.

CHAIRMEN OF SUB-COMMITTEES.

GEORGE M. BRACK, *Entertainment*.
B. H. SCHRIBER, *Finance*.
HAROLD G. LAINS, *Reception*.
PROF. H. E. PHILLIPS, *Music*.
J. GEORGE SMITH,
FRANK G. LISTER, } *Decoration*.
IRA C. OEHLER, *Registration*.
HENRY C. CAPSER, *Halls*.
JOHN K. ROBINSON, *Ushers*.
CHARLES A. ARNOLD, *Press and Publicity*.
OLIVER H. STEPHENSON, *Information*.
G. WINTHROP LEWIS, *Evangelistic*.
REV. M. D. EDWARDS, D. D., *Pulpit Supply*.
JOHN E. FRISBY, *Excursion*.
DEANE EDWARDS, *Printing*.
REV. HARRY NOBLE WILSON, D. D., *Educational Exhibit*.

7

A WORD OF HEARTY THANKS.

When one considers the number of meetings that are held during an International Convention, and the additional fact that many of these meetings were held simultaneously, the compilation of a report that will do justice to all is no easy task. The compiler takes pleasure in acknowledging with earnest thanks the services of Rev. Howard B. Grose, D. D., Rev. Elijah Humphries, Rev. Jesse Hill, Rev. Samuel McNaugher, Mr. William Phillips Hall, Rev. R. G. Bannen, Mr. John T. Sproull, Rev. F. D. Power, D. D., Rev. J. Stanley Durkee, D. D., Rev. James Francis, D. D., Rev. U. F. Swengel, Rev J. Spencer Voorhees, President George B. Stewart, Mr. C. F. Ensign, Mr. Walter R. Mee, Rev. S. H. Woodrow, D. D., Prof. Amos R. Wells, Rev. R. P. Anderson, Mr. George W. Coleman, Mr. William Shaw, Mr. H. N. Lathrop, Miss M. F. Murray, and Miss C. L. Heywood, and of many leaders of meetings and conferences whose helpfulness in reporting various sessions of the Convention has made the early publication of this report possible.

With the prayer that the reading of it may be spiritually uplifting to thousands of young people, and may give them many suggestions for the betterment of their work in the Master's cause, this account of the proceedings of the Twenty-fourth International Christian Endeavor Convention is sent forth.

GEORGE B. GRAFF,

Publication Manager of the
United Society of Christian Endeavor.

St. Paul, July 12, 1909.

CHAPTER I.

ON THE THRESHOLD.

C. E. at St. Paul signified Contagious Enthusiasm, Civic Elevation, Conspicuous Earnestness. It was Enthusiasm with a very large capital "E," and was in evidence everywhere,— on the trains, at the stations, in the hotel lobbies, on the streets, and in the Convention hall. Enthusiasm before sessions. But it was enthusiasm coupled with earnestness. That was what gave such an impressive character to the Convention. The Endeavorers had come together for a purpose.

Doubtless not a little of the enthusiasm was due, at the outset, to the eager and irrepressible advocates of the claims of rival cities which were after the Convention of 1911. They were after it hard and all the time, with megaphones, and ingenious badges, and all sorts of devices. There was a company of seventy-five young people from Indianapolis, equipped with a "zip, boom, bah" and "rah, rah, rah" yell that would do credit to Comanche or college, besides a special song and alluring banners. Then there was another group, larger and louder, from Kansas City, armed with megaphones, songs, a "pull-the-string" white badge, and an ardor not to be abashed or abated. The busy persuaders soon had badges for one place or another pinned on everybody that could be badgered, even to the bell-boy and the stranger. There was another company, also, that would unquestionably have added fire and fervor to a condition already aquiver with excitement and eagerness: but that unfortunate and unhappy Texas delegation, with the mayor of Dallas at its head, could only send in telegrams, which said pathetically: "Water-logged, floods behind us, floods in front of us; but we are coming. Wait for Texas." Not even floods could quench the spirit of Endeavor enthusiasm. Later, however, the Texas delegates arrived, headed by Mayor Hay of Dallas. The mayor made an eloquent plea for the city in the Lone-Star State. The charms of Atlantic City were also graphically depicted by Mr. J. T. Sproull, the president of the New Jersey State Christian Endeavor Union.

St. Paul had made all preparations for a characteristically hospitable entertainment. The reception committee had its white-capped representatives and messengers in abundance.

11

As the arriving Endeavorers poured through the station gates, they found State standards directing them where to gather. As company after company broke into song, the enthusiasm kindled and spread. The newspaper reporter and photographers were on hand, and before Dr. and Mrs. Clark had been five minutes off the cars they had to line up with a group of trustees for a snapshot, with certainty that their features would be wholly unrecognizable in the reproduction.

The streets were gay with flags and bunting, and the C. E. monogram, known around the world, was seen in store windows, on banners, and most effectively upon the great electric lamps at the street corners. The city plainly knew that Christian Endeavor was coming, and was worthy of the best welcome that tasteful decoration could symbolize.

All day Wednesday the delegates were coming in and being distributed through the city, in preparation for the opening session. The matter of registration had to be attended to, as the badge was necessary for admission. The weather was perfect, as it had been for several days. The conditions all favored a convention of spiritual power.

"THY KINGDOM COME."

This was the central theme of the Convention. Other Conventions have had their watchwords; Good Citizenship, Tenth Legion, The Quiet Hour, all have a special significance for Endeavorers; but the key-note of the St. Paul Convention contains all the others rolled into one,—a crowning of the past. These words from the one only perfect petition glowed and burned into the hearts of the delegates with an almost overwhelming sense of their meaning.

"Thy Kingdom Come." It greeted us upon arrival at the station. It greeted us from the city's decorations. It greeted us with the handclasp of the Twin Cities' Endeavorers. It greeted us in the business method underlying the work of each of the Convention committees.

"Thy Kingdom Come, in Civic Life." When before has a convention been graced by such distinguished citizens as Hon. William J. Bryan, Gov. John A. Johnson, Mayor Daniel W. Lawlor, and others? And when since "Washington, '96," has there been a greater outdoor demonstration than that held on the Capitol steps? How our hearts thrilled with patriotism as we listened to the burning words of that peerless orator, Mr. Bryan!

"Thy Kingdom Come, in Song." This was a singing convention. How could it be otherwise, with such leaders as E. O. Excell and Percy Foster? The new hymn-book, "Jubilant Praise," was used for the first time; and, as foretold in the Convention announcements, it was a "jubilant-praise" Convention throughout. The singing of the Hawaiian delegates, and of the chorus in costumes representing different nations, was a marked feature of the gatherings.

And now the delegates have returned to their homes to carry out the injunctions to which they have listened, and to be a part in working out the answer to the prayer, "Thy Kingdom Come." Down through the years God sends us the opportunity. It may be this year, this day, this hour. We know not when. It is our part to be ready.

CHAPTER II.

THE OPENING SESSION.

Wednesday Evening, July 7.

The early hour of seven was set for the pre-convention service of prayer Wednesday evening, but the people began to gather still earlier than that, and immediately the spirit that was prevalent manifested itself in singing. One group on floor or in gallery would break into a hymn, and another group would respond. Informal, happy, anticipatory, animating, it all bred enthusiasm, and made the best possible preparation for what was to follow.

The Convention Auditorium was one of the most satisfactory in acoustic qualities that has been found. Whether the seating capacity be ten or twelve thousand, as the St. Paulians put it, or something less, it is certain that a speaker with anything like a good voice properly propelled could be heard by all present. Yelling was not necessary. The decorations were in good taste. To quote a reporter:

"The Auditorium was gay with banners and flags. Everywhere 'Old Glory' hung, and draped close at hand were the colors of the Christian Endeavorers and the escutcheons of the States and Territories that have joined the great march. Over the platform two immense American flags were hung, and between them the Union Jack of Canada was suspended from a resplendent sign bearing the word 'Welcome'; and high over this on a red background were the letters of the Society monogram traced in electric-light bulbs. The effect was one worth going far to see, and made a worthy setting for the cheerfulness that pervaded the meeting and the bright badges and insignia worn by the delegates."

It certainly was an inspiring sight to look out over the audience, and note its quality as well as numbers. Quick, responsive, sensitive, earnest, reverent, orderly, expectant, full of the spirit of the occasion, it was a representative Christian Endeavor audience, and what more can one say? What more could any speaker desire?

A pretty incident came at the very start. President Clark was just ready to interrupt the informal song service to call the Convention to order, when Secretary Howell, of the local committee, stepped to the platform and said he had a pleasant

14

task to perform. The Minnesota Union desired to give the President a gavel. The idea was originated by an enthusiastic St. Paul Endeavorer, Miss Lucy Gunlach, who had been designated to present it. This was enough to start the applause, and the fair Endeavorer made this happy address:

"Years ago one of New England's greatest men made famous in one of America's greatest poems our own beloved State. He told how Gitche Manito, the Mighty, gathered the tribes of men together, how

> " 'From the mountains of the prairie,
> From the red pipe-stone quarry,
> With his hands he broke a fragment,
> Moulded it into a peace-pipe;
> Smoked the calumet, the peace-pipe,
> As a signal to the nations.'

"From the selfsame red pipe-stone quarry, set apart from common, petty, commercial use, was broken a fragment which was moulded into a gavel to be given New England's present greatest man, as a signal to the nations of the love of the Endeavorers of Minnesota, of the Convention city, and as a sign that we pray for the spread of the kingdom of Him whose coming brought peace on earth, good will to men."

Then there was a storm of applause as President Clark took the tomahawk, with the remark, as he held it aloft, that this was the first time a gavel of that form had been used, and they all knew what a tomahawk could do in case of misbehavior. There seemed to be no great sense of fear, however, and laughter was inspired rather than awe.

But in a moment the mood changed, as with a stroke of the red pipe-stone gavel the President opened formally the Twenty-fourth International Convention of Christian Endeavor. The devotional service followed, and at once the superb singing qualities of the Convention as a whole were proved, as "Abide with me," that grand hymn of the church, was sung. The chorus was there, perhaps two hundred strong, with various members of it dressed strikingly in Oriental costumes; but no chorus was necessary to make that body musical. How the Christian Endeavorers can sing! They put their hearts into it, and into the Scripture responses as well.

Then came the long but deeply interesting programme, with its several surprises as well as set features.

Dr. Clark said the Society had never had in all its history a speaker whom it welcomed more gladly than the governor of this commonwealth, the statesman and reformer, Gov. John A. Johnson. As the governor came forward, he was given an ovation, and the Chautauqua salute plainly moved him, as he stood bowing in return to the hearty and prolonged greeting. He looks like the published portraits of him, and has a face marked by serious purpose. He said in substance:

It becomes my very agreeable duty and very pleasant privilege to come to you on behalf of the people of this commonwealth, to extend to you the most cordial and hearty welcome.

Minnesota is indeed glad you are here, glad for two reasons. We want you to know Minnesota and her people, and Minnesota and her people are glad to know you all. We are anxious to have you know that we have taken an important position in the civic and industrial history of this nation. We are anxious to have you know that we produce more than fifty-five per cent of the iron of the United States and twenty-five per cent of that of the world. But we put it into industry, while the people in other parts of the country put the iron into the souls of the people. [Laughter and applause.]

We would like to have you look over the topography of this State, to sail about its waters, to walk in its vales, to wander through its forest primeval, and all the beauties of nature in which it abounds. But above all we want you to know that we take pride in the fact that, although we are one of the youngest of States, the whole world acknowledges us to be first in educational systems. Because of this we are building up a city which must commend itself to the country and the world, and we want you to go away feeling as we feel, that this is for all, and that we are glad to have you here.

We welcome you because of the things you stand for, the Christian church and the Christian religion, which have been the greatest force in civilization, and which are responsible for the present condition of mankind.

He said, further, that he sometimes wondered whether, with all our material progress, we had made the same strides morally and religiously. But he believed the world was better than ever before. We have, however, the ethical as well as the spiritual to cultivate. There is needed a finer sense of commercial and political honor. May that time be hastened when this country and its flag shall mean just what we say they mean, and there shall be no counterfeit anywhere.

Certainly the governor could find no fault with his reception. The young people appreciate the reformer and honest public servant, and they showed it unmistakably. Governor Johnson is a man of action rather than ornate speech, but his sincerity spoke with most eloquence.

President Clark next introduced Mayor Lawlor to speak for St. Paul and Minneapolis, as he gracefully included both in his welcome. He said there was really but one great city at the headwaters of the Mississippi; and for this greater city, with its half-million of people, he spoke. He rang with eloquence, and drew repeated rounds of enthusiastic applause as he welcomed the Convention because it stood firmly for something definite—for the Bible, for the old faith of our fathers and mothers, and for the preachings of the divine

INFORMATION BOOTH AT UNION STATION.

THE STORY OF OUR FLAG.

Master. It was fitting that this interdenominational and international meeting should be held in a city named after St. Paul, that great apostle to the Gentiles, who broke down all barriers of race and religion and saw in every man a brother. In closing he said: "In the name of half a million American men and women, including every known sect, in the name of Protestant and Catholic, Jew and Gentile, I welcome you and bid you God-speed in your great endeavor."

By this time enthusiasm was boiling over, and our old-time leader, Mr. Percy Foster, of Washington, came forward and had the audience sing a verse of "America," then one of the Christian Endeavor International Hymn, followed by a verse of "Blest be the tie that binds," and a verse of "All hail the power of Jesus' name." This gave vent for feeling, and it was singing that thrilled.

For the churches and the committee of arrangements welcome was extended by Mr. J. Powell Moore, chairman of the 1909 committee. The committee had taken a great deal of pleasure in the hard work of the months past, and now felt that the consummation of their hopes had come in this splendid gathering.

Again the Convention hosts lifted their voice in praise, after which the genial and much-loved secretary of the United Society, Mr. William Shaw, was introduced to give his annual report. As usual, he was greeted with a storm of applause, and the reading of his report was frequently punctuated with marks of approval by the audience.

LOOKING BACKWARD: CHRISTIAN ENDEAVOR GROWTH.

The Biennial Report of William Shaw.

The theme of this great convention, "Thy Kingdom Come," is the keynote of Christian Endeavor.

For two years, or since our last report, more than threescore and ten thousand societies and three and a half million members have been praying and laboring to that end.

We are here to-night to review in the briefest possible way the record of these years.

Growth Outward.

Each year, with the steady multiplication of our own and kindred societies, we feel that we have come to the end of any great numerical increase in our fellowship. And still we find that we have not yet taken possession of all the land.

At the Seattle Convention it was my privilege to report a total enrolment of 69,138 societies, with a membership of 3,456,900. This great host has. been still further increased by the addition of 2,355 societies, with a membership of 94,200, making our present net enrolment 71,493 societies. with 3,551,100 members.

Practically all the evangelical denominations are represented in this world-wide fellowship. The Presbyterians still hold the first place, with an enrolment, including Junior, Intermediate, and Young People's, of 10,198 societies. Next come the Disciples, who by the united, enthusiastic interest of pastors, church leaders, and young people, have captured the second place from the Congregationalists, with the magnificent total of 7,148 societies. The Congregationalists are now third, with 6,454 societies. After we get through analyzing and criticising the movement—I speak as a Congregationalist—which in the providence of God we had the honor of giving to the world, we shall take hold of it and push it in a way that will make the leaders look out for their laurels.

Next come the Baptists, with their splendid squadron of 3,497 societies. Neither time nor space will permit the enumeration of the long list of denominations and their subdivisions that are represented in our movement. When Christian Endeavor has done its perfect work their number will be smaller, but their strength and effectiveness will be greater.

Last year the United Brethren Young People's Union at its national convention voted to come into our interdenominational fellowship as the United Brethren Christian Endeavor Union. All hail, and welcome to these earnest young people; and may their action be a prophecy of the speedy coming of the day when all the denominational societies shall be federated under the broad, inclusive name of Christian Endeavor, and we all become united brethren in Christ.

This is coming on the mission fields; may it speedily come in the home field.

Christian Endeavor does not legislate for the local societies; we do not levy taxes or assessments; we exercise no authority; we stand for no dead level of uniformity; we ask only for the fellowship that shall reveal to the world our essential oneness in faith, in spiritual experience, and in practical service.

Juniors and Intermediates.

The growth in these two most important departments of Christian Endeavor has been most encouraging, but there is still much to be desired.

When will the church come to a full realization of the fact that the biggest thing in the world to-day is the child, that teaching must be supplemented by training, that one session a week in the Sunday school is not sufficient for the full development of the spiritual life, and that the only way to have trained men and women is to train the boys and girls?

Spirituality and Stewardship.

The growth of our young people in spiritual life, which must precede and vitalize all real service, is shown by the large increase in the Comrades of the Quiet Hour. The number of those who have covenanted to spend a few minutes each day in quiet communion with God through prayer and the Word is now 48,561.

Largely as a result of this emphasis upon the spiritual side of life during the past two years a great army of youth has passed through the ranks of Christian Endeavor into the church.

Equally encouraging has been the steady growth of the Tenth Legion, which now numbers 25,773 persons who have consecrated and set apart at least the tenth of their income for the work of the Kingdom in all the world.

When the majority of our church-members take the matter of giving out of the realm of the emotions, and make it a matter of principle, then, and not till then, shall we solve the problem of adequate financial support for our church and missionary enterprises.

Growth Inward.

Bnt more important and gratifying than the growth in members is the record of service rendered by our societies and unions during the past two years.

It is impossible even to name the different forms of service undertaken by our societies. They cover the whole field of social, civic, philanthropic, and religious work.

The spirit of Christian Endeavor is that of genuine democracy. We believe in working with others as well as for them. Class and caste must go; and the Christ standard of service and sacrifice for the individual, denomination, and nation must be accepted.

"What would Jesus have me do?" is not a question for a day, nor a week, nor a year, for one city or country; but it is the question for all time and for every man. It is the standard for the individual, for society, for business, for politics, and for religion.

I believe that our young people are more ready to accept this test and apply it to life now than they have ever been before. The application of this principle is shown in the record of the Philadelphia Christian Endeavor Union, which has just celebrated itd twenty-first anniversary, and the work of this union is typical of that of many others. Twenty-one years ago there were eight societies in the Philadelphia Union; now there are four hundred and eighty.

Then the work of the societies consisted largely of a prayer meeting and a social, and the work of the union was an occasional mass-meeting. Last year more than forty inspirational rallies were held in different parts of the city, and more than four hundred voluntary and unpaid workers were trying to help other young people to a vision of the larger life in Christ.

One hundred and twenty mission-study classes were organized, and conferences on mission work were held with one hundred and fifty societies.

Hundreds of evangelistic meetings were held in missions, homes, prisons, hospitals, police stations, street-car barns, and public parks, and on street corners.

The Floating committee extended a welcome to thousands of seafaring men, and distributed several thousand comfort-bags, tons of clean wholesome literature, and hundreds of Bibles, in many languages, and held meetings on shipboard and on the piers every Lord's Day.

In many smaller cities, and in the country as well, equally good work is being done. The foreigner who has come to our shores, and all too often has been treated as an alien, is now being received as a brother, and societies of Christian Endeavor, clubs for fellowship, and classes for instruction are being formed to make him an intelligent American citizen and an earnest Christian.

More of this work should and could be done if the unused power in our societies was called into service by sympathetic local leadership.

Thousands of societies have done splendid service in our Fivefold Campaign for Christian Endeavor Extension, Missionary Activities, Evangelistic Endeavor, Christian Citizenship, and the Circulation of Religious Literature.

Union Work.

The work of our Christian Endeavor unions has had the most gratifying increase, both in quality and quantity, that has marked any period in our history.

Our monthly magazine, Union Work, and our "Get-Together" campaign are largely responsible for this. The weakest are brought into helpful fellowship with the strongest, the poorest with the best. We are level-ling up, and the results are seen in the more definite and practical plans adopted; in the more energetic and businesslike way in which they are pushed; in the improved character and greater variety of the union meetings; in the emphasis that is being laid on conference and institute methods for the consideration of the practical problems that face the societies; in the rest that is being given to the old sermon and the sky-rocket oration; and in the actual work that is being done for the promotion of civic righteousness, temperance, Sabbath-observance, fresh-air vacations for the poor and sick, hospital ministries, and prison work, all in line with the spirit of the Master's message when he said, "Inasmuch as ye have done it unto one of the least of these my brethren, ye have done it unto me."

The International Building.

A long step forward in the accomplishment of this most worthy object has been taken in the purchase of a splendid site for the building on the corner of Huntington and Longwood Avenues, Boston.

This section is to be the institutional heart of Boston within ten years. Already many of the finest public buildings in the city have been erected within a few blocks of our lot, and others are being planned. Next year our building should begin to rise, stately and beautiful, an adequate expression of our appreciation of what Christian Endeavor has done for us. It should be a building built by the gifts of the young people and their friends, and consecrated to the work for the young people in all lands for all time.

Surely there is not a person here to-night who is not able to subscribe for at least one five-dollar share in this building. Have you secured yours? If not, do it now.

Is your society on the Honor Roll with a contribution of at least twenty-five cents a member, active, associate, and honorary? If not, put it there at once. Give to your secretary the privilege of reporting to the World's Christian Endeavor Convention at Agra, India, next November, the inspiring fact that the funds for the building have been provided, and work will begin on our return home.

May we not have an expression of your enthusiasm for Christian Endeavor in this practical form?

The Field is the World.

In addition to the regular office work your secretary has had the privilege of meeting the Endeavorers in local, district, or State conventions in thirty-four States and the republic of Mexico. The trip to Mexico was a memorable one, with three great conventions in Monterey, Mexico City, and Chihuahua.

I believe that Mexico is the key to the "Neglected Continent," and Christian Endeavor is helping to fashion it so that it may unlock the door of opportunity to the millions of people still living in the spirit of the fifteenth century.

A report of the office work would show personal letters to the number of more than fifteen thousand, and circulars to the number of more than one hundred thousand, sent out. Nearly twenty thousand changes in corresponding secretaries have been made, and about three thousand requests for organizing literature have been answered.

The 1908 campaign of Dr. Clark in Great Britain and on the Continent was a magnificent illustration of the strength and vitality of Christian Endeavor. No more successful series of meetings has ever been held in the history of the movement.

Of the lands beyond the seas, England leads, with Australia second,

India third, Germany and China a close fourth, followed by Africa, France, Japan, and eighty or more countries and islands that rejoice in the world-wide fellowship of Christian Endeavor.

The service to our cause rendered by Prof. Amos R. Wells, Mr. H. N. Lathrop, Mr. George W. Coleman, Mr. George B. Graff, Rev. R. P. Anderson, and Mr. A. W. Kelly, all busy men, earning their living in other ways, but living for the extension of Christian Endeavor, cannot be overestimated.

To these should be added the thousands of workers, trustees, and union officers who have given freely of time and money for the advancement of Christian Endeavor. Mention should also be made of the invaluable service rendered by our paper, *The Christian Endeavor World*, which merits the support of every Endeavorer.

The Future.

The future of this great movement is in God's hands, as all the glorious past has been.

We believe in it, and pledge ourselves to its advancement. We seek the sympathetic co-operation of every pastor and Christian worker, that its faults may be minimized, its virtues magnified, and its possibilities realized, so that all the youth of all our churches shall be in training for the King's business, in order that his kingdom may come and his will be done in earth as it is in heaven.

Dr. Clark sprung one of his surprises by introducing the Hawaiian quartette. One of them is a minister, one a banker, two are judges. All are fine-faced, well-built, most attractive men, and their voices are remarkably sweet, with something of the peculiar plaintiveness noticeable in the type of race to which they belong. Their rendering, in their native Kanaka tongue, of hymns the tunes of which were familiar, as "Saviour, like a shepherd lead us," caught the interest of the great audience, and the quartette had to sing again in response to an encore that was irresistible. They are a missionary object lesson.

Treasurer Lathrop took the audience at once by saying, "Blessed is the man who speaketh briefly, because he shall be asked to speak again." His clear presentation of the finances brought forth rounds of applause, and it was noticeable that his forcible appeal for the Headquarters Building met with an enthusiastic response. The Treasurer emphasized the fact that the United Society's publishing business had earned and contributed to the extension of Christian Endeavor more than two hundred thousand dollars. There is no parallel record.

Then Dr. Clark gave his second surprise, introducing the Japanese delegate, Rev. T. Makino, of Kyoto, pastor of a large native church, and a graduate of Yale College. He was received with the Chautauqua salute, and gave both in Japanese and English the following greeting:

"Japan to St. Paul, Greeting:
"City of Noble Name and Honorable History:
"May the missionary spirit of the great apostle of the Gentiles take full possession of your Convention; and may we all, Endeavorers from North America and eastern Asia alike, give ourselves unreservedly to the grandly glorious endeavor of practising the presence of God in our own lives, and of winning the world to loyal allegiance to the threefold cause of righteousness towards God, love of our brethren, and peace among the nations.
"Signed: "TASUKE HARADA,
                                      "T. SAWAYA,
                                      "JAMES H. PETTEE,
                                      "TORAJI MAKINO.
"Kyoto, Japan, May 10, 1909."

As the little Japanese delegate concluded, Secretary Shaw sprang to his feet and shouted, "Now, need we fear such men as these?" This brought down the house, and the brown man retired to his seat smiling with joy and receiving the embraces of the men on the platform as he passed them.

The chorus sang a hymn in Portuguese, and the audience was ready for the conclusion of the feast of good things, the annual address of President Clark, the beloved leader, who was introduced by Secretary Shaw in words that told of his own affectionate relations, recognized the love and honor in which the Father of Endeavor was held around the world, and called on the Convention to voice its sentiments, which it did with a will, prolonged applause being followed by the Chautauqua salute and then another outburst of applause, spontaneous and hearty. It was a noble recognition of a noble life, devoted to the highest ideals.

President Clark set high the mark in the address which follows, and which was received with deep interest and approval:

LOOKING FORWARD: "CHRISTIAN ENDEAVOR—1911."

Every organization that has a right to live has a mission, clearly perceives its mission, and strives to fulfil its mission.

Every other is worse than useless, and the decree has already gone forth, to be sooner or later carried out, "Cut it down: why cumbereth it the ground?"

The mission of the Christian Endeavor Society is as plain as the sun in the noonday heavens. It was written in its first constitution; it was perceived by its earliest members; it has been acknowledged by the churches throughout the world; it has been affirmed and established by the providential history of more than twenty-eight years.

That mission is to be *the training-school of the church.*

This training is along four great lines; they might be called the
"Four Major Courses" of Christian Endeavor.
1. The expression of the Christian life in deeds.
2. Its expression in words.
3. Its expression in loyalty.
4. Its expression in fellowship.
The boy who goes to college indicates his desire for an education.
The courses that he takes largely determine his future life. The boy
who joins the Christian Endeavor society indicates his desire for practical Christian education, and the thoroughness with which he takes its
courses will largely determine his usefulness in the kingdom of God. All
these courses in our Christian Endeavor college in the nature of the case,
and by reason of the constitution and requirements of the human soul,
are compulsory because necessary for the building up of a fully rounded,
symmetrical Christian character; none of them are optional.
    The first course, the expression of the Christian life in deeds, finds
its classrooms in our many committees; the second, expression in words,
is taught in our prayer meeting; the third, the expression of the Christian life in loyalty, is learned in all the multifarious services for the
church; and the fourth, the expression of the Christian life in fellowship,
is taught in the ten thousand Christian Endeavor conventions and union
meetings held every year throughout the world.

Service, Confession, Loyalty, Fellowship.

    Written over all the eight and twenty years of Christian Endeavor
history are those words. Blazoned across its sky in every land we read
as we look to the future, "By these signs we conquer."
    Then it is too plain for argument that we are fulfilling our mission as
a world-embracing movement just to the extent, and only to the extent,
to which we establish our principles and enlarge our boundaries.
    To these great ends let us address ourselves with renewed energy,
devotion, and confidence in the Master's leadership during the next two
years, before we meet again in biennial convention.
    We meet on this seventh day of July, 1909, in an all-North-America
conclave. Canada, the United States, Mexico, are together in Endeavor
convention assembled. Two years from now, in 1911, God willing, we
will meet in another similar convention in some city of this broad continent.
    In two years Christian Endeavor will be thirty years old. Then it will
have attained the riper years of early maturity.
    We may well fix our eyes on that date, and make our thirtieth year
a landmark in our history.
    In two years what may not be accomplished?
    In two years dynasties have risen and fallen.
    In two years nations have been born or born again, as has Turkey
since last we met in International Convention.
    In but little more than two years our Lord himself began and ended
his earthly ministry.
    So I propose that we fix our eye on the future, while we labor un-
tiringly in the present, and that we take for our motto,

"Christian Endeavor, 1911."

    Boston citizens have taken for their rallying-cry, "Boston, 1915;" and
they mean thereby a better, busier, bigger, more beautiful Boston in 1915.
We mean by "Christian Endeavor, 1911," a better, bigger, busier Christian
Endeavor movement in 1911.
    We mean better prayer meetings, better committees, better unions,

better conventions; larger societies and more of them; larger unions and more of them; we mean that we shall all be busier about the Master's business.

There is great advantage in having a definite ideal, a target, far off perhaps, but yet within sight, at which we can aim; and I further propose that in realizing our purpose and our motto, "Christian Endeavor—1911," we strive for a million new members before 1911; yes, let me repeat, *a million new members before* 1911.

Think what that may mean! Its full significance is glorious indeed. Its results stretch into and through eternity.

A million souls born into the Kingdom!

A million pairs of busy hands set at work for the Master!

A million hearts welded to the church in more loving loyalty!

A million mouths opened in confession!

A million lives brought into closer fellowship with other millions!

These, in brief, are some of the meanings of "Christian Endeavor, 1911."

How to Accomplish It.

It remains for us to consider *how* this can all be accomplished.

Again I would be very practical and definite.

As there are four great lines of training in the world-wide Christian Endeavor college, which I have already indicated, so there are four great classes in this Endeavor college, which we can and should enlarge and improve.

1. The Young People's Society in its active, associate, and honorary membership.

2. The Junior Society for the boys and girls.

3. The Intermediate Society, wherever needed, for the youths and maidens.

4. The Senior Society for graduate Endeavorers and older members of the church, where the principles learned in the younger societies may be carried out to the end of our days.

Young People's Societies.

Members of our Young People's societies, let me speak directly to you. You have not reached the limit of your growth by any means.

You have hitherto concentrated your attention too exclusively upon your active members; the most important element, to be sure, but not the only important element in your society.

Strive in the two years to come for more associate members and more honorary members, and make both of these classes count for more in your societies; give them something to do; put your associate members on appropriate committees; and give the regular meetings to your honorary members to conduct at least two or three times a year. You can, if you will, on the average, enlarge both of these classes by at least fifty per cent greatly to the advantage and enlargement as well of the active membership of your society.

Junior Workers.

Junior workers, you have not by any means reached your furthest boundary, and "Christian Endeavor, 1911," may mean great things to you.

Let me suggest as a way of simplifying the task and multiplying the usefulness of Junior superintendents that a course of instruction be prepared for Junior societies, to supplement, not to take the place of, the devotional meetings, which should never be omitted.

Why not devote half an hour each week to the Junior prayer meeting, and half an hour to definite instruction in the many lines which build up a well-rounded Christian character, and for which instruction there is no such place and opportunity as that furnished by the Junior Endeavor society?

This instruction might embrace the common doctrines of Christianity, the history of the church, and the underlying principles of morality.

It might include also, in the series of years in which the children remain in a Junior society, the specific teaching not only of temperance and missions, now partially provided for, but of good manners and good health, of kindness and gentleness to man and beast alike, of good citizenship, and even of peace and comity between the nations.

It might embrace, in summer rambles or autumn outings, Christian instruction about God's great universe in earth and air and sky.

So infinite a variety of subjects comes within the scope of Junior Endeavor, and may lend perpetual interest and vigor to our Junior societies.

The United Society during the coming years will strive to be particularly helpful to Junior superintendents along these lines.

Intermediate Endeavor.

Intermediate Endeavorers, these coming twenty-four months may, if you will, double your members.

You hold a strategic position in Christian Endeavor.

You stand between boyhood and manhood, between girlhood and womanhood, "where the brook and river meet."

The years that you influence are the decisive years. Thousands more of our larger churches need this society to bridge the gap between childhood and early maturity.

Whoever undertakes this great work for adolescents may well feel that he is helping to save the nation and the church.

Senior Endeavorer.

There is but one more branch of our work to be considered, but that is the most neglected of all, the Senior department of Christian Endeavor.

Too long we have allowed our older members to drift away from us in activity and sympathy; too many of them have felt that their Christian Endeavor obligations were ended when increasing cares or duties prevented their regular attendance at our meetings; too few of them have made their Christian Endeavor training count in the prayer meetings and activities of the older church.

Let us set ourselves resolutely, during the next two years, to remedy this defect.

One way of doing this is by forming Senior societies whose weekly meeting shall be the weekly prayer meeting of the church, and whose committees shall fill any gaps and till any neglected corner in the church garden.

"Give me a *pou sto*," a place to stand, said the ancient Grecian sage, "and I will with my lever move the world." The Senior society should afford a *pou sto*, a standing-ground for all older friends who have had the training of Christian Endeavor, or who believe in its principles; a standing-ground, and a lever as well, with which to serve the church and move the world.

This it may and should do in many churches, and always without taking away a single needed member from the Young People's society.

The same person may belong to both Young People's and Senior society when needed in both.

The Midweek Prayer Meeting.

How much this might mean to the midweek prayer meeting, to mention but one field of activity for the Senior society! The midweek church prayer meeting has fallen upon evil days. It is being given up, or lives at a "poor dying rate," in many churches, terribly to their loss. An evangelical, non-liturgical church that cannot sustain a weekly prayer meeting already has the seeds of death in itself. The Christian Endeavorer movement, the child of the prayer meeting, may well make it one of its great objects during the next two years through the Senior society to rejuvenate and revivify the midweek prayer meeting, as a quarter of a century ago it rejuvenated the young people's prayer meeting.

If it should do this, grateful pastors and churches the country over would rise up to call it blessed.

Ten Thousand New Societies.

Here, then, are our great fields for growth and usefulness; the Young People's society in all its important classes of membership, active, associate, and honorary; the Junior society; the Intermediate society; the Senior society.

To make our aim still more definite, let us set our mark for the next two years at

Three thousand new Young People's societies.
Three thousand new Junior societies.
Two thousand new Intermediate societies.
Two thousand new Senior societies.
Ten thousand new societies in all.

But it is equally important that the existing societies should be strengthened and enlarged.

There are few churches where intelligent, consecrated effort could not increase the total number of local Endeavorers by fifty per cent, counting the possible additions to be obtained through associate, active, and honorary membership of the Young People's society, and through the formation and enlargement of Intermediate and Senior societies. This, allowing a reasonable percentage for deaths and removals, would give us more than our million new members; indeed, it would mean a million net increase.

This, then, is the reasonable, attainable ideal I set before you.

We do not forget that North America is not the only continent in which Christian Endeavor has obtained a firm foothold; so into our friendly rivalry for larger and better things we will invite our brothers and sisters of all lands; and, when we meet for our World's Convention in India next November in the historic city of Agra, I will repeat these suggestions, and will ask Europe and Asia and Africa and Australasia to join in one motto and one aim in this two years' campaign.

"Christian Endeavor, 1911," Means Ten Thousand New Societies and a Million New Members in Two Years.

How shall we signalize this advance if God gives us the courage and persistence to make it, as I believe He will?

I would suggest three ways.

1. By weekly or monthly reports of the progress of the campaign in *The Christian Endeavor World* and other Christian Endeavor papers and publications.

2. By a special "Christian Endeavor, 1911," meeting of thanksgiving and rejoicing at our Convention two years hence.

3. By a souvenir certificate or diploma, worthy of a place on the chapel wall, for every society that within two years increases the present number of its Endeavorers in any or all of the societies I have suggested by at least fifty per cent.

Not Merely a Numerical Increase.

I hope that by 1911 our new International Headquarters will be well on its way to completion, a worthy monument to a great undertaking and another landmark for "Christian Endeavor, 1911."

Remember, I beg of you, that I am not pleading merely for a numerical increase.

I have suggested an aim and a motto, a souvenir and a meeting of jubilant praise at the end of our campaign, simply to make definite and concrete a mighty, concerted, continent-wide, and world-wide endeavor for the advancement of our Master's kingdom, for the upbuilding of his cause, for the reviving of the social prayer-service of the church, for the fulfilment of his petition for unity. *We can do it if we will; we must do it if we can.*

It is no mean or paltry or selfish aim that we have before us. It is important, if religion is important. It is worthy, if to seek the souls of men is a worthy quest.

In it we are encouraged by his promise, "I am with you." In it we are inspired by His command to us as well as to the children of Israel, "Speak unto the children of Christian Endeavor, that they go forward."

We have had our Increase Campaign before. It added thousands of societies to our ranks and hundreds of thousands to our membership.

"Christian Endeavor, 1911," brings it down to date, yes, two years ahead of date; brings it to every society, and not simply to our unions; gives every one of us a part in it, and extends it throughout the world.

Who will join me in this campaign for more societies and larger societies and better societies, for larger and better prayer meetings, for more Christians and better Christians?

Who will join me in this campaign for church and native land, for God and every land, for "Christian Endeavor, 1911"?

Rev. Dr. S. H. Woodrow, of Washington, from the committee on resolutions, offered the following, in the line of the President's suggestions:

Whereas the year 1911 will mark the thirtieth year of the life and work of Christian Endeavor: and Whereas our beloved President, Dr. Francis E. Clark, desires that the next two years shall be the best yet in Christian Endeavor growth and fruitfulness, therefore

RESOLVED, That we, the representatives of the International Christian Endeavor Union, assembled in convention at St. Paul, Minnesota, pledge our fervent prayers and our earnest efforts to the work of adding ten thousand new societies and one million new members to the International Christian Endeavor Union during the next two years. We also pledge anew our allegiance to our President and his associates, and promise renewed efforts in our State and local unions for the accomplishment of this great object.

This was passed with ringing applause. "Bringing in the sheaves" was sung with fine effect, and the benediction ended an opening session of the most impressive character. a session rarely exceeded in interest, prophetic of a convention of power.

CHAPTER III.

"THY KINGDOM COME," IN THE INDIVIDUAL.

The Auditorium, Thursday Morning, July 8.

The first full day's session in the Auditorium opened under most favorable circumstances. The weather was ideal. From the sectional meetings the great crowds marched toward the Auditorium singing the familiar choruses. With clock-like precision the genial face of Mr. Excell appeared on the platform as the hands on the dial pointed to ten. The leader that can bring music out of anything found an especially responsive chord in this great expectant throng. "Help somebody to-day," and "I am here on business for my King," are strains that can never again die out of the memory of those to whom they brought a vision of the King and his kingdom that morning. The theme for the morning was "Thy Kingdom Come, in the Individual." Dr. Clark introduced the first speaker, Rev. Jesse Hill, pastor of Williston Church, Portland, Me., who spoke on "How to Win Young People for Christ." He said in part as follows:

The kingdom which Jesus Christ came to establish was not composed of any one class of individuals. But a man might be fairly charged with short-sightedness who did not recognize the distinct enthusiasm he created among the young.

No approach to this question can be successfully made that does not recognize two things. First, that the point of power is the individual. God's favorite number is one. And that one appeal and method of procedure will not fit all cases. Fishing for trout with bait designed for salmon spells an empty basket. The diversity of nature and human nature is one of the most noticeable features of the world.

"Win young people"; I like the statement of the theme. That word "win" lifts the whole problem of Christian service out of the realm of the negative to the breezy heights where it becomes a tonic and an inspiration. It suggests the young man with dancing blood and beaded brow contending for mastery. It suggests the lawyer before the jury. All the foresight, energy, persistency, patience, tact, and enthusiasm found in these illustrations are wrapped up in that word "win."

My theme deals with methods. Three things I have found to be helpful.

A persistent policy of trying to discover young people to themselves. Every person is a continent of unknown values. He is a mine of unrealized possibilities. The most joyous impulse that ever comes to an individual is to discover that he is good for something. This kind of service often calls for a patience that is willing to wait until need develops a sense of appreciation of what Christ has to offer. It is easier to

29

appreciate a chart, a compass, and a lighthouse when the sea is choppy and the roar of the surf is heard. To discover the man and to harness him to his task is to awaken the sense of stewardship and to give the world a different aspect.

Another factor of value is a persistent policy to utilize the latent leadership in the society. Power is never easy to define, and the hiding of power is even more difficult to discover. But the one fact that stands out distinct and clear from all the rest is that all moral power is personal.

The third factor of value is to recognize that the only royal road is that of work. There are too many spectators in some games. This is one of the fields where proxies do not count and sponsors are not admitted. The greatness of our task is the measure of its cost. We are tempted to want men saved by wholesale. We should like to see the world Christianized by edict. We forget the divine Saviour, who was content to be spent on a single woman at the well and a single man in an upper chamber. Sacrifice can never be reduced to the terms of personal comfort. A man is not a Christian until he is willing to be a savior in the form of a servant.

A hearty applause greeted the next speaker, when Dr. Clark introduced Rev. Henry F. Cope, of Chicago, Ill., secretary of the Religious Education Association. His speech was punctuated with apt illustrations, which were cheered again and again. He brought a greeting from the Religious Education Association, and pointed out the parallel lines on which the two societies are working. Said he:

There are two kinds of young people in this world, those good for something and those good for nothing.

The good-for-nothings are simply parasites and putterers. The good-for-nothings are those who aspire so much that they never have time to perspire. There are those who dream so much that they have no time for doing.

The religious life is a life of aspirations and a life of ideas. No man does any great thing without some great vision. The best thing of being young is that you have new visions. I am sorry for young men and young women who do not believe that somehow God called them to some big place in life. Let them believe that God has given them a great mission among men.

I believe in the prayer meeting, the place where men get together in vision. The religious life is often the dream, the aspiration, of an ideal character.

Some people say, "O to be nothing, nothing!" and then sing, "Dear Lord, I give myself away." It is mighty easy when you become nothing to give it away. We have too many people who are talking of laying their lives down upon the altar. They haven't any life to lay down.

The first thing that you will want to do if you express an ideal character is to reach out to the high visions that come. Realize and be that of which you dream.

We want full lives, not little lives, but larger lives, visionary lives, lives that measure up to "the fulness of the stature of Christ."

If you are going to do any work in this world, the first thing you must do in order to get ready for this work is to put your feet upon the facts of the work that you are going to do.

I am afraid a lot of people do Christian work without any plan. They are trying to do work without knowing how it is done. Get your feet upon the facts.

What about the facts of the place where you do your work in your community? In your Sunday school you have a map of Palestine. It is a good thing to have. It is a good thing to know about it, but I want to say that every Sunday school should have a map on its walls of the section of the city where they live.

I believe in Christian Endeavorers' trying to help our United States to do things in Christian citizenship. I believe in the laymen. I was educated for the ministry. Your business may be in the pew to drink in the sermon and to digest the sermon. People often suffer from spiritual dyspepsia, due to undigested sermons. I would rather have a congregation that *did* one sermon a month than *enjoyed* eight a month.

The church has a job. This job is worth doing well. Men will be in the church when there is a job in the church for the men. It is up to us pastors and other leaders to see that there are courses of study and courses of preparation for men who want to do work in their church. There are things for men to do. Have they got to be content to take up the collection and to stand up in front while God's blessing is asked on the offering? There are thousands of things men will find to do when they get the spirit of Him in their hearts.

"The Big Brother Movement."

There is always work in making your church count in your community. That would be the natural expression of your religious life. Whenever there comes to you an impulse to do any good thing, then that is the time to do it.

If you have an impression, the worst thing you can do with it is to bury it inside of you. God is stirring us. We must stir ourselves up, and do his bidding. May we lay a strong, full, developed life on the altar of service for the Kingdom.

Rev. Samuel H. Woodrow, D. D., pastor of the First Congregational Church of Washington, D. C., and trustee of the United Society, responded to the topic, "What Should be the Attitude of the Pastor and Church toward the Society?" Dr. Woodrow's personal presence commands attention, and gives one the impression of poise, sanity, and reserve power. Frankly and kindly he pointed out the weakness in places where the society had not thrived, and set forth a constructive programme, which, if followed, would result in a blessing such as his churches have always received. He said:

Modern thought is laying strong emphasis upon the importance of environment. The biologist is aware that favorable environment has much to do with the growth of all living organisms. Luscious oranges do not grow amid the rocks and glaciers of the arctic, but gather their golden glory from the warmth of tropic suns.

A fold is built for the sheep, but the lambs are not left outside the fold to prove by their powers of enduring cold and storms that they are worthy of being admitted. If there is a warm, comfortable place in the fold, it is given to the lambs. Proper food is given them that they may gain strength in the fold to withstand the evils without the fold.

Social reformers are directing their attention to environment as never before. They are coming to see that children are born in the slums of our cities under conditions that render healthy bodies, clear minds, and pure hearts well-nigh impossible. An environment of vice is not a school of virtue.

All this has a direct bearing upon the relation of the church and pastor toward the young people. They are young people. The term itself implies that they are yet immature, that they have many lessons to learn in the hard school of experience, and that the discipline of life has yet to do its work for weal or woe.

If the young people were all mature, wise, self-controlled, and able to express perfectly the powers they feel struggling within them, they would need no home training, no schools, and no Christian Endeavor.

The society is a young people's society, and the very name implies that there will be the same immaturity that we find in other young people of the same ages in the home and in the school. Too many churches and pastors expect the blossoming and the ripe fruit without the irrigation and culture.

The church must furnish a congenial environment and an atmosphere of sympathetic interest. There are churches where the cold breath of carping criticism prevents any fruit from coming to perfection. The pastor should be the wise, sympathetic leader of his Young People's society, the friend and helper of every boy and girl in his parish. If he is afraid of the society, suspicious of its action, and doubtful of its sincerity, then probably his fears will be realized. Let him neglect his pulpit preparation, his prayer meeting, his Sunday school, and see whether it is not followed by similar results.

The society is a means to an end, as the church itself is a means to an end. The society is for training of young people in regular habits of Bible-study and daily devotion; it is for training men to give expression to their faith and love through worship and testimony; it is to train men for service in church and state. Its endeavor is that men and women of the future may be "throughly furnished unto all good works." This aim is surely a worthy one, but it does not accomplish itself.

The Young People's society is the pastor's opportunity. There he can discover the undeveloped talents of the boys and girls. One has executive ability; one has power to arouse enthusiasm; another, gifts of teaching; another, fervor in prayer; another, gifts of song; another, unusual gifts of speech, and you can get him to college and into the ministry or out on the mission field.

The wise church and pastor are training workers and leaders; and, though these go elsewhere to live, they will still be leaders and workers for the Kingdom.

Nothing ever succeeds in any church but by the wise oversight and direction of somebody who is competent to direct and interested in the object.

You can't even get up a "rummage sale" without thought and work; much less can you train young people to be useful Christians without patient, long-continued effort.

Young people are sometimes thoughtless, self-willed, and bumptious, but no more so in the Christian Endeavor society than they are in the home and in the school. We do not abolish the home because some parents and children are failures. We do not abandon the school because there are failures, and more than forty per cent of those who enter fail to graduate.

The Society is plastic, and can be adapted to local conditions and needs. A pastor and church should use it gladly till by thought and prayer they can devise something better. The relation of the pastor to the society should be that of wise, patient, sympathetic oversight and direction. The church should furnish the environment and atmosphere necessary for the shepherding of the lambs of the flock that the Good Shepherd carries in his bosom, upon his very heart.

THE INTERIOR OF THE ARMORY.

After the singing of a hymn, Rev. Charles H. Hubbell, secretary of Christian Endeavor for the Methodist Protestant Church, and for many years the State secretary for Ohio, conducted the Open Parliament. Dr. Hubbell wears the smile that won't come off. When the Ohio delegation caught sight of him, they made the Convention conscious of their presence by their welcome to an old-time leader. He skilfully summarized the addresses of the three speakers, as he said:

"We have just heard three strong and stimulating addresses on three of the most important themes that will be discussed during the entire Convention.

"Each address may be put in one word: First, emotion; second, motion; third, promotion.

"Each address ended with an interrogation point. We want this parliament to end with an exclamation point of achievement and optimism. Let us hear from you. Make your responses pertinent, pleasant, profitable, pointed, pithy, polite, prayerful, praiseful, and prompt."

Then the optimists' club had a most hilarious and helpful session. Reports of splendid endeavors came thick and fast. One hundred and sixty-five new societies organized in the African Methodist Episcopal Church in six months. One hundred converts were made through an evangelistic committee. A local-option campaign won through Christian Endeavor support. Missionary books read in large numbers in a society contest. More than one hundred members received by a local society. Bigger and better prayer meetings. These are only a few of the splendid samples given.

From every section of the great hall they came pouring forth in an unreportable way, the dominant note being the missionary activity of local and State societies. Looking over the audience, one could not help noticing the splendid proportion of young men, the use of note-books, and the enthusiastic response to every practical suggestion that was made.

CHAPTER IV.

CHRISTIAN ENDEAVOR FUNDAMENTALS.

The Armory, Thursday Morning, July 8.

The first simultaneous meeting held during the Convention was held in the Armory, a building admirably adapted for convention purposes. The hall has a seating-capacity of about three thousand people. Like the Auditorium, it was very tastefully decorated in the Convention colors. Around the walls of the rooms were various exhibits, which always attracted the earnest attention of the delegates when the meetings were not in progress. The opening session was presided over by Mr. H. N. Lathrop, the treasurer of the United Society of Christian Endeavor. He conducted the meeting in his own unique manner, while Mr. Percy S. Foster was in charge of the singing.

The four Christian Endeavor fundamentals were the Prayer-meeting, the Pledge, the Committee Work, and Our Fellowship, all of which were treated in an able manner by four distinguished speakers.

"The Prayer Meeting: Its Place and Power in the Society," was treated by Rev. Samuel McNaugher, pastor of the First Reformed Presbyterian Church of Boston, Mass. He said:

We are considering Christian Endeavor fundamentals, and very significantly the very first topic is the prayer meeting: its place and power in the society.

The first point for us to remember is the importance of the prayer meeting in every Christian Endeavor society. It would be a misnomer to call a society a Christian Endeavor society that did not have a weekly prayer meeting. All the members of the society should be led to believe in the fundamental place the prayer meeting holds, and contribute of their very best efforts to its success. The Christian Endeavor prayer meeting is the training of the young in the use of the Bible, in the expression of the longings of the soul in public prayer, and in the ability to bear testimony before others to the goodness of God. What could be more important than just this training that is given in every true Christian Endeavor prayer meeting?

Secondly, if what I have said is true concerning the prayer meeting, then it follows that a new emphasis must be placed upon this branch of our work. The personality of the members of the prayer-meeting committee will make either for failure or for success. This is specially true of the chairman. This committee, in my judgment, is the first and chief committee. It is the business of such a committee to see that the leaders are selected with great wisdom and care, to volunteer to help the leaders by

34

suggestion, and to watch over these meetings with the utmost watchfulness.

"The element which is most universally lacked in the average prayer meeting is careful and prayerful preparation; and yet, while this element is most often wanting, it is perhaps the most essential of all." The prayer meeting should be a meeting where there is much prayer and testimony. It should be a meeting for missionary and evangelistic inspiration. It should be a meeting of Christian fellowship in the things of the spirit.

Third, it remains for us, finally, to speak of the power of such a prayer meeting in the society. The prayer meeting, vitalized by the Spirit of God, has an inherent power in itself. You can feel it at once as you are privileged to attend such a meeting. It also exerts a wonderful influence on all the other branches of the work. Things are made to go in such a society. The electric car goes because the car receives power from the wire by way of the trolley. In like manner the prayer meeting is the arm which connects the work with the throne of God and of power. This is the only explanation that can be given for success. Wherever there is failure, it can be traced to the lack of this power. Here is power for the asking. "Ask, and it shall be given you." The early Christians experienced this power, and so may we. A society of Christian Endeavor with such a prayer meeting is to be congratulated. It has come to the Kingdom for such a time as this.

The second address of the morning was on "The Pledge: Its Reasonableness and Helpfulness." In treating it the Rev. Elijah Humphries, D. D., pastor of the Primitive Methodist Church, Fall River, Mass., said:

All civilized society is held together by compacts. States have their constitutions; political parties, their platforms; corporations, their laws; clubs, societies, lodges, their mutual obligations. The foundation of the home is laid in the marriage vows. The church has its covenant, and membership therein is rightly conditioned on a reasonable compliance with its requirements.

No one will for a moment question either the reasonableness or helpfulness of these compacts. No sane mind would advocate the abrogation of these pledges merely because they are occasionally violated or treated with indifference. Yet there are those who admit the propriety and utility of these obligations, and question the wisdom and usefulness of the Christian Endeavor pledge. They say that larger numbers of young people would unite with the Christian Endeavor Society, were it not for the pledge, and that young people do not always keep the pledge, and this laxity reacts unfavorably upon their character.

As to the latter objection, it may be observed that a quarter of a century of experience and observation fully proves that the Christian Endeavor pledge is far more faithfully kept by the young people than the church covenant is kept by their elders.

As for the former objection, our answer is that the young people that are unwilling to indorse the splendid purpose and programme, and sustain the lofty standards and aims, of Christian Endeavor as set forth in the pledge would be no real gain to the cause. Numbers do not always stand for strength. The Christian Endeavor Society is not a mutual admiration society, or a social club, or a go-as-you-please association. It has a purpose. It stands for something, for something definite, something worthy. It stands for the attainment of high Christian character and noble achievement for Christ, the church, and humanity. It has no room for idlers or dress-parade soldiers. It wants young people of high purpose, of moral fibre, of noble aims, willing to attempt great things for God and man, willing to assume obligations involving self-sacrifice and strenuous living. There is something in the Christian Endeavor pledge that appeals to the heroic element in young people of the right stuff. Shirkers and jerkers have little use for the pledge, but whole-souled, consecrated workers are attracted by it.

The flexibility of the pledge also evidences its reasonableness. It is not a cast-iron law, not, like the laws of the Medes and Persians, unalterable. There are now four different pledges approved and commended by the United Society, not one of them compulsory. All of them are merely suggestive, and may be accepted, altered, amended, at will. All may be even rejected and an entirely new and original pledge substituted, adapted to local needs and conditions.

The duties enjoined in the Christian Endeavor pledge are fundamental to Christian life. The pledge does not create, but simply voices, them, is a constant reminder of them and an inspiration to their fulfilment. The pledges suggested by the United Society have behind them the weight of long years of experiment and test, which gives value and worth to them. They should not, therefore, be easily tossed aside.

A pledge of some sort is essential to a genuine Christian Endeavor society. We have said that the Christian Endeavor Society has a definite purpose, aim, standard. In the pledge that purpose and aim are clearly defined. It is the aim of Christian Endeavor to cultivate Christian character, and to teach that character how to spend itself in the service of humanity in its physical, mental, social, industrial, political, and spiritual development. The pledge most certainly conduces to these noble ends. Take the oldest of the four pledges referred to. What splendid gems flash in the sunlight as we uncover this precious jewel: The supremacy, the Lordship of Jesus Christ, confession of human weakness and divine strength, acceptance of the will of Christ as the law of life and service, daily prayer and Bible-reading, absolutely essential to the Christian life, witness-bearing, definite service, church-attendance and church-support; and the latest form of the pledge adds generous giving, soul-winning, Christian patriotism, and Christian brotherhood, and all these according to the measure of the will of Christ, as it may be discovered by an enlightened Christian conscience. Who can question the reasonableness and helpfulness of such a standard? The elimination of the Christian Endeavor pledge will mark the decline and fall of Christian Endeavor.

"The Committee Work: A Definite Task for Each," was treated by Rev. Ernest H. Tippett, pastor of the First Congregational Church, Hamilton, Ontario, Canada. He said:

The key-note of this Convention is "Thy Kingdom Come." This kingdom is the rule of righteousness, purity, and love. It is not limited to heaven, but is to be built on earth: "As in heaven, so on earth." *We* have the honor of being called of God to co-operate with him in bringing this to pass. It is no small task. The dense mass of heathenism in our country is to be evangelized and reclaimed; the drink traffic, the gambling iniquity, the white slave trade, and kindred evils must be stamped out. Unholy monopolies must become impossible. Graft and greed must be driven from the political and commercial arena. Seeing the immensity of this task, we feel like saying with Jehoshaphat of old, "We have no might against this great company that cometh against us, neither know we what to do, but our eyes are upon thee."

We are not to hold services, but render services. The devotional meeting should be the feasting-place where nourishment is taken and strength obtained to go out and serve. To arouse emotions in the prayer meeting and fail to supply a means for these emotions to express themselves in action is criminal.

The committee work of the society supplies that means. Efficient committees forever refute the charge that we are an impractical, emotional organization.

On the Eddystone lighthouse there is an inscription which should be inscribed on the face of every society: "To give light and to save life." In doing this there is a task for every one. One of our weaknesses at present is the lack of the sense of individual responsibility on the part of many members.

To fulfil the mission of the society every active member should be on a committee. That marvellous organization, the Roman Catholic Church, finds a place and work for every person; recognizing that every one possesess at least one talent, it supplies the opportunity for its use. The same kind of generalship should characterize our societies. The executive should be students of human nature, discoverers of the various abilities of the members. The one who could not attack a saloon can hand a flower with a smile to the sick. The one who is too timid to offer the glad hand at the door can place a chair in the best position. The one who could not organize an open-air meeting can correspond with a missionary and keep the society in vital touch with his work. I mention these just to illustrate the hundred and one things that have suggested themselves to you while I have been speaking. There is work for all to do if the committees are properly organized. The officers can, if they will take the trouble, soon develop the gift of putting the right person in the right place.

The convener should see that his committee meets and works. For him to do the work to save calling a meeting is a fatal error. He should bring plans for something aggressive to every meeting. He should procure for his members literature upon their department of work.

Every member should endeavor by reading books, by clippings from papers, by conversation and observation, to become an expert in his line. A lot of energy is wasted for lack of knowledge of facts, methods, and the experience of others.

In speaking of "Our Fellowship: How to Enlarge It," Rev. W. F. Richardson, D. D., pastor of the First Christian Church, Kansas City, Mo., said:

Our fellowship is a present and increasing fact. Let us not forget that. If the Roman Church boasts of her unity as against our divisions, we may rejoice in our freedom, to which her people are strangers. But we ought to seek both union and freedom, for only through the marriage of the two can the family of God find their true ideals realized. How may we so enlarge our fellowship through Christian Endeavor as to make effective what we already enjoy, and hasten the day when we shall realize the full measure of unity for which our Lord prayed?

First, by our mutual appreciation of one another in Christ. Many of the things that hinder our fellowship are trivial and a mere matter of names.

Second, by our mutual co-operation in Christian work. If, as Paul assures us, "All *things* work together for good to them that love God," is it not possible for those who love God to work together for good? It is time we were at least practising our fellowship more, if we talk it no less. It is possible to know the time-card, and yet to miss the train; and we may be talking together and working apart. A law of Wales requires every keeper of bees to distribute, once a year, part of his honey to his neighbors, on the ground that his bees have fed on their flowers. We are so deeply indehted to one another that we must share with others all that comes to us. The church has been engaged in the work of transportation, when she ought to be busy in that of transformation. Instead of taking men to heaven, she would better fit them for it, and the chariots of God will take them up. Such transformation is impossible to the selfish or sectarian soul. Let us make the deed fit the word, and practise the fellowship we preach. I wonder whether the reason why so many pins are lost is not that they are pointing one way and headed the other. Let's not be pin-headed.

Third, by mutual courtship. We shall have to love one another when we get to heaven. Why not begin to cultivate it here? "By this shall all men know that ye are my disciples, if ye have love one to another," said our Master. How can we find one another attractive over there, if we cannot be drawn toward one another here? When Robert Louis Stevenson heard of the death of Matthew Arnold, he quietly observed, "He won't like God." Shall we like him, if his children are not dear to us now? Shall not the Christian Endeavorers of the world erect their monument of universal peace on the border-line of every nation? and where is a better place to resolve upon this high aim than in this noble city, bearing the name of that apostle who saw the vision of a universe gathered into one through the fellowship of the regal Christ?

These addresses were followed by an Open Parliament, conducted by Mr. Walter R. Ceperly, of Chicago, Ill., president of the Illinois Christian Endeavor Union. It proved to be a very spirited and interesting hour. A great many helpful suggestions were offered by those present. In closing, Mr. Ceperly warned all present against getting into a rut, claiming that this was one of the most dangerous mistakes in the Christian Endeavor work. The meeting closed with prayer and the benediction by Rev. W. F. Richardson, D. D.

CHAPTER V.

ADDRESS OF HON. WILLIAM JENNINGS BRYAN.

Metropolitan Opera House, Thursday Noon, July 8.

Noon evangelistic meetings were planned for the Metropolitan Opera House each day during the Convention. The Hon. William Jennings Bryan had promised to reach the city in time to speak at the Thursday noon meeting, as well as to address the Convention at two other places in the afternoon. The theatre was filled from pit to dome, and it was noticed that in the audience were not only many Endeavorers, but also business men, men from the street, and many that sadly needed a service of this kind. The meeting was in charge of that well-known business-man evangelist William Phillips Hall, of New York. After prayer and reading of the Scriptures by Rev. James A. Francis, of Boston, Mr. Bryan was introduced. The audience arose to their feet amid tumultuous applause, thereby signifying the pleasure and honor they felt in having the great Commoner's presence. Mr. Bryan's address was so strong and helpful that we think it is well worthy of a chapter by itself, and we publish it herewith in full:

There are two things that the Christian is interested in,—his work with others, in the first place, to bring others to the Christian profession of faith, and, in the second place, his work to develop the Christian spirit into larger activity.

The work of the evangelist is to bring the unbeliever or the non-believer to the point of accepting Christ. I am not an evangelist, but each one of us has his own ideals as to how this work can best be done, and it is necessary that all of the ideals shall be presented and be tried in order to reach the various people who are to be reached. The thoughts that I suggest here may not commend themselves to all of you; you may have a different point of view; your method of work may be different; but all that I can do is to present this subject as it appears to me, and suggest a line of work that I believe will be effective with some at least.

I want to assume that the one whom we are approaching has no secret reason for not becoming a Christian. If a man has a secret reason which he will not give you, it is very difficult to reach him; and I am persuaded that many have a reason that they do not give when asked why they do not become Christians. I think that very often it is an unwillingness to give up some particular thing that in the mind of the person stands in the way of a Christian life, a thing that he feels that he cannot do and live up to the profession that he would be required to make.

I recall an instance of this. A lady asked me to speak to her husband, for she was much interested in bringing him to the point of making

39

a profession of faith. I knew him very well, and went to him at her
request. He very frankly told me that it was not necessary to argue
about Christianity; he admitted all that. "But," he said, "I am in a
certain business, which I cannot give up, and in it I am required to do
things that I ought not to do if I was a member of the church; and that
is the only reason why I do not become a member of the church."

There was another man whom I approached with a request that he
teach a Sunday-school class. Mentioning a form of amusement of which
he was very fond, he said, "What would my scholars think if I did that?"
"Are you more interested in that than in teaching?" I asked. "Yes," he
said; and he did not teach.

Often there is a secret reason why a person will not become a Christian, and until you know that you are not in a position to present an
argument. But, assuming that the person is open to conviction, but presents objections, how ought he to be answered? I remember a sermon
by Mr. Moody, whom I have always regarded as the most powerful
speaker in appealing to those who are not Christians whom I have ever
heard. His text was, "And they all with one consent began to make
excuse." He took up the excuses, and showed how frivolous they were.
One man had bought a piece of land, and must go to see it. "That was
absurd," said Mr. Moody, "because the man ought to have gone to see
the field before he bought it. After he had bought it there was no
necessity for haste in seeing it." It was the same in regard to the man
who had bought a yoke of oxen; there was no haste to test it after he had
made the purchase. And as for the man who had married a wife—why
did he not bring her along?

Then Mr. Moody took up the familiar excuses that we all hear whenever we talk to men about salvation, analyzed each, and showed how without foundation it was. And so, if we are going to appeal to people in
regard to their souls' salvation, let us first show them Christianity in the
life; let us show them that the first and most essential thing is for a
man to get right with God, to see the relation between himself and his
Creator, that that is the fundamental thing in life. I was impressed by a
sentence in one of Tolstoi's letters in which he spoke of the possibility
of making an extended improvement in the condition of people, but said
that the most important thing is for a man to find out God's will concerning him and do it. This is to be presented as the first thing, to get
right with God.

But suppose the man presents an objection. Suppose he brings up
the fact that there are hypocrites in the church. That is a weak objection;
for, if the man were really disturbed because it seems to him that so
many church-members are hypocrites, the best thing he could do would be
to go in and increase by one the number of those who are not hypocrites.
There is a reply that we might make if it were not so impolite. When
he says that there are so many hypocrites in the church, we may answer:
"That is none of your business. You are not responsible for them, but
for yourself. You see that you are free from the hypocrisy and evil-doing
of those church-members."

And suppose that this man with whom you are talking sees a good
many things in religion that he cannot understand. I admit these perplexities. When a man tells me that there are mysteries in religion, I do not
try to deny it, but I tell him that there are mysteries everywhere else.
I know not where I can go to escape from mysteries. If a Christian has
doubts and fears, the unbeliever has more. If he will not become a
Christian because he cannot understand all the mysteries, why is he
willing to live without understanding the mystery of life? Who knows
this mystery? We are thrust into being without our volition. We come
we know not whence, and we go out we know not whither. How mysterious is life! How mysterious is everything! After six thousand years

of human history, who knows the mystery of the span of a human life? The man to whom you are talking this minute in half an hour may pass far away. In a moment the change may come over any one of us that will convert a living, breathing human being into a mass of lifeless clay. What is it, that, having, we live, and, having not, we are as the clod? We know as little of the mysteries of life now as at the dawn of creation.

What man has a right to say he cannot believe that a multitude was fed with a few loaves of bread? Every spring, when the sun comes forth in its power, it melts the ice, and not a few thousands, but hundreds of millions, are fed with the products of the soil. And how many of those that eat and are satisfied understand the chemistry of the soil and the processes of vegetable growth? How is it that you plant a few seeds in the spring and gather a bountiful harvest in the fall? If a man should refuse to eat anything till he could understand the mystery of food, he would die of starvation. But mystery does not bother us in the dining-room; only in the church. What can a man explain if you demand an explanation? All the processes of nature are mysterious. We know how to raise a vegetable, but we do not know why we can raise it in that way. Thus it is with everything that we deal with. Science has discovered much, but there is an intellectual pride that I think stands in the way of Christianity. Intellectual pride in the main does not like to admit that there is anything it cannot explain.

We may answer such a man by declaring that there is nothing of importance that he can explain. If he tells me that he cannot accept the Bible plan of the univeres, I ask him to give me a plan that is more easily understood. If he denies the Bible statement of creation, let him present another that will stand the test of his reason. Do you know any theory of creation that is better than the Bible one? I remember that when I was a young man I studied what was called the nebular hypothesis. It begins by assuming that certain things existed before the theory begins to work. What does it assume? First, that matter existed. How? In particles infinitely fine. Why not make them finer? Because that is as far as our imagination can go. Where? Infinitely separated. Why not push them farther apart? Because out imagination cannot go any farther. But the theory does not explain how matter came there, and the theory does not explain how or why the forces acting on matter came to be there. It assumes that there was in force a tendency acting upon matter, and in matter a willingness to be acted upon. There is no explanation; but, beginning with the assumption of these things, the theory begins to work, and, according to the theory, force working on matter created a world.

The man who invented that theory is not the only man who has a right to guess. I have a guess coming, and I have as much right to assume as he had; and I prefer to assume a Designer back of the design; I prefer to assume a Creator back of creation. It is easier for me to believe that a God can create matter than to believe that matter can create a man. We have to begin somewhere, we have to commence with something; and the Christian begins with God.

I had a difficulty with this subject when a young man. It was a difficulty that, like measles and other childish diseases, I had when young, and got over with it. I had difficulty with the origin of things, and I went back to Genesis. I found it written there, "In the beginning God created the heavens and the earth." That was something solid, and I decided to just get up on that and stand there until man found some other theory of creation that should go back to the beginning. And I am still standing there.

Then I had difficulty with the miracles. Stop and analyze this matter of miracles, get acquainted with it. When a horse scares at anything, if you drive him around it, he scares at it the next time; but, if you drive him straight up to it, he won't scare again. I found two questions only in regard to miracles: Could God perform a miracle? and, Would he want to? As to the first, I had no difficulty in answering. A God who can make a world can do anything he wants to with it. You cannot deny that God can perform miracles without denying that God is God. But would he want to? The question gives the most trouble to those who know God so well that they can tell quite without investigation just what God would and would not do. This is intellectual pride, this unwillingness to believe anything beyond my power to know. Who am I that I should attempt to measure the arm of the Almighty by my puny arm? Who am I that insist that my finite brain shall comprehend the mind of the Infinite? Who am I that I dare fix by metes and bounds the Creator's power? And yet the man who denies that God can perform a miracle denies and disputes the power of God; and the man that says God would not perform a miracle assumes to know the mind of God, and declare just what God would or would not do. I find it so difficult to decide each day what God wants done to-day that I have not presumption enough to look back through the ages and attempt to decide without the possibility of mistake what he may have wanted to do thousands of years before I was born.

And then, my friends, we are constantly increasing our knowledge, learning things of which men were totally ignorant a few years ago; and it is easy for me to believe that there may be forces and laws in nature of which we have as yet no knowledge. A few years ago men knew of the lightning only as it flashed across the sky, only as something to fear. Who dreamed that that invisible fluid, imprisoned in man-made wire, was to light our streets and homes, carry our messages, and drive the wheels of commerce? And more recently man, peering into nature, has discerned another unseen force whereby messages can be sent through space without any wire. It seemed impossible a few months ago, but since a sinking ship has been rescued by the system of wireless telegraphy we cannot doubt that it is an accomplished fact.

If Christ was divine, we must assume that he had all knowledge and all power, and it is easy for me to believe that he may have acted by laws to him well known, but laws of which we are ignorant and must forever remain ignorant while we are in the flesh. But shall these mysteries prevent my accepting religion? If we just apply to religion some of the common sense that we apply to other things, we shall have no difficulty about it. I have mentioned some of the mysteries of science. I could occupy the whole of the hour, the whole of the day, the rest of my life, talking about mysteries that will not be explained. What a mystery is love! What is it that brings two hearts together, and welds them together, and makes two persons walk through life as partners? It is an invisible thing, but the invisible things are eternal. We know that love exists in this world, but who can explain it? Who can explain a mother's affection for her child? Can the scientist weigh it? Can he measure it? Can he tell where it is? It is as large as the world. It is the imperial force in her life and in the lives of her children. These things are not only invisible; but they escape every effort to analyze them, explain them, or understand them.

I repeat, we are surrounded by mysteries. Everything with which we deal is mysterious. Water has been necessary to human existence from the beginning, and I have sometimes thought that man would have been better off if he had cultivated a more intimate acquaintance with it; and yet we found out just the other day that this which we call water is not water at all, but a gas; two gases got mixed together, and they cannot get apart, and we just call it water. But infinitely more important than that knowledge is the fact that we have water to drink. Man needed water before he found out that it is only gas; and, while the knowledge that it is gas has done the world some good, yet the value of water would have been much the same if we had never known what it is.

No one can explain why water contracts as it gets cooler until it reaches the freezing-point, and then expands. That is not the law with other things. We do not know why it is so, but we know it is very important that it should be so. It is infinitely more important that water should cease to contract as it freezes than that we should know why it does.

And so, my friends, God has given us the things we need and the knowledge necessary to use them; and the truth that he has revealed to us is infinitely more important than the mysteries that he conceals from us. So I would say to an unbeliever, if he asks, "Can you understand everything?" I would answer: "No. If I only try to live up to the things I understand, I shall be kept so busy doing good that I shall have no time to worry about what I do not understand. And it is my observation that those who spend the most time looking for contradictory passages in the Bible spend the least time trying to live up to the things that are easily understood." I should tell him that, judging from the principal use that such people make of the knowledge they have, I wonder if they would make any better use of the knowledge they seem so anxious to get. If a person complains' of the mysteries, the best answer we can give him is that he lives in the midst of mysteries, and that it is very inconsistent in him to spend so much time on religious mysteries when all other mysteries seem to worry him so little.

I would not begin with the non-believer by discussing mysteries with him, only to answer his objections; or miracles, unless the matter is brought up by him; not even the theory of the atonement, though I have my idea regarding it. If asked why I think the plan of salvation was adopted by God, I should tell him that it is not necessary I should understand the reason why it was adopted, but only necessary that I should accept it as it is. Yet, if any reason is needed, I have one which satisfies me; namely, that love is the greatest thing in the world, and sacrifice is the language of love; and that Christ could not have found a better plan of reaching human hearts than this of expressing his love in sacrifice, being willing to die for the world, and thus giving the best evidence of his love for the world; and that thus he has touched the hearts of the human race wherever the story has been told.

But I should not attempt to discuss such questions with an unbeliever. In the first place, when you attempt to meet him on that fundamental proposition of Christ's divinity, he denies it. "I do not know that Christ was divine," he says. You bid him look at the miracles, look at the resurrection; and he says, "You have not proved that they occurred; I deny them all." Then you may meet him half-way if you will get him to consider what are the admitted facts regarding Christ. First, Christ lived; and he must admit it. Then take the facts of the life of Christ, the death of Christ, the words he spoke, the great truths he enunciated, and the surprising growth of the Christian church. I would show how Christ, reared in a carpenter's shop, never had access to the wisdom of the past nor contact with the sages of other lands, yet at the age of thirty he spoke by the lake and on the mount majestic sentences whose truths the world has not exhausted in centuries of study; how he gathered around him a few disciples, most of whom were soon put to death, but his royal spirit marched on until it had seized upon nation after nation until hundreds of millions had taken his name, and millions are ready to die rather than surrender their faith in him. I would also show how this religion takes the selfish man, and converts him from one who would sacrifice the world for his self-gratification into one who would give his life for a principle. I would show him how this love of Christ put into the heart has taken hold of the lives of young men. I would show him a young man starting in the practice of medicine, feeling the touch of that love, sacrificing his chances for advancement, fame, and fortune, crossing the ocean and burying himself in the Dark Continent, to give his life for a people of whom he has only heard. I would tell him that Christianity is the greatest fact in history, that this character put into the world nineteen centuries ago has been multiplying itself with increasing power in the thought and lives of men, and is to-day the mightiest influence in the world.

Now it is my time to ask a question. "What will you do with Christ? What will you think of these facts of his life? What answer can you make to this question? What explanation of these facts can you give?" It is easier for me to believe that he was divine than to explain in any other way what he said, and what he did, and what he was; and I should ask him what his explanation was. I might have gone farther. I might have shown how from the beginning the prophecies pointed to Christ. I might show how Christians are the salt of every community in which the Christian spirit is manifested. If he points to somebody in the church who is doing what a Christian should not do, I tell him that that is the best evidence that Christianity is right and good, because even an unbeliever can see the difference between a man who does not live according to its teachings and a man who does.

Christianity calls on every follower of Christ, according to his opportunity, to go to lands where other religious rule and challenge them to a comparison. They go to the lands of the Prophet, the countries of Mohammedanism, and, except where they have borrowed from Christianity, they are scarcely beyond where they were fifteen centuries ago. The lands where the philosophy of Confucius and the doctrines of Buddha hold sway, except where the have borrowed from Christianity, have made no progress in two thousand years. Tell the unbeliever to take the lands where Christianity is the dominant religion, and he will find that in a thousand years it has taken a nation that then was in barbarism and has lifted it till its civilization surpasses all that the world has ever known. Christianity not only solves the problems of its own lands, but, sending Christian teachers and physicians to all heathen lands, it solves their problems also, and becomes the saving salt of the whole earth.

To describe it I would turn back to the Old Testament and read the first Psalm: "Blessed is the man that walketh not in the counsel of the ungodly, nor standeth in the way of sinners, nor sitteth in the seat of the scornful; but his delight is in the law of the Lord, and in his law doth he meditate day and night. He shall be like a tree planted by the rivers of water, that bringeth forth his fruit in his season; his leaf also shall not wither, and whatsoever he doeth shall prosper." I would tell the unbeliever that he can take the Christian people of this land and measure them against an equal number elsewhere, and he will find that prophecy and promise made good. Where do you find the best education of the world? Among the Christian people. Where do you find the largest wealth *per capita?* Among the Christian people. What is the reason why Christianity has made such progress? Because it has the only philosophy that fits a human being, the teaching that greatness is to be measured by service; and, when a man gets hold of that doctrine, he gets ready to serve. And Christian civilization is the highest the world has ever known, because it rests upon the conception of life that makes life an unending progress toward the higher things; for there is no limit to human development and advancement.

Yet all the conversions that are made are made not so much by what we say as by what we do. We are told that we should be living apostles, known and read by all men. We are a sort of book in the world's circulating library; and, if the world does not heed us so much as we could hope, possibly it is because there is so much fiction in the library, and not enough history. Speech is necessary; sermons are necessary; but no one has yet lived who could answer a Christian life; that is the unanswerable argument. When you find one who disputes what you say and will not accept your arguments, the best answer is this: "You live your plan, and I will live mine; and we will decide by the way we live which is the best plan for living." The only trouble is that those who live moral lives outside the church are borrowing their morality from the church without giving credit to the source of it. Those who are held up as examples of what a man can be without being a member of the church have been in almost every case the products of Christian homes. Christianity is so valuable a thing, so powerful a thing, that a Christian father and mother can give to their boy a momentum that carries him a long distance after he leaves home, even though he denies that from which he got his impulse. But, even so, the best final answer we can give to an unbeliever is to say to him: "You live as you believe and I will live as I believe; and let us see which life is the best. By their fruits ye shall know them."

If he tells you that you put too much emphasis on faith, tell him that without faith it is impossible, not only to please God, but to do anything else. Faith goes first; works come afterward. Come to believe that you can do something, and because you have that faith you are willing to undertake anything you believe to be right. If you have not that faith, you will lean and fall; but you will stand if you believe that you are standing for the right. This belief gives you the power to do all things that are worth doing in life.

And so, to recapitulate, if I were talking to one who was not a believer, I would simply present to him Christ, his life, his teachings, and show what Christ and his example have accomplished. And if he answered me by pointing to mystery and miracle, I would silence him by showing how little attention he pays to the mysteries all about him. And then, if I could not reach him in any other way, I would challenge him to make the test and see which can produce the highest, the best, the noblest life, the theory of the non-Christian or the theory of the Christian; and I believe, as I have said, that that Christian life is sufficient to demonstrate the right of Christ to our hearts and to our lives. And after visiting the lands where missionaries are at work I return with this conviction, that, if we could not find ministers to send abroad to preach the gospel, teachers to instruct the people of other lands, and physicians to heal them in the name of the Master, it would be sufficient to send Christians abroad merely to live before the heathen, and show how Christ's conception of life can make men live; and their lives would be a spring pouring forth constantly of that which refreshes and invigorates.

CHAPTER VI.

"THY KINGDOM COME," IN THE HOME AND SOCIETY.

Auditorium, Thursday Afternoon, July 8.

The meeting in the Auditorium was presided over by Dr. Clark in his usual happy way, and the subject, "Thy Kingdom Come, In the Home and Society," was one that was near to every Endeavorer's heart. After the service of praise and prayer, the Rev. William M. Anderson, D. D., pastor of the First Presbyterian Church of Nashville, Tenn., spoke on "The Influence of the Home in Bringing in the Kingdom." He presented the' subject in a masterful way, and was listened to with rapt attention by the large audience. He said in part:

The individual and the home are the units in God's calculations for the race. They are the basis for his plans in working. The solution of their problems will solve the problems of the race.

My exact theme is "The Influence of the Home in Bringing in the Kingdom." This will lead us to examine into

1. *The nature, character, and conditions of the Kingdom.*
2. *The nature of the relation of the home to the race.*
3. *The nature of the relation of the home to the church.*

The kingdom of God is the end and motive of all divine manifestations and institutions of the Old and New Covenants; yea, of the creation and promise from the beginning.

Now the greatest human agency for the solving of all problems that concern mankind and ushering in the Kingdom is the home. The home is God's conception. He designed it. He prepared for its related parts. He adjusted its every relationship. He thus planned for the limitless and irresistible influence which it was to use in the life of mankind.

The home is a place—the place—the only place of abiding happiness. As Robert Burns said:

> "To make a happy fireside clime
> To weans and wife,
> That's the true pathos and sublime
> Of human life."

If one cannot be happy at home, one cannot really be happy anywhere. God is a happy God. He desires and designs that we should be happy, and he has so arranged it that unless we or those about us are at fault, our home life can and will be made happy. To Adam, our first parent, Paradise was home, and to all his righteous descendants home is Paradise.

We should do well to study the sanctity of marriage. Marriage is a social compact because civil society is builded upon the purity and perpetuity of marriage, and recognizes the relationship as soon as it is established.

46

Marriage is also a civic contract, inasmuch as the state for the welfare of human society must recognize and enforce it in its civil relationships and consequences. But marriage is more than a social compact or a civil contract,—it is a divine ordinance. It is a religious contract under a divine constitution.

Such a conception as this reveals the gigantic character of God's purpose when he set the home to perpetuate the race, and in large measure solve the problems confronting it, and thus form the conditions of ushering in the Kingdom.

The home is a school. In its ideal form it is admirably fitted with excellent teachers, who have an abundance of love and a sufficiency of wisdom for the discharge of all their duties. Within the home the greatest lessons are taught; and the enduring principles of truth are implanted like seeds in the characters of the children. The facts of life, science, and truth are taught and demonstrated in a way to make permanent impressions. And all this teaching is done in the most impressionable and most valuable period of the student's life. Ideas of order, system, economy, and courtesy are implanted and nurtured into the healthy growth of a well-rounded character.

The home is also a state—the germ state—wherein are begun the development of those elements which mature into good citizenship. Within the home they learn of law and its enforcement; they learn that individual welfare is coupled with the welfare of others. They learn one of the most valuable lessons of life, that is, obedience to law. An obedient child in the home will develop into a law-abiding citizen; while a reckless, wilful, spoiled child in the home will become a dangerous citizen.

The home is also a church—the germ church—wherein are first taught the lessons of prayer, devotion, and worship. Every home ought to be consecrated to God. Its daily life ought to include a time of worship. The relation of its inmates should be established and controlled by a religious devotion to each other. As a church it ought to furnish systematic instruction along the lines of truth and practical living. It ought to demonstrate practical righteousness.

In the thought and plan of God, the home is a kingdom. God has arranged to have preside there the best king and queen of all earthly sovereigns. That prevails in the home kingdom which does not prevail in any other earthly kingdom—namely, the subjects are all blood kin. Cords of love bind them together. Love rules on the throne and leads the king and queen to become the servants of the subjects.

The home and the church are the means which God has ordained to prepare citizens for the Kingdom.

The church is a body of believers banded in love for service. It is the high school of religion.

Now the home is the primary school of the high school, the church. It prepares for and should lead up to the church. It virtually gauges the standard, type, and degree of religion in the church. There cannot be more religion in the church than there is in the home. The stream cannot rise higher than its source.

Our great desire and aim should be to develop religion in the home. This demands that the father and mother shall be practical working Christians. And the central institution of the home must be a family altar, where religious devotion is nurtured, and religious knowledge is imparted. The daily conduct of the parents must speak a louder religious message than any words they could utter. There should be established the fullest, freest confidence between parents and children.

If we can bring our home life up to a high religious but reasonable standard, we will have lifted the life of the church up to a high plane, and begin to answer in fact our oft-repeated prayer "Thy kingdom come."

The conditions of royal citizenship are developed in the heart, manifested in the home, effective in the work of the church, and prophetic
to the race of a coming kingdom.

Dr. Clark requested the singing of the convention hymn
of Great Britain, "Let the tide come in." It was new to American Endeavorers, but in a few minutes, under the leadership
of Mr. Foster, they were singing it heartily. Then followed a
short season of prayer for God's blessing upon the home life,
and singing softly a verse of "Home, sweet home."
The Hon. William Jennings Bryan, of Lincoln, Neb., was
the next speaker. Dr. Clark, in introducing him, said, "On
such a platform as this he belongs to every one of us, and we
all belong to him."
Mr. Bryan's subject was "Religion and Life."

I esteem it a privilege to meet with you this afternoon. In coming
to take part in these proceedings I am but paying a small part of the debt
that I owe to religion. If there is anything in me that is worth having, if
there is anything in me that is worth keeping, if there is anything in me
that will outlast the years, it is the religious convictions, the religious principles, that were deeded me by a Christian father and mother when I
was but a child. If by coming here and presenting my testimony with
yours, I can render any service at all to the church, to society, and to my
God, I am only doing my duty when I give and render that service.
The subject assigned to me is "Religion and Life." I am not sure
that I should have written it that way if I had been writing it. It seems
to me that the subject is too long; why put the word "and" in there?
for religion and life are really one and the same thing. Take religion
out of life, and there is nothing left worth living; and you cannot separate
life from religion. Tolstoi says that religion is the relation that man
fixes between himself and his God, and that morality is the outward man-
ifestation of that inward relation. We know of our relations to God by
our own feeling, by our own experience; but man knows of our relation
to God only by our lives. Morality is, I believe, the outward manifesta-
tion of that inward relation that man fixes between himself and his God.
There are those who think that morality can be built upon a material-
istic foundation. There are those who think that reason is a sufficient
guide. There are those who think that one can argue himself into the
conviction that it pays to do right. But there are several objections, if
you would have a morality without a religion. In the first place, there
never was a system of morality resting upon reason alone. In the end
of things, there cannot be, for there are no people anywhere, who have
knowledge enough to talk of a system of morality, who are not already
so saturated with the morals derived from a religious system that they
are not in a position to frame a system with religion left out.
And then, again, we cannot analyze a man's decision to do a thing,
or not do it, and determine how much rests on reason, and how much on
other things.
Still again, we have not time in this busy life to stop and investigate
each case and decide how a good deed to some one else will come
back in blessing to us. You cannot build a noble life upon arithmetic.
We have dwelt upon this text. The point I want to make, the
thought I want to leave, is that religion is the dominant end in every
human life, and just in proportion as that note sounds true, the life is
a success. It makes all the difference in the world whether a man is

TORAJI MAKINO, OUR JAPANESE DELEGATE, AND HIS FAMILY.

THE FOUR HAWAIIAN DELEGATES.

simply trying to conform his life to the public opinion about him, or endeavoring to formulate his life to a definite standard. The man who does right only when he thinks people are looking is sure to find a day sometime when he thinks the people are not watching; and then he takes a vacation, and falls. I am not an old man, but I am old enough to have seen many start out with brilliant prospects and fall, and I have yet to see the first real failure in life that was not traceable to a breakdown in morals of the man. Man needs the inner strength that comes from the conscious presence of an all-seeing God.

In the brief time that I have this afternoon—and it is a brief time—I want to suggest some of the things that I believe we can put into a Christian life at this time with advantage to ourselves, and with advantage to society, and advantage to our country.

A Christian life implies a willingness to abandon anything and everything that is wrong. Does that mean that one must live a life of sorrow and sacrifice? No. When Christ was defining his mission he said that he has come that we might have life, and have it more abundantly; and the world is learning that Christ came not to narrow human life, but to broaden it. God does not require of us the surrender of anything that contributes to man's highest good. A Christian life does not require the abandonment of anything that really makes for man's highest and best development. Christianity requires us to leave off some things that might be temporarily pleasant, but I do not regard it as a real sacrifice to give up an evening of pleasure that leaves a headache in the morning. I do not believe that one should envy the evil-doer. I repeat that religion does not require of a man the sacrifice of things material to his welfare.

The great Swiss, Carl Hilty, has written a book on "Happiness." He says in this book on "Happiness" that happiness is impossible unless one has some regular stated occupation that furnishes work for the hands, activity for the mind, and satisfaction for the conscience. Is it happiness that one wants? Then there is no surer way to secure it than to live a Christian life. For Christ gave us the ideal of service.

Service is the measure of greatness. It always has been true, it is true to-day, it always will be true, that he is greatest who does the most good, and service is the measure of happiness as well as greatness. If God had so arranged it that our happiness depended on what people would do for us, we should be apt to be disappointed; but, when he makes our happiness dependent on what we do for others, it is our own fault if we are miserable. If a man's happiness depends on what he gets out of the world, he is to be disappointed; but, if his happiness depends on what he puts into the world, then there is so much to do, he has no idle time on his hands, and only regrets he has not the time to do all his heart would prompt him to do. My friends, I believe that just now we need more than anything else in this country the exemplification of Christian teaching in Christian life.

If I attempted to show in how many different ways a Christian conscience can busy itself in correcting dishonesty, I should exhaust the time at my disposal, but not exhaust the subject. I simply suggest it; let me apply it in another direction.

I believe that one of the things that the Christian conscience has to deal with is the drink habit. It is not sufficient for the Christian to say that he can drink in moderation without injury to himself; that is a physical question, and a great many people have been mistaken about their capacity for drink. There is a moral question that is larger than the physical question. Again, no Christian drinks without injury to people who accept his example and follow his example to their own injury. if they are weaker than he is. I do not say that taking a glass of liquor, wine, or beer is a sin. We have never affirmed that it is a sin for a

man to take a glass of liquor, but I do say that a man whose appetite
for liquor is stronger than his love for his fellow man cannot say with the
apostle, "If eating meat make my brother sin, then I will eat no meat."
If I were talking with Christians on the subject of temperance, I would
impress this idea upon them, that, if a Christian loves his fellow man, he
must try to help him, and I know of no better way to help than to set
an example. So live that others, seeing your good works, may glorify
the Father, and where can we better begin than in setting an example in
regard to total abstinence? I think we ought to cultivate such a sentiment in this country that the fear of offence would be on the other side,
—in offering the drink, not in refusing it.

I do not want the Catholic Church to be ahead of the Presbyterian
Church. I want the Presbyterian Brotherhood that is recognized in this
country to have a total-abstinence committee. I believe in conscience. I
think it is a good thing to have different churches. I would not, if I
could, bring all the Christians of this country together in one church. I
think it was Beecher who said that God might have made all the flowers
of one color; but he liked variety, and the world was more beautiful because there were flowers of different hues and different shapes. And so,
my friends, I believe that these churches are reaching the people.

My friends, I have faith in conscience. I believe it is the most potent
force of which man is possessed, and the church is the power to reach
the conscience. The pastor in his pulpit, the layman in his work, and the
members working through various organizations, are in a position to take
hold of the young life of this nation, and by starting it aright save millions of lives from the wrong that creeps on almost unconsciously with
the drink habit.

Then there is another direction in which I think the Christian spirit
can manifest itself; it is in the matter of gambling. In my own opinion,
it is harder to reform a gambler than a drunkard. A man who gets into
the habit of getting money for nothing, of wanting the things of chance,
is finally incapacitated for any honest, honorable employment, and I believe
one work that we can do in this organization is to show up the vices of
gambling. We must teach our children that the whole spirit of gambling
is wrong. If I understand what Christianity means, it means that you
must give something to the world when you take something from the
world. If I understand God's law of rewards, it is, that a man is entitled
to draw from society only in proportion as he renders a service to society.
If the Christian church is not big enough to array itself against gambling,
it had better resign and invent a religion that can touch the hearts of men
and govern them.

CHAPTER VII.

JUNIOR AND INTERMEDIATE INTERNATIONAL UNION SESSION.

House of Hope Presbyterian Church, Thursday Afternoon, July 8.

One of the largest and most enthusiastic conferences of the Convention was that of the Junior and Intermediate International Union. In a lecture-room crowded with that bright and happy class of Endeavorers who are always to be found in the ranks of Junior and Intermediate workers a most interesting programme was enjoyed. After a service of song led by Prof. E. O. Excell and an opening prayer by Mr. William Shaw, general secretary of the United Society, who presided, the usual business of the Union was transacted.

Much to the regret of all present, Rev. William T. McElveen. Ph.D., of Evanston, Ill., who was to have delivered the opening address on "The Relation of our Bodies to Soul-Growth—What Our Boys and Girls Ought to Know, and How Shall They be Told?" was unable to be present on account of the serious illness of his wife.

Miss Lillian E. Hayes, Junior superintendent of the Indiana Christian Endeavor Union, took charge of the conference, and introduced Mrs. Charles Hutchison, Junior superintendent of the Ohio Christian Endeavor Union, who gave a most interesting address on "The Kind of Religious Appeal to Make to Children." Mrs. Hutchison, using as an illustration the deep and underlying foundations of the Singer Building of New York City as the means by which the safety of the entire superstructure was safeguarded and made possible, showed how the religious life and training of the child are absolutely essential as the foundation of the future church. Amongst other things she said that this feature of the life of the boys and girls is very little understood and appreciated, that we must get in touch with it by studying their various needs in connection with their varying ages; study their mental capacity, making much of their inherent powers of imagination, so as to present by illustration religious truths, thus making them real; and, further, we must study the heart life of the child, and by the power of love win him or her into a love for his Father in heaven, and by the life of the Junior

51

or Intermediate superintendent furnish the best living example of what it means to love and live for Jesus.

Mother Endeavor Clark, in her inimitable way, and enlivening her address by many a pointed illustration, gave a most helpful talk on "The Kind of Religious Service to Place before Children." Among the many practical suggestions given were the following:

The meetings of Junior or Intermediate societies, whenever held, should be orderly and reverent all through the service, and especially at the commencement, as the beginning most frequently determines the character of the whole meeting. Use a regular planned and printed service whenever possible. Meetings should always, of course, be intensely interesting. The use of the blackboard and object-teaching was emphasized as one way of impressing a truth through holding the attention. Stories, and especially Bible stories, were also urged. The children are always to have some definite part or thing to do in the meeting, and especially in leading it; but only those who are honestly trying to keep their pledge being allowed to lead (thus putting an emphasis on faithful pledge-keeping), and also only after such leaders shall have had a quiet personal talk with the superintendent on the topic; thus not only helping the leader, but also enabling the superintendent to get into the heart of the child. In the meeting they should always have an opportunity to express their own thought, or answer some question previously given, or read a verse. Always give the children a part in the planning of the meetings and of the work of the society. Mrs. Clark especially emphasized the point that all of this work should be done with the underlying thought of winning the child to Jesus Christ.

Miss Lillian E. Hayes conducted an open parliament, bringing out from the audience the following helpful suggestions for the work:

On "How to conduct Junior meetings" among the answers were, "Through object-lessons, costumes, maps, blackboards, etc."

"How raise money?" "Have the children earn what they give, giving as examples the raising of chickens and selling of eggs, and also the raising of garden truck where practicable and selling the same."

"How arouse interest in hot summer months?" "By holding the meetings in the open air, using the back yard of the superintendent or some worker, with the added inducement of lemonade and a wafer."

"When hold business meetings?" "Whenever will best suit the circumstances of the children, and always combined with some social feature."

"How secure the pastor's help?" "By his attendance at the prayer meeting, at socials; by using the Juniors in his church service; and by once a year devoting a special service in the church to the Junior work."

On "What should Juniors do outside of their prayer meeting?" the illustration was given of the example furnished by the St. Paul Juniors, who not only made pictures and scrapbooks, but were given the privilege of taking them to the hospitals and cripples' homes and giving them themselves and spending an afternoon in the various institutions.

"What special religious features for the children?" Amongst other things were "premiums for bringing in new members, special revival services for the children," and, along the line of instruction, sending a special Junior or Intermediate regularly to the business meetings of the older society; and without making it at all compulsory give an opportunity for voluntary attendance (when the meetings are held Sunday afternoons) for the Juniors to attend a prayer-meeting service during the week.

In the discussion on what new plans should be advanced for the coming year it was felt that it would be more advantageous to improve the weak places of last year. The time of the session was all too short for all who desired to participate in this meeting, and after the Mizpah benediction the workers dispersed, realizing that the most necessary as well as the most promising work of the Christian Endeavor movement is with and for the boys and girls.

CHAPTER VIII.

THE WOMAN'S CHRISTIAN TEMPERANCE UNION AND ITS WORK.

The Armory, Thursday Afternoon, July 8.

Rev. Frederick D. Power, of Washington, D. C., presided, and introduced the speaker, Mrs. Bessie Laythe Scovell. He said that half of America to-day is "dry"; thirty-eight million are in prohibition territory against six million in 1893. Last year fifteen thousand saloons were put out of business. Besides this, "coercive prohibition" covers many thousands, where great corporations, railroads, for example, will not allow their employees to drink either on or off duty. The great forces that have wrought this revolution are in large measure such organizations as the Anti-Saloon League, the Christian Endeavor Society, and the Woman's Christian Temperance Union.

Still, we need to gird our loins and keep our faces toward the foe. A single State, the Empire State of New York, pays $17,000,000 for license to sell rum to eight million people, while all Protestant Christians give but $17,000,000 to send the gospel to one billion heathen people. Washington, the United States capital, is yet without prohibition, and there are signs that the full spirit of the great apostle has not yet fallen upon St. Paul.

Mrs. Scoville, president for twelve years of the Minnesota Woman's Christian Temperance Union, delivered an able address as follows:

It seems most fitting that this great, broad, large-hearted Christian Endeavor organization, whose very name includes every effort to Christianize the world, should hold this "Exposition of Civic, Moral, and Religious Progress" in its International Convention. As president of the Minnesota Woman's Christian Temperance Union, and on behalf of the four thousand women whom I represent, I greet you and bid you welcome to the capital of our State. May your coming to us be an inspiration to every young man and woman in Minnesota to make the highest Christian endeavor, that His kingdom may come and His will be done in this "land of waters." As one of the vice-presidents of the National Woman's Christian Temperance Union, and on behalf of the 300,000 followers of this great organization, I greet you and wish you God-speed. On their behalf, on behalf of my own State, and in the name of the Christ, who died for poor bruised humanity, I ask your co-operation in helping to remove the greatest hindrance to the coming of his kingdom—the licensed liquor traffic, that soul-corrupting, man-destroying business.

"Thy Kingdom Come" is your Convention motto, and is the prayer of all our hearts, but it never will come until Christian men everywhere shall quit voting damnation to the souls and bodies of men by voting for the saloon. In heathen India, with 300,000,000 souls, 22,000 human lives are destroyed on the average every year by poisonous snakes, which bite and kill the people. Heathen India worships the snake, and protects its life. In the Christian United States, with only 86,000,000 souls, we kill on the average every year 100,000 of our splendid citizens with our licensed saloons. We protect the saloon, and do not allow its destruction.

Thirty-six years ago in this nation there burst forth the Woman's Crusade, from the pent-up agony of women's hearts. Women have always suffered more than men from the liquor traffic, physically, mentally, and financially. On an average about 3,000 wives are murdered annually by drunken husbands. Then there are a vast number who escape death who are battered and bruised. The husband, who is seeing snakes and all the demons of the infernal regions, from delirium tremens, surely suffers mentally, but not as the wife suffers, with her clear brain, who can see the physical, mental, and moral degradation of her loved one. Her mental suffering is keener by far than that of the one whose sense of suffering is in every way blunted by the alcohol which causes all this misery.

No wonder, then, that women have organized to fight the foe of their own and their children's happiness.

The National Woman's Christian Temperance Union was organized in 1874, and is the organized outgrowth of the Woman's Crusade. Miss Frances E. Willard was the first corresponding secretary, and laid the plans of the organization. Wherever a few women believed in total abstinence, a union was organized. In 1879 Miss Willard was elected the president of the National Woman's Christian Temperance Union, and served in that capacity for nineteen years.

Eleven years ago last February 17, Frances Willard swept through the gates of glory, saying, "How beautiful it is to be with God!" The liquor men then predicted that in ten years after the death of Frances Willard the Woman's Christian Temperance Union would be dead. They hoped it would be true. But from then till now there has never been a national convention but there has been reported a net gain of from 3,000 to 20,000 new members. We are not dead, nor will we die as an organization until the last saloon is outlawed, until the manufacture and sale of intoxicating liquors for beverage purposes are stopped. Mrs. Lillian M. N. Stevens, of Portland, Me., has been the efficient national president since the home-going of Frances Willard.

There are two great branches of the Woman's Christian Temperance Union: The Young Woman's Christian Temperance Union and the Loyal Temperance Legion.

The Woman's Christian Temperance Union has six great lines of work, under which are grouped forty departments, each with a capable national superintendent who is an expert in her department.

I. Organization, under which line we seek to organize the Christian womanhood of the nation into active, aggressive warfare against the saloon.

II. Preventive, under which come two great departments, Health and Heredity, and Medical Temperance. Under the first we give instruction in the laws of health in relation to dress, food, air, exercise, cleanliness, sanitation, ventilation, mental and moral hygiene. The Medical Temperance department presents the teachings of eminent physicians who discard alcohol as medicine. It also seeks to educate the public as to the dangers of self-medication with powerful drugs, especially in the form of patent or proprietary medicines.

III. Education, under which are grouped fifteen departments, including the Bureau of Scientific Temperance Investigation and the Department of Scientific Temperance Instruction in\ Public Schools and Colleges, Physical Education, and Temperance Work in the Sunday Schools.

IV. Evangelistic, with fourteen departments.

V. Social, under which head are grouped Social Meetings and Red-letter Days, Flower Missions, and Fairs and Open-air Meetings.

VI. Legal, with the following departments: Legislation, Christian Citizenship, Franchise, and Peace and International Arbitration.

The following is our Declaration of Principles:

"We believe in the coming of His kingdom whose service is perfect freedom, because his laws, written in our members as well as in nature and in grace, are perfect, converting the soul.

"We believe in the gospel of the Golden Rule, and that each man's habits of life should be an example safe and beneficent for every other man to follow.

"We believe that God created both man and woman in his own image; and therefore we believe in one standard of purity for both men and women, and in the equal right of all to hold opinions and to express the same with equal freedom.

"We believe in a living wage, in courts of conciliation and arbitration, in justice as opposed to greed of gain; in 'peace on earth and good will to men.'

"We therefore formulate and for ourselves adopt the following pledge, asking our sisters and brothers of a common danger and a common hope to make common cause with us, in working its reasonable and helpful precepts into the practice of every-day life:

"*I hereby solemnly promise, God helping me, to abstain from all distilled, fermented, and malt liquors, including wine, beer, and cider, and to employ all proper means to discourage the use of and traffic in the same.*

"To confirm and enforce the rationale of this pledge, we declare our purpose to educate the young; to form a better public sentiment; to reform, so far as possible, by religious, ethical, and scientific means, the drinking classes; to seek the transforming power of divine grace for ourselves and all for whom we work, that they and we may wilfully transcend no law of pure and wholesome living; and finally we pledge ourselves to labor and to pray that all these principles, founded upon the gospel of Christ, may be worked out into the customs of society and the laws of the land."

In the thirty-five years we have been organized we have originated the idea of scientific temperance instruction in the public schools, and have secured mandatory laws in every State in the Union, and a federal law governing the District of Columbia, the Territories, and all Indian and military schools supported by the government. Three hundred and fifty thousand children are taught scientific reasons for total abstinence in the Loyal Temperance Legions, and become trained temperance workers through that branch of the work.

Since 1898, twenty-five thousand purity meetings have been held, and sixty thousand White Cross and twenty-eight thousand White Shield pledges have been signed. Twelve million pages of literature have been distributed by this department alone.

There have been held more than fifty thousand medal contests by our young people, which have given as many evening programmes of recitations and songs advocating total abstinence and prohibition before large audiences. The number of prohibition votes made by these and the essay contests cannot be estimated.

Wherever there is a State campaign for statutory prohibition or constitutional amendments, the Woman's Christian Temperance Union has been one of the chief working factors. We have petitioned for and secured the raising of the age of protection for girls in nearly every State in the Union. Anti-cigarette laws have been secured in many States.

The Woman's Christian Temperance Union will continue its work of organization, agitation, and education until public sentiment is raised to the power of the prohibition of the manufacture and sale of intoxicating liquors, until the homes of the land are protected from the ravages of the liquor traffic. When the death-knell of the last saloon is sounded, we believe the church of Jesus Christ on the earth will move forward by leaps and bounds. Woman will then be freed from at least fifty per cent of the charity work she now must do. She will be freed from the money-making schemes to raise funds to support the minister and the missionary. When the $1,400,000,000 which now goes annually into the saloon tills is kept in the pockets of the citizens, we feel sure some of it will find its way into God's treasure-house in tithes and thank-offerings until there will "be meat in mine house, saith the Lord," and woman will be free to be the spiritual aid to the church which she ought now to be. So we ask the co-operation of every Christian Endeavorer in helping us sweep this evil from the land as quickly as possible, that "His kingdom may come." We want your prayers, your love, and your ballots. We want you to help make this great map of ours "all white." Sing this song with us until it becomes your song.

CHAPTER IX.

PATRIOTIC MEETING ON THE CAPITOL STEPS.

Thursday Afternoon, July 8.

Mounted police, police on foot, an automobile in which rode Dr. and Mrs. Clark, Mr. Bryan, and several Christian Endeavor leaders, followed by thousands on thousands of Christian Endeavorers by countries and States—such was that great march to the State Capitol.

Had there been a marshal every forty feet to keep the line and lead in singing, what a mighty impression that march of thousands of young people would have made! But they did make a mighty impression even with their uneven marching and intermittent singing. The favorite song was "Onward, Christian soldiers." You could hear it from the front ranks, back, back, a half-mile back, "Onward, Christian soldiers," answered by "Like a mighty army moves the church of God." As the procession swept around to the front of that beautiful Capitol, one felt as if the architectural grandeur of marble and stone were challenging the young men and women of the race that had conceived it and given it birth. How stately it is! How calmly the great dome looks down upon the coming thousands, but how exultantly!

Up to the speakers' flag-draped stand come the men of yesterday, to-day, and to-morrow; men who have a message to these thousands, and men who will live in their message and their deeds for long. There is Governor Johnson. How one's heart thrills as he remembers the life-story of early struggle and later victory. William Jennings Bryan is there. Great Bryan! Never defeated! Others fail in political struggle, and go to oblivion. He never will. He has a message. He has a gospel of good citizenship that must be preached. Dr. Clark, the Father of Endeavor, is there, the man through whom millions of young people have discovered themselves. Others are there—but they begin to sing, that great multitude, "I'm here on business for my King." Are they? What King? Who calls them? Another song bursts forth, "Where he leads me, I will follow." Wherever their King leads shall they follow? Then they march to victory, for their King is King Jesus.

Still the procession comes on, State following State with

banners flying. One State sings, "Glory, glory, hallelujah." Another sings, "I will go with him all the way."

From the Capitol front comes the Coronation hymn, "All hail the power of Jesus' name." Ah! that is the song. Blessed Jesus! Regnant Jesus! Take our praise, thou blessed Saviour!

But Indianapolis comes up cheering. Duluth answers. Tennessee sweeps by, and echoes the words:

> "We'll join the everlasting song,
> And crown him Lord of all!"

Listen! What is that?

> "My country, 'tis of thee,
> Sweet land of liberty,
> Of thee I sing."

Who sings it? Ah! Massachusetts and Maine and New Hampshire, heart of old New England. How they sing! The vast audience catches it. Minnesota knows it, and Texas. The plains have heard it before and loved it. Majestic Mississippi sings bass in the choir. What a country! What a heritage! What soldiers of the cross! O church of Christ, see! see! And use this army, and win this nation for its Christ. The hope of the conquest is in your young people! The anthem rolls on;

> "Let music swell the breeze."

It is swelling. Eyes have grown bright; hearts have gained strength. But a new note creeps in;

> "Our fathers' God, to thee,
> Author of liberty,
> To thee we sing!"

Did you see that upward glance of the moist eyes, that new light on those faces? A quartette of native Hawaiians sing their national anthem.

Bishop Fallows prays. "And at last may we be among that great throng which no man can number, gathered about thy throne." How the mind leaps from this great throng of earth to that vastly greater one of heaven!

Secretary Shaw reads letters from Hon. George Nicholls, M. P., of London, England, and Ambassador Bryce, both expressing deep regret for their forced absence. Well might they regret. It is a life-opportunity to speak to such a company.

One might not hear all the words they wrote. The great crowd and great Capitol were speaking, though silent. Those stone eagles, perched on the base, where rested the dome of the building, were looking off over the throng and the city and the river and the hills, and were looking up to the blue. We followed their look with understanding, swelling hearts.

Once again the crowd is singing, this time the "International Hymn":

"Two empires by the sea,
Two nations great and free,
One anthem raise."

Not more heartily do they sing than when "America" was flung to the breeze, but somehow there is a deeper note:

"One race of ancient fame,
One tongue, one faith, we claim,
One God, whose glorious name
We love and praise."

You get the meaning of the deeper note when the leader swings that song into "Blest be the tie that binds our hearts in Christian love." Not that we love America less, but that we love Christ's kingdom more.

Dr. Jones of India brings the greetings of three thousand fellow Endeavorers.

Dr. Clark rises to introduce the man that great throng is waiting to hear. "We have come to hear an eloquent voice, our Christian statesman, William Jennings Bryan." How they cheer! How the flags wave! One man to speak to thousands and thousands. Can he hold them?

"This great gathering has a significance that ought not to be lost on this country. This great Christian organization means the application of religion to the social order."

It is the voice of a virile statesman speaking to the heart of this strangely virile young nation. "If the things we plead for are wrong, it is better for us to be defeated. If we are right and are defeated, we ought to have faith to believe that right will triumph yet." So he goes on teaching the gospel of good citizenship. How that great throng held on to his words! They knew their teacher, and were eager to learn, those splendid young thousands.

The speaker's face glows with intensest earnestness. The lines deepen to passion, as he pleads for righteousness in the government of this great, new land.

The people's faces have grown tense with emotion. They see the vision. They will respond.

Far above them on the Capitol the golden horses, eager for the plunge forward, are held in check by strong arms, picture of the powers and passions of this host of young men and women, ready and waiting.

Clouds come up, and sprinkles of rain fall; but the crowd does not move, for they hear him saying, "I have faith in the cause in which you are enlisted, and am with you."

His closing words are a challenge, a call, a prophecy, and, when the cheering has hushed, Mr. George Coleman, superintendent of the Patriots' League of Christian Endeavor, says, "I think I can pledge three and a half millions of Christian Endeavorers to the kind of doctrine Mr. Bryan has been preaching." An outburst of cheers tells that he makes the pledge not in vain.

Secretary Shaw, that inimitable leader, wanted a picture of that throng to be hung in the new Christian Endeavor building, soon to be erected in Boston. He told the crowd so, and asked it to face about. It did so. He wanted Governor Johnson to the front of the speaker's stand, and Mr. Bryan, with Dr. Clark standing between them. They stood there.

When the photograph was taken, that vast throng turned away to face life again. What ideals were formed, what visions seen! Now go, young men and women. Yes, go to work out your visions. East, West, North, and South, go! Go to the wheat-fields, to the mines, to the factories, to the colleges, to the homes. God goes with you, and America awaits your visions translated into deeds.

Mr. Bryan spoke as follows:

This gathering has a significance that ought not to be lost on this present age of the country. The men and women here assembled represent a mighty army, two and one-half millions of Christian Endeavorers in the United States, and three and one-half millions throughout the world; and this body represents but a part of the Christian activity and the enthusiasm of our country. Besides this organization we have the Epworth League, and we have various similar organizations representing denominations. We have the Young Men's Christian Association that is interdenominational, and we have the Knights of Columbus, representing the largest branch of the Christian church; and the main thought, the largest purpose, of each one of these organizations is the application of Christian ideals and Christian thought in the daily life, the social work, to politics and to government. I think I see evidences of a great awakening that is world-wide.

Charles Wagner with his "Simple Life" that was translated into almost every tongue was a strong protest against the materialism that has been making man a slave of his passion. What will be the result? No human being can tell the metes and bounds to a moral awakening. It begins with the individual, and is spread to all about him. An idea can revolutionize a man; he can revolutionize a community, a State, a nation, a world.

I believe that this great movement is destined to work in the home, in business, in politics, in government, and in international relations; and I am glad to take a humble part in this great gathering, and to extend my hearty sympathy with the work of the Patriots' League, which is a part of this Christian Endeavor movement. The application of Christian thought and of Christian purpose to life means the rejuvenation of the individual man and woman. It means that the home will be a higher type and better realization of what a home ought to be. It means that business shall be made more honest, that conscience will not be an outlaw in the counting-room or stranger in the marketplace. It means more than that. It means that the conscience will become a factor in the party life of the nation.

When nineteen hundred years ago Christ weighed the soul against all things else, and asked that question, "What shall it profit a man if he gain the whole world and lose his own soul?" he asked a question that arises wherever man deals with his fellow man, or wherever man comes into contact with his brother.

I am not a minister; if I were, there is one text that I would probably use more than any other. But, my friends, when I have a really serious case, when I have some wrong of gigantic proportions, and want to smite it with a blow that will tell, I always go to the Bible to get a quotation. There is no other book that contains so much of truth, and there is no other book in which truth is so justly expressed; and I might give another reason; there is no other book with which people are so familiar.

If I were a minister and seeking for a text, I should find it in the passage that says, "If a man say, I love God, and hateth his brother, he is a liar." The text is short, but the sermon would be long if I tried to show you how many liars there are. How can a man show his hatred of his brother? By his testimony? No. Very few men are convicted of crime on their own testimony; it is generally on the testimony of somebody else, and that testimony usually describes not what a man said, but what he did; and so, my friends, if I should try to show how many there are who falsely declare they love God, and prove the opposite of the declaration by their hatred of their brothers, I should show not only indifference to their brothers' welfare, but actual hatred against their brothers' welfare, and I could show it in many ways; but as we are here this afternoon under the auspices of the Patriots' League, I am only going to show it in politics and government.

We need parties in this country. We cannot get along without them. There must be organization among those who think alike if they would make their opinions effective. But, my friends, there is an honest plane upon which politics can be conducted, and I believe that, when this Christian spirit applies itself to political life, we shall find two things:— First, charity and respect for one another's opinion; and, second, honesty in the conduct of politics. No matter how sure we are that we are right, we ought always to recognize the fallibility of human judgment, and the possibility of error; and we ought to recognize in others the right to differ from us, and the possibility also that they are right and we are wrong.

And there is one way by which we can bring ourselves to be reconciled to the defeat of our party and our ideas. I do not mean in a personal and individual sense we can be reconciled, but it ought to be easy for any man to be reconciled if defeated in a country like ours. I had one touch of conscience this afternoon. We were to have a speaker, and I was anxious to hear him, and we find him attending to official cares. There is some consolation that official cares never keep me away. [Laughter.] There is a consolation that I think we could all find in defeat, and it is this: if the things we plead for are wrong, it is better for us to be defeated, and have our errors discovered while we are out of office, than to have been successful, and had our errors discovered in office. And, if we are right and are defeated, we ought to have faith to believe that right will triumph yet.

My friends, I believe that one of the results of this movement will be the purification of American politics, and I see signs already. Twelve years ago last fall it was considered perfectly proper for great corporations to contribute to campaign funds; now there is a law on the statute-books that makes it a penal offence for any corporation of any kind to contribute to a national campaign fund. I do not know what influence this organization may have had in bringing about that law, but I do believe that every word spoken for righteousness has its influence, and that no word for good government can be lost.

But this movement has gone farther. We have not only a law that prevents bribery and corruption, but we have a sentiment that demands publicity as to individual contributions; and this sentiment is so strong' that in the last campaign for the first time in American history the two leading parties recognized the right of the people to know what was going on, and the two leading parties through their organizations have opened their books and given the names of contributors.

But, my friends, the application of this principle of government means a reformation in the methods of government. We have seen people acting as if the government could be sold at auction, bid in, and then used by those who bid it. If I understand this movement of Christian patriotism, it means that there is going to be a clearer recognition of the fact that this nation must be just if it is going to be strong or have length of days.

Now, my friends, what is the application of this thought? It is that, when a city council has to act, the question is not what particular person will be benefited, but whether it is just or not; and, when a legislature has to act, the question is not what particular party will receive the greatest advantage, but whether it is just or not. I should not apply the thought to any party question; but it must be applied to every question, no matter what its kind or character, and I believe that one of the results of this great ethical movement is that we are going to lift our legislation to a higher plane.

But I shall not occupy your time longer. This is the third opportunity that I have had to speak to you to-day, and I do not want to take so much time as to recall the campaign days when I began in the morning and talked until morning came again.

I am here as one of your well-wishers, as one who wishes to stand shoulder to shoulder with you, and to march side by side with you in this work in which you are engaged. I believe that this Christian spirit is so large and so broad that we shall not only enlist all those who take the name of Christ and are followers of his example; but we will teach the world that Christianity is so broad, and its work so large, that all whose hearts are touched by the plea that Christianity presents have a higher manhood and womanhood, and the whole world are welcome to come and help us in the conversion so devoutly to be wished; and, if I mistake not, the results of our work will be so great that the cup of blessings will overflow the Christian nations, and all the sons of men will share in the good that is done.

CHAPTER X.

"THY KINGDOM COME," IN CIVIC AND SOCIAL LIFE.

Auditorium, Thursday Evening, July 8.

With Dr. Clark in the chair, Mr. Excell in charge of the music, and the Minneapolis Convention choir leading the vast Auditorium audience in the singing of the hymns, this session opened with the large promise for a profitable meeting that had characterized the preceding sessions. The promise was fulfilled as the meeting progressed. Dr. Clark, who has a fine facility for treating the Convention to surprises, had an unusual supply of them for this evening. They successfully filled the large gap in the programme due to the enforced absence of Mr. Nicholls, whom official duties in Parliament detained in London.

The many telegrams and cablegrams of greeting which Mr. Shaw read from Germany, France, England, Spain, Italy, Hungary, Iceland, Macedonia, Costa Rica, British Guiana, South Africa, Samoa, Australia, Cuba, the Philippines, and many places and organizations in America were a practical demonstration of the world-wide character of Christian Endeavor. This brotherly hand-shake from everywhere, this girdling the world with a fraternal hand-clasp, is one of the best things in Christian Endeavor. It reveals that this Society is one of the active and potent agencies for realizing the dream of the great apostle to the nations, to whom so many references were made in the Convention, when he said, "There is neither Jew nor Greek, there is neither bond nor free, there is neither male nor female, for ye are one in Christ Jesus."

Dr. Floyd W. Tomkins, of Philadelphia, who is so devoted to Christian Endeavor and every other good movement, and who is beloved by multitudes who have come under the spell of his great personality, made the one formal address of the evening. His theme was "The Kingdom Ideal Expressed in Social Life."

The newness of this ideal is evident when we reflect that it is within the memory of some of us that the main ideal of the Christian life was for each man to believe in God, love him, obey him, and finally to get to heaven. This ideal involved separation from the world, which was expressed in many various ways; but in whatever way it was expressed it meant,

64

MR. BRYAN AND HIS DOUBLE — The Rev. W. F. Wilson, D. D.,
one of the Trustees of the United Society.

UPON REACHING ST. PAUL.

"Come out from the world, and let the old world gang its own gait to its own destruction." Now all this is greatly changed. The Christian to-day sees that he belongs to his brother man, and with him is bound up in the bundle of life. The men who differ from him have a claim upon his love and sympathy. Even when he goes to non-Christian lands he no longer antagonizes the religious belief and life that he finds there; but he seeks to utilize it, to find what common ground it may offer for him and its adherents to stand upon, to employ its best on which to build the better things of our holy faith.

Thus Christianity is socialized, not to its degradation or loss of power, but to the widening of its horizon, the increase of its opportunities, and the vast extension of its influence and good repute.

Dr. Tomkins called especial attention to the new opportunities brought to the church along four lines by this social ideal of the Kingdom. They are opportunities in political life, opportunities presented by labor problems, opportunities in connection with morality, and opportunities presented by the advanced movements for the uplift of mankind.

Ministers are still criticised for "meddling in politics," but nevertheless politics offers them a great sphere for the application of the ethics of Jesus. It is their business and that of their fellow Christians to bring to bear upon their own political life and that of their community their Christian principles. Surely our daily prayer should include prayer for our own guidance in the performance of our political duties, and for all our rulers that they may be wise, holy, just in their official and private life.

The industrial world is the scene of the hand-to-hand struggle between mighty forces, represented by labor and capital. The church must show itself sympathetic with each side in so far as it may be right, but for many reasons the sympathy of the church for the laboring man should be made especially apparent. The church is really friendly to the working man, and he ought to be made to know it. The working men are not alienated from the church, and this will be more and more conspicuous if the church will work out the social ideals of Christianity. The Christian ought to seek for a fair, clear belief as to where the right lies in the various phases of this conflict, and aim to make the working man see the same.

In dealing with the moral issues, Dr. Tomkins called particular attention to temperance, social purity, especially as involved in the frightful prevalence of divorce, and dishonesty as shown in speculating and gambling habits, sweat-shop practices, and grinding the faces of the poor. He paid his respectful compliments to the wealthy women who go off to Europe and forget to pay their dressmakers and milliners before they go. He called attention to the fact, in discussing temperance, that there is an army of two and a half million of Christian Endeavor total abstainers in this country, and to the further fact that in the great prohibition reform which has swept over this country the Christian Endeavor hosts have borne an honorable and, in many places, a conspicuous part.

If we are to face our opportunities and responsibilities, Dr. Tomkins said we must have four characteristics. We must have high ideals, especially of the church and its work; we must have a broad, catholic love, which will embrace all classes and characters; we must have a magnificent consciousness of the power that we have through God for this work; we must have a magnificent hopefulness as to the issue of our endeavors.

Have a vision of God's great concern in all human affairs and every human interest. This is God's world, not the devil's. Everywhere are men and women for whom Christ died. Not one thing you do to bring in the Kingdom shall fail.

When Mr. Walter D. Howell, the secretary of the St. Paul committee, arose after Dr. Tomkins's address, to give some notices, he was accorded a reception that for heartiness amounted to a "demonstration," and must have been to him a gratifying appreciation of his great and efficient service in the interest of the Convention.

The traditional reputation of the Twin Cities for friendly rivalry had a beautiful illustration in the presence of a splendid choir of several hundred voices from Minneapolis, which sang with fine effect "Loudly unto the world is a chorus resounding," and "When peace like a river attendeth my way."

One of the surprises of the evening was the presentation by Dr. Clark to the Convention of seven members from the Williston Congregational Church, of Portland, Me., the original society of Christian Endeavor. Dr. and Mrs. Clark stood with them while on their behalf Mr. Hill, their pastor, spoke a few felicitous words.

Mr. George W. Coleman, superintendent of the Patriots' League, called attention to one of the banners on the wall, "Close the saloons in the national capital," and suggested that Endeavorers all over the country use their influence with the members of Congress from their districts. This movement to make our capital city a worthy example to the rest of the country received the enthusiastic approval of the whole audience of several thousand.

Rev. S. G. Inman, from Mexico, brought formal greetings from the national Christian Endeavor union of Mexico, then in session, reading a telegram just received from that convention. In citing evidence of the interest of these Mexican Endeavorers in their conventions, he said that many of them would walk three, four, five, or six days over mountains and plains from their homes to the convention city. There are now three thousand members of the Society in their republic, and the churches are taking a deep interest in this movement. One church has allowed its pastor to give the entire time of one month in three to the promotion of this work. He called attention to the fact that next year the republic of Mexico would celebrate its centennial, and stated that the Endeavorers were planning to make the celebration notable by securing the abolition of bull-fighting. He intimated that visiting Americans by their patronage did much to keep up this barbarous custom.

Mr. Inman brought with him as a gift to Dr. Clark a beautiful silk Mexican flag from the Christian Endeavor society of Monterey, which he presented to Dr. Clark on its behalf. This church has one of the largest Junior societies in the world, its membership being more than three hundred. In making the presentation Mr. Inman gave Dr. Clark a most loving embrace, the same being the salute common to his country. In accepting the banner Dr. Clark said it would be hung in the museum of the new Headquarters Building.

The evening, which might be styled the international night, was enriched by the brief but ringing message brought by Rev. Edward Marsden from his fellow Endeavorers, "For we are not ashamed of the gospel of Christ" being its key-word.

The meeting came to a close with a striking testimony from Rev. Daniel A. Poling, general secretary of the Ohio Christian Endeavor Union. He stated that he joined the first Christian Endeavor society west of the Rockies, and that, of the seven members that composed that society at that time, one is a missionary, one is the wife of a missionary, one is a minister, one a Christian Endeavor secretary, and the other three are active in church-work.

CHAPTER XI.

Central Presbyterian Church, Friday Afternoon, July 9.

A conference of the union workers in attendance at the Convention was held in the Central Presbyterian Church on Friday afternoon at two o'clock. Mr. William Shaw, general secretary of the United Society, was in the chair; and his presentation of the speakers was one of the most interesting features of the conference. The body of the church was well filled with a splendid audience.

At the beginning, at Mr. Shaw's request, many arose and introduced themselves to the othérs, representing most of the States and Canada. Prof. E. O. Excell led the singing. First of all a paper was read by Prof. Amos R. Wells, the editor of "The Christian Endeavor World" and various Christian Endeavor publications. His subject was "How to Get Together." Mr. Shaw introduced him as an animated fountain pen attached to a big head that was full. Prof. Wells spoke as follows:

I am to talk about how to get together. And first we must find out what is meant by getting together, for, like many other common phrases, people are likely to use this one in a general way that signifies nothing in particular.

In a word, getting together is helping one another. You cannot help one another unless you sympathize with one another's purposes, join in one another's plans, bear one another's burdens, co-operate in one another's work. Husband and wife get together when they seek the same goal hand in hand. Business partners get together when each is willing to defer to the other's judgment, and all pull as a single man for the welfare of the firm. Church and minister get together when they love each other, believe in each other, and sacrifice for each other and the great cause they both love.

This is the romance of human life, this getting together. This is the dynamic of existence, this getting together. This, in the highest sphere, is the supreme of religion, God and man getting together in the atonement. This is the climax of history, the nations getting together at the Hague. This is the perfection of society, men of all classes and occupations getting together in an effective human brotherhood. Getting together? Why, when you come to define it, what is getting together but the millennium?

After all these centuries, men are only beginning to get the idea of getting together. More than three millenniums since the Tower of

68

Babel, and only the past few years have seen any comprehensive and hopeful attempt at a universal language. Nearly two millenniums since Christ came into the world, and only within the past few years have his churches made a serious attempt at federation. All these ages of warfare among the nations, and only within the past decade has the beginning of the parliament of man become established at the Hague. Since the creation of man labor and capital have existed side by side, each for himself in selfish competition, and only recently have laborers begun to get together in profit-sharing establishments. These are the most important of human interests, and it is only in our lifetime that men have begun to get together in them. We are living in great days, days when for the first time the principles of Christianity have a chance to get tried on a large scale among men.

Who are to get together in Christian Endeavor, and how can we help them do it?

For one thing, certainly the societies are to get together. If they do not, who will? And the way to do that is to form Christian Endeavor unions. It may seem superfluous to say that to a set of union officers, but it is not. The number of Christian Endeavor unions in this country could be doubled in a year if all the unions already existing were awake to the opportunities for forming other unions that exist right around them.

So much for the societies. Whom besides are we to bring together? The Endeavors and the pastors. Most of them, I believe, are together already, but enough are apart to make this one of the most necessary and important tasks for Christian Endeavor unions. I know of no better way to bring the pastors and the Endeavors together than to appoint a live, sympathetic, influential pastor as the pastoral counsellor of your union. Then, having appointed him, utilize him. Get him to bring the pastors together in a conference on Christian Endeavor. At that conference talk it all out. Answer criticisms. Remove misunderstandings. Show the true spirit of Christian Endeavor. Keep up these conferences till the Endeavorers and the pastors understand one another, believe in one another, and work heartily toward the same ends; that is, till they have come together.

Whom besides are we to bring together? The denominations. Not all are represented in Christian Endeavor, but nearly all are, and more and more are coming in all the time. I firmly believe that some day the denominations will be one in Christian Endeavor, just as now they are one in the Sunday school, the Y. M. C. A., and the Young People's Missionary Movement. How can we best bring this about? By making the best use of the splendid denominational fellowship that we now enjoy. Let us make it so enjoyable and profitable that no denomination will want to remain out of it. Magnify this year our interdenominational fellowship. Have exchanges of leaders. Have union prayer meetings of neighboring churches of different denominations. Have union socials of these societies. Make much of your denominational representation at every union meeting. Set the Endeavorers to studying other denominations than their own, to learn from them. Do what you can to bring the denominations together, and, my word for it, the results of your consecrated and brotherly labors will be great beyond your highest imagining.

Whom besides are we to bring together? The Christian Endeavor forces of our States. We are to focus the local societies, the city, county, and district unions, and the State unions, upon our Christian Endeavor enterprises, whatever for the time they happen to be, and we are to make of the whole one splendid tool for the Master's service. To do this, correspondence is fine and a printed State bulletin is fine, but if you were to start out theoretically to devise the ideal plan for unifying the State work you would discover precisely the instrumentality that lies already at hand, namely, our State Christian Endeavor conventions. Let us go home, therefore, to push our next State conventions.

Whom besides are we to bring together? The States themselves. There are many things in which the State unions should be co-operating. We should come together in the dates of the State conventions and in our arrangements for speakers. Neighboring States should plan to have their conventions follow one another so closely that speakers may go from one to the other in an easily managed tour, and then the officers of the State unions in each group should agree upon a few leading speakers who will visit all the conventions in a circuit. For such a tour you could obtain speakers of the greatest eminence and ability, and at far less expense than if each union went at it alone. The States should lend their best workers to one another. The State workers should tell one another about their best plans, and consult one another about their difficulties.

Whom besides are we to bring together? All the Christian Endeavor forces and the United Society. That is the last point I shall make. I have saved it for the last because it is the most important. The United Society is the keystone of the arch of Christian Endeavor; upon the firmness of its relation to all the other Christian Endeavor forces depends the stability of the whole. Through all these years the United Society has originated many of the most fruitful plans for the work. The United Society is continually gathering up from the local societies and the various unions the very best plans that the workers have devised and proved. These collections are useless unless the United Society is in close touch with the workers everywhere and can communicate its discoveries to those that need them. Every enterprise must have a head, and the United Society is the head of Christian Endeavor; but the head must be in closest touch with the body. Even the separation of a fraction of an inch is fatal. If you don't believe that, try it.

And now how are we to bring the Christian Endeavor forces and the United Society together? Through Secretary Shaw and the United Society's paper for that express purpose, *Union Work*.

First, get in touch with Secretary Shaw. It is not easy for him to get and keep in touch with twenty thousand, but it is easy for each of the twenty thousand to get and keep in touch with him. It costs the United Society two hundred dollars to send even a postal card to each union officer, and the United Society has not many two hundred dollars to use for postage. A postal card will cost each of you just one cent. On a postal card you can put an interesting piece of union news. On a postal card you can report some method of work that you have found helpful. On a postal card you can put your latest statistics. If every union officer would write Secretary Shaw one postal card every three months, four postal cards a year, the cost in time and money would be very little to each, and the efficiency of the United Society in its work for the unions would be multiplied by ten at least.

And then, answer his letters! If you were in the same room with our beloved general secretary and he were to ask you a question, not one of you would be so boorish as not to answer, and answer at once. What do you call it when he asks you a question in writing, and you answer it ten weeks afterwards, when it is too late, or do not answer it at all? Ordinary politeness calls for the prompt answer of letters: but more than ordinary politeness, the kingdom of God calls for the answer of letters. Letters and their answers constitute one of the surest ways of getting together.

The other way of bringing your union work and the United Society together is through our monthly magazine for workers, *Union Work*. It is made up, from first page to the last, of little articles from the union officers themselves. Officers of all kinds of unions write for it,—city unions, Junior unions, foreign unions, county unions, district unions, State unions. And all kinds of officers,—presidents, secretaries, treasurers, superintendents of all sorts of departments, chairmen of all kinds of committees. They describe their best methods of work. They ask questions about their perplexities, and the questions are answered. They tell of their inspiring successes. It is simply impossible for any union worker to invest fifty cents to better purpose for his work than by subscribing for this paper.

And now I can sum it all up in Paul's famous saying, "We are members one of another." And we are to be the body of Christ. Oh, the inspiration of the thought—the body of Christ! Not his worn-out Palestinian body, wearied with the hard roads, wasted with hunger, racked with cruel pain, but the splendid body of his ascension glory, swift and strong and beautiful, ready for any task, equal to any burden, victorious over any foe. Then our plans will seek the same goal, for they will all be his plans. Then we shall work in harmony, for we shall be attuned to his will. Then we shall see eye to eye, and labor hand to hand, and the joy of one will be the joy of all, for we shall enter into the joy of our Lord. When may all this happen? Not when we get to heaven. Not in the millennium. Not next year. It may happen to-day. It may begin in this room.

The conference consisted in the main of what Mr. Shaw called "target practice with five-minute guns."

The first speaker was Mr. William Ralph Hall, field secretary for Michigan. He spoke on "The Christian Endeavor Union as an Educational Institution." He said that Christian Endeavor as an educational institution is to develop, first, the latent power in all the societies in the union along the lines of loyalty to Christ in prayer and Bible-study and mission-study and service; secondly, loyalty to the church in all its activities; and thirdly, loyalty to Christian Endeavor as an organization to be extended everywhere. The Christian Endeavor union should help the local society to the most efficient committee work, and should inspire personal work in every individual and society. This educational work may be extended by larger use of Christian Endeavor literature, especially "The Christian Endeavor World" and "Union Work," also through conferences and rallies and by State and national conventions.

The second speaker was Mr. H. Gordon Lilley, field secretary for Manitoba and Saskatchewan. His subject was "The Christian Endeavor Union as an Evangelistic Force." He discussed the aim of the church, and defined the church as God's agent for proclaiming the gospel in the world. The Christian Endeavor Society is one of the factors to train for this purpose. He spoke of the importance of the observance of the Quiet Hour. It is the business of our unions to see that societies are awake to this·purpose and active; to see that our lookout committees are soul-winning committees, and are not simply striving to add members to the society. This is the real object of the lookout committee. There might be planned and carried out a campaign for soul-winning led by the union, in which all the societies are enlisted. He asked, "Are you making your local-union rally for the unchurched as well as for Christians?" Here is something that may be accomplished in connection with our local-union conventions. He told of the success of outdoor gospel meetings in Winnipeg.

The third speaker was Rev. J. P. Anderson, president of the South Dakota Union. His subject was "How to Get Things Done." He said: "Doing things is the spirit of the age. Some things can be done in a hurry. It takes the Lord six weeks to make a squash, but a score of years to make an oak; that which is most worth while takes time. God expects us to do our best. For this we are to work, think, and pray. It is the persons of faith who do impossible things. It is wise to aim to get busy people on committees, for they will do things. Keep in touch with others who are doing things. To this end take 'Union Work' and other helps of the United Society. Get into touch with conventions, local, State, and international. Study methods, and· get the executive committee together to plan and then to do. Young people are ready to work when they are shown how. If you are to have failures, make failures in trying to do, and not in doing nothing.

The fourth speaker was Rev. Daniel A. Poling, field secretary for Ohio. He spoke on "Union Finances." He advised that the financial campaign for the union be carefully planned and then persistently worked. It was important to have a budget, and then get the money needed. In Ohio they have an apportionment of the county, and then raise the amount needed by card pledges. A considerable proportion was subscribed by Juniors. They had found it profitable to secure a band of volunteers to raise the money by personal solicitation, each agreeing to raise some definite amount. Finally he said that, if we allow the Spirit of God to vitalize the financial campaign, there will be no trouble in getting the money needed for his work.

The fifth speaker was Mr. A. J. Shartle, field secretary for Pennsylvania. He spoke on "Definite Campaigns, and How to Push Them." He said: "Christian Endeavor, whether in the local society or in local, district, or State unions, is an insurance against failure in the development of young people for the larger work of the church. It is well to concentrate the power of the local society in the local union, and use it to organize other societies throughout the State. In Pennsylvania in six months six county unions were organized, and one hundred and thirty-six new societies. Mr. Shartle believes that Pennsylvania will organize a thousand societies in the next two years, aiming to have a society in every community or church.

The sixth speaker was Mr. Karl Lehmann, field secretary for Colorado and New Mexico. He spoke on "Christian Endeavor in Print." He said there are three things that Christian Endeavorers are not doing. First, they are not utilizing the secular press as they should. He finds the press always ready to give space generously. Secondly, they are not using the Christian Endeavor papers as they should, especially "The Christian Endeavor World," "Union Work," and "Junior Work." And, thirdly, they are not using as they should the Christian Endeavor literature that is published. He said that in Colorado he had sold in one year more than five hundred dollars' worth of Christian Endeavor literature.

The seventh speaker was Mr. George W. Coleman, superintendent of the Christian Endeavor Patriots' League. His subject was "Our Unions and Civic Problems." He said that saloons and street corners are developing grafters and corruptionists all the time. Christian Endeavor is developing the finest types of citizens, who are to do something to rid the world of these. Politics is vital to each one of us, local, State, and national. To run a city government from the partisan standpoint is a failure; and a business administration, which so many are clamoring for, is not just what is needed. What is needed is a home administration. The city should be administered in the interest of the home. Water and light are furnished to all homes by the city; city government is housekeeping on a larger scale, so that all women should be interested, and must realize their responsibility in the matter as well as men. Then we must all learn to work with other people who are aiming for the same thing, with Jews and Gentiles, Catholic and unbelievers and every one who wants what is right.

The last speaker was Rev. Julian C. Caldwell, D. D., general secretary of the Allen Christian Endeavor League of the African Methodist Episcopal Church, Nashville, Tenn. His subject was "Christian Endeavor and Our Afro-Americans" He said: "I have been a member of the Christian Endeavor society since 1886. One year ago I was elected as head of the Allen Christian Endeavor League, which has 1,006 young people's societies in thirty-seven States and Territories." He said that one of the cardinal principles of the Christian Endeavor movement is fellowship in Christ. "I represent twelve million American citizens, who are in this country to stay because we were brought here, and it would be discourteous to go away. We are not asking for any special privileges, but simply a chance. Christian Endeavor has given us a chance to develop and grow and show the possibilities of men. It has taught us that one is our Master, even Christ, and all are brothers."

At the close of this "target practice" the cause of "The International Headquarters Building" was presented by Rev. R. P. Anderson, superintendent of the Builders' Union. He said that a most desirable lot had been secured and paid for. He showed the picture of the building proposed to be built, and asked that a campaign be started that would bring in the money to go ahead and build, for which one hundred and fifty thousand dollars is needed. This is something which is to be done at once, and must be done well. This building will bring a permanent income for the extension of Christian Endeavor around the world. The international headquarters is a personal affair, and the State unions can work through the district and local unions until every Endeavorer is reached and invited to co-operate.

Mr. William Shaw closed the conference by a heart-to-heart talk that was impressive and winning. He said that since he had been an Endeavorer he had seen Christian Endeavor grow from twenty-eight societies to the present worldwide organization, but he was sure that we had not yet had a vision of the possibilities in Christian Endeavor if all were unanimous in doing the things that need to be done. He told us that the officers of the United Society earn their own living, and that he himself, the general secretary, is the only paid officer; that the United Society has earned two hundred thousand dollars, which it has put into the extension of Christian Endeavor, and now it asks for less than that amount for an international headquarters that will enable them to do greater work in the future. Less money is asked for the headquarters building than one city spends for its Young Men's Christian Association building for the young men of that city, while this building is for all the world and for a society that develops Young Men's Christian Association workers and officers, and workers for all churches.

Mr. Shaw also spoke convincingly of the value of "Union Work," a most needed help to all union officers, which should be paid for out of the treasury of each local union and placed in the hands of every union officer.

He said that he considered "The Christian Endeavor World" a necessity for each Christian Endeavorer if he is to be the best success that he can be as an Endeavorer. He said in closing: "Let us be unanimous to win the young people of the world to Christ. Let us stand together."

The hearty applause that followed Mr. Shaw's earnest appeal ought to mean a speedy response along these lines.

CHAPTER XII.

THE JUNIOR RALLY.

Auditorium, Friday Afternoon, July 9.

The Junior Rally was one of the great events of the great gathering. The scene prior to the opening, the children in white, and wearing costumes expressive of the parts they were to take, and seated in companies in various parts of the hall, happy as birds, produced a pretty effect. The spectators cheered them over and over. At the moment for opening Mr. Percy S. Foster stepped to the front and announced the national hymn, "My country, 'tis of thee." The children joined in the song so heartily as to make the immense hall ring. Then came the children's song, "Jesus loves me; this I know." No sweeter song was rendered in that hall. Mr. Foster led in the opening prayer. Dr. Clark presided in his usual happy manner. He spoke of Christian Endeavor's hope through the Juniors. The Minneapolis Juniors gave the " Message of the Nations," in which the children of Great Britain and America sung their purpose to win the world for Christ; and, as they sang, representatives of the nations began to come with their appeal.

The " Bow of Promise," executed by five hundred children, members of the Junior Christian Endeavor societies of St. Paul, in the presence of several thousand delighted and enthusiastic spectators, turned out to be all that its name indicated and a great deal more. All the colors of the rainbow, painted on capes worn by the youngsters, and many varied combinations thereof, produced a kaleidoscopic effect of dazzling splendor. Marches and countermarches, which at the beginning gave promise of nothing but chaotic endings, suddenly and with the utmost precision turned out to be most picturesque arrangements of letters and figures.

Minneapolis, too, had no small part in the rare treat furnished. From the twin city came several hundred boys and girls, garbed to represent many countries. Happily and handily they went through their evolutions on the big floor of the Auditorium, and were rousingly applauded for their part in the entertainment.

The St. Paul boys and girls were led by Harold G. Lains.

Prof. Pease led the singing, and to him must great credit be given for the sweet music that came from the young, untried throats. The entire performance was conducted with the utmost care, and the result was all that St. Paul could have hoped for.

Ranged on either side of the stage were the boys and girls, the former in red capes and caps and the latter in multicolored capes hidden by a white top-piece. The caps of the girls were gold on one side and white on the other.

On the big stand in back were the girls who were to form the human rainbow. Their caps were of a color to match that which they were to represent in the showing of the spectrum. The performance began with the showing of the first color of the rainbow. At a signal from the floor a row of capes and caps were turned and the glowing red first appeared. As it did so the youngsters recited a verse from Scripture appropriate to what was being done.

Then came the orange, yellow, green, blue, indigo, and violet. And, as each color appeared, a verse of Scripture accompanied it. When all was completed, the effect was beautiful, and the audience broke into loud and prolonged hand-clapping.

Then came the singing of hymns, following which the boys and girls on the side seats, at a word from Mr. Lains, marched upon the floor, and after turning and twisting there for a minute or two suddenly formed the most realistic breathing monogram that Christian Endeavor has probably ever beheld. The applause that followed well repaid them; for it was spontaneous and sincere, and lasted several minutes.

The two stars came next, and these were formed just as carefully, with the same splendid result. The boys with their red formed the smaller of the two stars, and the girls in gold and white the larger. This was followed by the singing of several hymns, which was encored by the audience, and had to be repeated.

Then came the final outburst of color, which Dr. Clark, who presided, proclaimed the best work of the sort he had ever seen, and he asserted that he had seen many juvenile exercises of the kind in many lands. The boys in red marched up to places on the stand, half of them going way up in back and taking seats on a line perpendicular to other seats taken by more of the boys lower down. This formed the upright of the cross, and the line of red in the rainbow formed the bar.

The formation of the cloth of gold came next, and the girls who had taken part in the floor manœuvres found places around the cross and beneath the rainbow. When all was completed and the youngsters burst forth in one grand chorus that had been specially prepared for the occasion, the audience rose to its feet, and the applause was thunderous.

The effect was wonderful. From way back in the parquet it looked like a flood of light after a rainstorm, with the rainbow showing through the mist, and then, piercing its very middle and extending above and below it, was the blood-red cross. Backing up the whole was the golden hue of pure virgin gold. Directly back and to either side of the stand two crosses had been suspended from the balcony. They were made of a dull, soft green, and over them shone out the word "Duty" in electric-light bulbs. This added to the effect produced, and the whole was as dazzling and splendid a sight as St. Paul has ever beheld.

As the singing finished Dr. Clark arose to his feet, and with both hands extended on high asked the Almighty to bless the children and the kith and kin who had brought them into this work. This made the scene all the more impressive, and the audience joined in the prayer.

At the conclusion of the exercises Dr. Clark presented to the Knox Presbyterian Junior Society the banner of the St. Paul Christian Endeavor Union for the largest percentage of increase and the largest average attendance during the year. The increase of this society was 200 per cent, the attendance was 56 per cent, and 40 per cent of the Juniors took some original part in the meetings.

After prayer by Dr. Clark the meeting was closed with the use of the Mizpah benediction.

CHAPTER XIII.

"THY KINGDOM COME," IN CIVIC AND CHURCH LIFE.

Auditorium, Friday Evening, July 9.

"The Voices of the Denominations for Christian Fellowship" was the predominant thought at the Christian Endeavor meeting at the Auditorium, and fellowship was indeed the keynote, the genesis, and the exodus of the meeting, which began with the voice of the Presbyterians, uttered by Rev. Harry Noble Wilson of the Central Presbyterian Church, followed by many denominations represented by ministers of the respective creeds, and at the end the entire audience rose to their feet and every man grasped his neighbor's hand as each repeated:
"The Lord bless thee, and keep thee; the Lord make his face
    shine upon thee, and be gracious unto thee;
The Lord lift up his countenance upon thee, and give thee
    peace."
Men and women repeated it word for word with evident feeling and sincerity. On the platform ministers of every Christian denomination repeated it, and, standing on the very edge and directly facing the big crowd, Dr. Clark on the one side and Mr. Foster on the other clasped the hands of Bishop Fallows and repeated it.

The meeting abounded in beautiful sentiment. Fellowship, friendship, and citizenship, as suggested by Rev. J. H. Garrison of Mobile, Ala., who talked as the voice of the Disciples of Christ, was in the spirit of all that was said. The elimination of denominational lines and the unification in one church of all the peoples who follow the cross were the prophecy and hope of all the speakers.

More than a mere hope or prophecy was the resolution read by Rev. Howard B. Grose, who spoke as the voice of the Baptists. A movement that will probably have great significance in the religious world was announced when he made public the resolution passed at the First Baptist Church yesterday by the conference held there. It read:

"Resolved, That it is the sense of the Baptist young people, assembled in conference at the International Christian Endeavor Convention in St. Paul, Minn., July, 1909, that it would be to the advantage of our denominational life to take such steps as are necessary to bring about a close organic union among Baptist young people who are now organized as the Baptist Young People's Unions and Christian Endeavor societies.

"We believe that this end could be naturally and speedily secured if the Baptist Christian Endeavor societies would add the words 'Baptist Young People's Union' to their name; and all Baptist Young People's societies add 'Christian Endeavor' to their name, giving the common name 'Baptist Young People's Union of Christian Endeavor,' thereby opening the way for a united Baptist movement that will fully safeguard our denominational interests, and at the same time give us the added impetus of the world-wide movement that brings together the Christian forces of all denominations.

"We therefore express our cordial approval of such a course, and devoutly hope that this end may be achieved.

"Resolved, That this matter on our part be placed in the hands of a committee of three that shall carefully consider the details and confer with the Baptist Young People's Union and any other organizations that might be affected by such change."

The reading of this resolution brought the wildest enthusiasm. It means the beginning, was the report after the meeting, of a movement that will add hundreds of thousands of members to the Christian Endeavor societies all over the country. Dr. Grose expressed the opinion that the amalgamation would come speedily.

A pretty incident of the evening was the bringing of the heads of the Kansas City, Indianapolis, and Dallas delegations to the platform to say a word in praise of Atlantic City, their more fortunate rival in seeking the next convention. Orbison of Indianapolis, Willis of Kansas City, and Hay of Dallas all made pretty and warm-hearted talks congratulating their lucky rival and offering their support for the 1911 convention.

Another chord of sympathy was struck when a collection was taken up for the Christians of India, that they might be able to attend the World's Convention at Agra next year. Rev. J. P. Jones, the Indian missionary, had just spoken of that country when the collection was started. Two hundred and eighty-five dollars was the sum contributed in all manner of coins, small and large, and the announcement of the sum was cheered again and again.

The principal address of the evening was made by Rev. Charles R. Brown, D.D., of Oakland, Cal., whose subject was "America's Awakened Civic Conscience." He said:

THE PROCESSION TO THE CAPITOL.

MR. BRYAN SPEAKING ON THE CAPITOL STEPS.

The city is man's masterpiece. In all the history of the world he has attempted nothing so great as the highly organized, richly developed life of a modern city.

The city is God's masterpiece. When you open your Bible, the scene is laid in a garden, but at the other end of the Bible we find human life trained, matured, enriched, now making its home in a city whose walls are great and high. The clean, beautiful, healthful city is the outcome of these sublime moral processes indicated in the Scripture.

The realization of that vision held before us by the hand of God demands a finer and more heroic form of patriotism than we have ever seen. It is not difficult to bring about a moral spasm in any city; a strong, stiff dose of exposure touching the corruption that exists will accomplish that. But men in spasms, though they show an amazing amount of physical energy, cannot be depended upon to render continuous service. Only as the city is lifted into a higher mood, and kept there, only as the citizens gird themselves for a nobler public service, can these high ends be attained.

The problem is made harder to-day by the character of some of the enemies with whom we have to deal. The rascals are not all saloon-keepers, gamblers, and purveyors of vice. The representatives of certain interests intent upon special privileges for private profit are eager to corrupt the organized life of the city or the State or the nation.

We have had some frightful experiences in our chief city in California. The terrible thing was not that Mayor Schmitz, yesterday an unknown fiddler, was to-day indicted as a felon in high office. The terrible thing was not that certain other city officials sold themselves for money; they were poor political hangers-on at best. The terrible thing was that men who represented reputable corporations were concerned in the shame of the city as bribe-givers. In the face of the greatest disaster that has ever befallen this dear country of ours, before the ashes of San Francisco were fairly cold, and while the wires to the East were still trembling with expressions of sympathy and promises of generous relief, these respectable men were trafficking in the honor of the community. This was the horror and the shame of it all.

And San Francisco stands by no means alone. The expressions of contempt in certain Eastern newspapers for the municipal corruption in the city by the Golden Gate might well be kept for home consumption. The main difference between San Francisco and a dozen other cities I could name lies in the fact that, while we have taken off our dirty linen, and are engaged in the humble but necessary task of washing it out in the open where the world can see, many other cities are still covering theirs up and wearing it.

But in the face of the awakened civic conscience of the country the outlook is promising. The people are not dishonest; they are ignorant of the real conditions oftentimes; they are sometimes sinfully indifferent; they are frequently incapable by reason of that awkwardness in civic activity which springs from inexperience; but they are not dishonest. Make the issue clear—decency against indecency, honesty against theft, the defence of the home and of legitimate industry against the attacks of vice and of graft; and the plain people can be relied upon every time to come up to the help of the Lord against the mighty.

CHAPTER XIV.

"THY KINGDOM COME," IN BUSINESS LIFE.

Auditorium, Saturday Morning, July 10.

The topic "Thy Kingdom Come in Business" drew to the Auditorium a larger proportion of men than was seen in any other session of the Convention. Although it was a smaller crowd than was gathered at most of the sessions, the interest shown in the topics treated was exceedingly keen. Every one present seemed to be intent on getting light on a difficult and important subject.

After a praise service, led by Mr. Excell, Dr. J. C. Caldwell, of the board of trustees, led in prayer. Dr. Clark then introduced Mr. George W. Coleman, superintendent of the Patriots' League to speak on the topic, "The Golden Rule a Business Rule." Among other things he said:

The Golden Rule means Christianity. But it is also the moral law upon which human society is built. And the imperfections in the present order of things are the results of our failure to apply the Golden Rule. We idolize this principle of life in theory, but apply it only where it will not make too much of a disturbance.

Can the principle of doing unto others as you would that they should do unto you be made a vital factor in business life? Business is simply the exchange of something you have for something you want. It involves bargaining as to quantities and values. The question is then, Shall we bargain in the spirit of gain, getting as much and giving as little as possible, or in the spirit of the Golden Rule, which would see to it that each party to the transaction received and gave a full equivalent? There is nothing inherent in the nature of this exchange of things that dictates the spirit in which it may be conducted; that is determined entirely by the spirit of those who are engaged in the transaction.

But suppose the two parties to the transaction are not of the same spirit, and one seeks to do business in the spirit of the Golden Rule and the other in the spirit of the rule of gold. If they are men of equal ability, the man working in the spirit of gain will get the advantage. But, to add to the confusion, it is undoubtedly true that most of us who are actively engaged in modern business use both rules more or less. Under compulsion, or long habit, or through sheer selfishness, we follow the rule of gold and, upheld by our ideals, we hold to the Golden Rule.

I believe with all my heart and soul and mind that the root of all our present-day social and economic troubles is the lack of the application of the Golden Rule to business. Notwithstanding there perhaps never was a time when the Golden Rule was applied to larger areas of business life, it is equally true, I think, that there never was such a desperate need for a still wider application than there is to-day.

In all our Sunday schools we hold up the Golden Rule as applicable to every phase of life. And our young men are ever asking us if it is compatible with successful business. And we have never given them a complete and satisfactory answer.

The truth of it is that there are conditions in business where it works, mainly the minor and superficial conditions, but there are other conditions large and vital where it is not worked, and rare indeed is the man who pretends to work it. If he does, and works at it, and succeeds, he becomes famous thereby, as in the case of the Golden Rule Jones of Toledo.

Business, like love, is a thing entirely natural and right in itself, but they can both be either idealized or brutalized according to the spirit of those who enter into these relations. The Golden Rule is just as practicable in one case as in the other. Our inheritance of long years of commercial greed is no greater hindrance to an ideal business life than has been our long inheritance of animal passions a hindrance to ideal family life. What ought to be done can be done. What has been done in the one case will be done in the other.

Following this Rev. Charles Stelzle, D.D., the Presbyterian representative of their Church and Labor Department, made a ringing speech on "The Church and Labor and Capital," of which the following is a brief abstract.

Twenty-five years ago a famous French statesman said that the social question is a fad, upon which serious-minded statesmen should waste no time. To-day, no serious-minded man will question the fact that it is the most important problem which confronts us.

The labor question is the matter of giving the other fellow a square deal. The American working man is the finest working man in all the world; but, compared to what he produces, he is the poorest paid working man in the world. With us it is not so much a question of production as one of distribution. To this industrial and economic struggle the church cannot remain indifferent, because she herself is responsible for much of it.

But, having brought the masses of the people to their present spirit of social unrest, the church must not leave them in the hands of unscrupulous agitators. What the people need to-day is unselfish direction in their struggle toward democracy. For many years the masses fought for religious democracy, and they won. Then for four hundred years they fought for political democracy, and they conquered. To-day they are fighting the battle for industrial democracy, and no human power can stop their onward march. Just what the nature of that democracy shall be no sensible man dares prophesy.

If the church is to lead the people in their battle for all that is just and fair, they must be made to believe in the church's sincerity. Betrayed so often by those who have posed as their friends, the working men have become suspicious of every movement that pretends to be in their interest; and sometimes the very men that have betrayed them in political and in economic life have been prominent in the work of the church. Let's talk less about building up the church and more about building up the people. The church is simply a means to an end, and not an end in itself.

There must be found in the church itself the spirit of democracy. No patronage, no paternalism, can ever attract those who are accustomed to the freedom of the lodge, the labor-union, and even the saloon, where a five-cent piece puts a man on an equality with every other man in the place.

There must be more of the social spirit. When our young men go to the average theological seminary to study for the ministry, they study about the social life of the Israelites, the Jebusites, the Hittites, the Hivites, and all the other "ites"; and, when they become our ministers, they preach about these most interesting people, who lived thousands of years ago, and we listen to them with great pleasure. But, when a man studies into the social life of the Chicagoites, the Pittsburgites, or the Brooklynites, and preaches about it in precisely the same manner in which he preached about the social life of the Jebusites, he is reminded that he might better preach the "simple gospel." But it is easier to get the facts concerning the Chicagoites than it is to get them with reference to the Jebusites, and the Chicagoites need our preaching very much more, because the Jebusites have been a long time dead.

What the church needs more than anything else is the spirit of prophecy. Too long have we been boasting about our glorious traditions, with the making of which we to-day had not a thing to do. We need to concern ourselves about the duties of our day and generation. When the hour strikes that shall proclaim the victory of the people, it will not suffice for us to pat them on the back and commend them for the splendid struggle which they made and for the magnificent victory which they achieved. They will scorn us, and remind us that in the bitterest hour of their affliction we never so much as raised our voices in their behalf; and they will go on to even better and nobler things, indifferent to the church, which might have been the champion of the people, but which lost the greatest opportunity of her history.

President E. W. Van Aken, of Parker College, Winnebago, Minn., although a clergyman, showed an acquaintance with business life that enabled him to speak from experience as to the "Opportunities of the Christian Layman." He said:

The shortage of men for the ministry, so pronounced in many of our communions, is but another indication of the shifting of responsibility to the laymen. Men of power and devotion, whatever may be their specific calling, must take their full share in the promotion of the kingdom of heaven on earth; and the opportunities for laymen in religious work and in the varied places of the life of the Kingdom were never so great as they are to-day.

Just as the educators of our land are learning to adjust the mental training and discipline of our youth to the necessities of every-day life and the upbuilding of character, so we in the training of our young people in religion must ever keep in mind that a facility in conducting religious services fails of the full meaning and value unless it culminates in power and ability to render specific service to mankind in the every-day walk of life. We have ever to remember that, just as religion in its fulness is synonymous with life, so business is synonymous with life; and there must be no artificial destructions or barriers maintained between them. Herein lies an immense field of opportunity, which is peculiarly the layman's own, if he but understands how to draw from his religion the motive for doing business.

There is a great field for service for the layman in all our country districts where there is the greatest need of proper pastoral work, based upon territorial rather than denominational or faith lines. Only the laymen can do the work that will make possible the necessary conditions for such pastoral work.

A recent sermon of Dr. Aked's made plain that in New York, at least, our churches are suffering a serious loss in their failure to bring into the fold a larger proportion of the children who are born in the homes of their constituents. This same condition prevails in a greater or less degree throughout the country. Here is the greatest opportunity of all for the layman, for doubtless he more than any other is responsible for this serious leakage in our resources for the day to come.

Right here Dr. Clark presented to the Convention Mayor Hay, of Dallas, Texas, who in speaking of the motive that brought him to St. Paul at the head of an enthusiastic company of Endeavorers to secure the Convention for 1911, said that he would rather see the fires in every furnace in Dallas put out than see the Spirit of God depart from its people, and he was more concerned for the spiritual advancement of his people than for their material prosperity, which is already coming to them in superabundance.

The last speaker was Rev. Avery A. Shaw, of Winnipeg, Manitoba, who made a telling address on "The Principles of the Kingdom Applied to Life," in which he said:

We should not need to take time to argue the necessity of applying the principles of the Kingdom to life, for what is the Kingdom but the life of God applied to human society? As in the time of Christ, so to-day, the Kingdom is to some merely a future beatific state. To others it is purely a present practical social reality. It is both. Until the whole human race attains the goal of its perfection the Kingdom can never be perfectly realized.

It will help us to understand the application of the principles of the Kingdom to modern life if we will first of all listen to the challenge of modern life to the church.

There is first of all the challenge of the social need. This need is seen in the industrial situation with its pressing problems. We see it in the realm of public life and national affairs. We face it in the social vices that pollute the fountains as well as the streams of our common life. We feel the pressure of the social need in the problem of the immigrant. And finally the challenge of the social need is heard in the manifold problem of the city.

In the second place, we are insistently challenged to-day by what we might call the church outside the church. I mean by the large number of men who are really striving to do God's will who have lost faith in the power of the church to meet the problems and realize the Kingdom.

Again we are challenged from within the church by the host of godly men and women who grow heart-sick at the long delay in realizing Christ's ideals, and who say almost in despair, "Art thou the church that shall be, or look we for another?"

Still further we are challenged in a ringing call of the present-day opportunity. If we find the church often discredited, we never lived in a day when Christ was more universally revered.

Now, with this many-sided challenge ringing in our ears, we may well ask ourselves what may be reasonably expected of the church in response. The primary function of the church must always be recognized as the regeneration of individual character. But that is only the beginning of her duty. Our first duty is *to see the actual*. It is very easy and very tempting to see what we wish to see. The evils of a slum are not so very grievous to us if we derive revenue from it.

Our next duty is social repentance. The finest scenes in the Bible are where men repent not for their own sins, but for the sins of the society of which the speakers are a part.

Our third duty is to get a vision of Christ's ideal.

Then we must set ourselves to realize his ideal in and through the churches of which we form a part.

The individual church must become a miniature kingdom. The pulpit must become a centre and source of social evangelism. And in all departments of our young people's work especially, there must be begun and carried on a campaign of social education.

But in addition to all this there must be furnished an outlet for the social energies thus derived. In every church, or, where it can be more effectively done, in an affiliation of churches, influences should be set in operation to improve public health, to improve home conditions, to furnish and foster wholesome recreations, to drain the sources of crime, to train children in the duties of citizenship and social service, and to bring the church into living touch with both sides in the industrial world.

Further, every church should maintain or help to maintain a life-saving station where the human wreckage multiplies. Every family in every church should link itself wisely and lovingly for effective ministry to some needy family or individual. Every individual member of the church should link his life as big brother to some "weak brother for whom Christ died." It will not be enough to give our gifts or our service; we must give ourselves. Doing this, we shall hear our Master say every day, "Inasmuch as ye have done it unto one of the least of these, ye have done it unto me."

CHAPTER XV.

The Armory, Saturday Morning, July 10.

For missionary workers, the missionary-committee conference proved one of the most practical sessions held during the entire convention. It was in charge of Rev. Willis L. Gelston, the superintendent of young people's work in the Presbyterian denomination.

The opening service was conducted by Mr. Percy S. Foster, after which Miss M. Josephine Petrie, the secretary of the young people's department of the Presbyterian Board of Home Missions, of New York, was introduced. Miss Petrie's subject was "Missionary Meetings That Are Worth While," and she made her talk very practical by giving suggestions as to the kind of missionary meetings that have proved the most helpful in young people's societies. "It is a good plan," said she, "always to plan missionary meetings that will make a lasting impression upon the hearers. For this purpose secure helps from the denominational boards, but in doing so do not forget to send postage. Be sure to advertise the meetings. Make the singing a special feature of every meeting. Let the social committee follow up the meetings by getting hold of all who are interested in missions. Among the different styles of meetings that have proved the most profitable are meetings on tithing. At the conclusion of one missionary meeting, of fifteen speakers, the society was divided into two parts, and questions on the meeting were asked, a pansy being given to each person that answered the question correctly. Do not throw open the missionary meeting; control it yourself." Miss Petrie also spoke of the great help received from the reading of missionary books, from meetings for contests and quizzes, and from travel meetings. In conclusion she asked that the workers be definite in plans, be loyal to their denominational boards, and always remember in earnest prayer the volunteers and missionaries on the frontier.

"How to Secure Missionary Enthusiasts" was the subject of the talk by Rev. A. D. Thaeler, pastor of the Moravian church in Bethlehem, Penn., who eloquently showed how a powerful motive and thorough conviction are necessary for enthusiasm, and how this can come only from the love of our Saviour. To be interested in missions is no ninety-day affair; it is an enlistment for life. It is not for political, social, or humanitarian reasons, but for the love of Christ that constraineth us.

The question before us is one that has been the concern of the church of Christ from the day when Christian disciples first began to apprehend the vast and imperative Great Commission of the Captain of our salvation. But never before in all the nineteen centuries of our era has there been such an awakened sense of responsibility and opportunity as to-day.

It is a far cry from the Jewish mob howling for the death of the apostle who was declaring his call to give the gospel to Gentiles, to a convention like this embracing thousands of young people studying, as we are now doing, the problem of aggressive missionary enthusiasm.

Back of all enthusiasm, if we use the word in its highest sense, there must be two things: first, an all-powerful motive, sufficient to move the depths of life and defy all obstacles; secondly, a thorough conviction of the value of what is to be presented. .Without both of these there can certainly be no abiding enthusiasm for any sort of *gospel* mission. And let me lay all stress upon that word, "abiding." Abiding enthusiasm must be more than a form of nervous tension, or a straw fire, blazing hot, but soon burning itself out. True enlistment is enlistment for life, and there must needs be a corresponding stability and impulsive power that will last through life. Secure these, and you have kindled the right sort of enthusiasm.

Missionary enthusiasm must go beyond abstractions, beyond "business propositions," as we might call mere philanthropic eagerness. The New Testament has pictured for us the first mighty enthusiast of the church, who lost none of his ardor in the test of a third of a century. Paul has revealed the fire which generated his power, "The love of Christ constraineth us." Let me further venture the assertion that, were you to examine *any* life completely given over to service under the Great Commission, and blessed by God, you would find that it has been wholly and consciously dominated by this supreme motive, "the love of Christ."

First, therefore, to secure missionary enthusiasts we must develop a personal love for Jesus Christ. No one has any business in any field of Christian service in whom there is not a definite personal conviction of the power of the gospel, developing a strong inward impulse.

But again we hear St. Paul: "If any man have not the spirit of Christ, he is none of his." What *is* the unmistakable sign of the spirit of Christ? Can you picture Jesus without the eager passion for saving souls? "God *so loved the world* that he sent his Son." That Son was love incarnate, and he was the Christ in that he had been anointed to preach the gospel to the poor, to give deliverance to the captives, to proclaim the acceptable year of the Lord. To bear his name means possession of the same spirit, or it means nothing. Jesus forgot his utter fatigue, sitting at the well of Sychar, in speaking of the Father to the lost child of God. Paul cried, "I am become all things to all men, that I may by all means save some." Carey declared, "My business is to preach the gospel of Christ." Surely we have not the first experience of the living gospel

ONE OF THE EXHIBITS IN THE ARMORY.

ANOTHER VIEW OF THE PROCESSION TO THE CAPITOL.

within us if we have not known the impulse to bring this one, that one, every one, within the effective sweep of the grace of God.

Therefore, secondly, to secure missionary enthusiasts we need only to arouse within the church, and every member of the church, the spirit of Christ. Missionary aggressiveness is not the extraordinary duty of the body of Christ, but its very life.

We come now to our third proposition: Missionary enthusiasm will be the mark of a church that demands of itself universal expansive effort. In no congregation should missionary interest be confined to a single society, or even several societies, within its membership, permitting the inference that one may be a good member of the church of Christ without being concerned with the commission, "both in Jerusalem, and in all Judea and Samaria, and unto the uttermost part of the earth." Missions are not a separate and subordinate department. They are vital and comprehensive business of the church, which, failing here, eventually fails everywhere.

And yet again, missionary enthusiasts will arise among those who have been learning to pray for missions. Jesus told his disciples: "Pray ye therefore the Lord of the harvest, that he thrust forth laborers into his harvest." From the midst of those who look upon the whitening fields, who beseech the Lord because they have studied them intelligently, who have with the heart heard the bitter cry of need, who pray for even a thrusting forth of reapers—from such come our enthusiasts. We begin to pray when we learn enthusiasm. Correspondingly, we begin to be enthusiastic when we learn to pray. Let the church bow its knees, and calls will swiftly be answered.

Have we time to mention a few of the God-blessed means that have raised up and sent forth indomitable missionary enthusiasts? First, the inspiration of home influence. You remember how Hannah, in the Bible story, gave her little child to the service of the Lord in his tabernacle, and Samuel's wonderful life honored her devotion? That story is retold in the experience of Dr. Jacob Chamberlain, of India, recently published. He testified: "I drank in the spirit of missions on my mother's breast. My parents were one in missionary interest. It was their hope that God might honor them by calling one of their sons to be an ambassador of his to heathen peoples."

Secondly, missionary information should be given to the church constantly, wisely, patiently. Paul and Barnabas did this, showing inspired common sense. Returning from their first missionary tour, "they gathered the church together, and rehearsed all things that God had done with them, and how he had opened a door of faith unto the Gentiles." The event proved that they were preparing the church to send them out for a second and wider campaign.

We are to-day at a crisis in the battle. Let the church summon all its strength for a confident and swift advance. It must be made to see the opportunity. Workers from the field, at home on furlough, are always ready to help feed the flame of zeal with fuel. The celebration of anniversaries of missionary significance can arouse deep feelings. Farewell services for those who have offered themselves for the distant service forge a strong link of personal concern for both the missionary and his field. Mission festivals, in which sometimes two or more congregations unite, with a presentation of the great cause from several points of view, have developed many a volunteer. Missionary literature, mission libraries, chatty letters read before the whole congregation from friends who represent the congregation abroad, lectures on each field, with stereopticon illustrations, and the constant use of the church papers for the informing of friends at home—all these means can be used, have been successfully used, for the sowing of missionary seed.

And, finally, we mention that which will be increasingly true of a church which has *begun* to respond to the Lord's call. If the departing missionary is no stranger, but a brother, sister, son, daughter, the tugging heartstrings, the praying, the giving, the encouraging, will ever become more eager and intense, a steady-burning enthusiasm. The enthusiasm needed must be of that enduring type that does not let go because of financial deficits, nor shrink when reverses come; but it should glorify Him to whom all love and devotion are due, and so confidently believe in his ultimate victory that it is ready to dare all and endure all things, so that spoils may be brought to him from every tribe for which he died.

Mr. Guy M. Withers, of Kansas City, always a prime favorite, gave an address on "How to Promote the Reading of Missionary Books and Magazines" in his usual breezy style. He said :

The American people read; they read everything. It staggers us when we think of the carloads upon carloads of five-centers and ten-centers and fifteen-centers that come out every week and every month; not to speak of the daily press, which somehow or other we devour every day. We get up in the morning, and commence with reading. We get down to breakfast, and immure ourselves each behind his favorite paper. We bolt a hasty breakfast, or Fletcherize between paragraphs, and board a street-car, everybody looking straight at his paper for fear he should see somebody he should give his seat to.

The American people read; they are great readers. I wish they were good readers. I wish they were as well read as their newspapers. Our task, then, seems not to be to teach people to read, but to teach them what to read; but, the minute you approach them with a book that is good for them, they get a taste in their mouth like castor-oil.

The people you will work with divide very naturally into three groups.

In the first group are those that will read missionary books from the love of them. These you must help by very tactfully suggesting the wisest plan for their reading, and the best books for the course.

Another class of folks are just learning to read; they have not formed a fixed habit, but are browsing around, nibbling here and there, as a calf does before he settles down to eat grass and grow into a splendid fatling. With these you have great opportunity, because you will be forming habits to stay with them through life. You must be careful of the first choice, and give them something interesting. Don't suggest it as if you were prescribing a dose of medicine. They sometimes take it better if you don't label it too heavily "Missionary reading."

The third class are the hardened old sinners, so thoroughly addicted to the sensational literature of the day, or the heavy classics of the other day, that they don't take up readily with the new style of missionary literature. Very much of your failure in the past, particularly with this class of people, has been because you have been using out-of-date literature, which will not work at all now.

Take, for instance, "Uganda's White Man of Work." That first chapter, beginning with the newspaper reporter's interview with the black king, would hold any boy that ever had the wild West fever, even through the solid chapters that follow; and his father would be enamored, if he was at all thoughtful, in the same way with the "Frontier," whose first chapter leads you wonderfully into God's plan for the building of the American republic.

And for thinkers such books as "Where the Book Speaks," by Archibald McLean, or Bishop Bashford's "God's Missionary Plan for the World."

If our societies are to be up to date, if they are to have part in the great present movement of the missionary fields at home and abroad, we must educate them in this way to their responsibility and opportunity; not only must we supply them with a missionary literature, but we must never forget that it is one thing to get it ready and another thing to get it read.

A delightful interlude was introduced into the meeting by a series of songs from the missionary chorus. Charmingly grouped in the costumes of many lands, the girls made a brilliant spot of color in the large assembly. Some were in the brilliant Japanese style; some looked prettily out from Turkish swathings; and some wore the more sombre hues of India and Persia. They gave the national hymns of different lands, those of China, Cuba, and Japan especially, together with some beautiful songs in our own language.

Rev. Edward Marsden, who early became the leading native Endeavorer in Alaska and who was the first native Presbyterian missionary in that great region, was the next speaker, on "Alaska's Opportunity." He said:

The native tribes of Alaska to-day are receiving many blessings from on high through the labors of self-sacrificing men and women, and in spite of some unfortunate results from our contact with the march of civilization we are happy to acknowledge that God has been very kind to us in the North.

In the days past, when we were without the gospel of the Lord Jesus Christ, we were a dark and dangerous people. We practised sorceries; we killed one another for sport; we had no code of laws to restrain our evil passions; we bowed down to graven images; and in short we were a degraded and lost people in the sight of God.

But, in the words of the apostle, with us in Alaska to-day "the night is far spent, the day is at hand"; and I assure you fellow Christians that we are struggling to cast off the works of darkness; and we wish, yea, we plead, yea, we strive, to put on the "armor of light."

There are some things that you have done to our northern country whereby our plea for the blessed gospel is made stronger to-day than ever before. You have explored almost every part of our native country. You have traversed it up and down. The snow and ice, the high mountains, the swift rivers and uncomfortable climate in some of its sections, do not discourage you at all in your work of exploration.

Then you have brought that northern land within your very gates here. You have stretched your wires across it. You are laying your rails into the interior of it, and your elegant steamers ply between there and your Pacific States. You even can chatter by your firesides down here, and be heard up there. We are now assured that you will soon take the wings of the morning and fly up there. All of this is wonderful to us, and is a source of serious thought on our part.

Again, you have introduced and organized in our midst an orderly system of government with a certain code of laws. Out of chaos you have brought a well-regulated life. We respect you for this.

and it only creates in our dark hearts a desire for something higher and better.

Therefore, in the light of these things of which I speak we realize that it is useless for us to resist. We know that the time has come for us to cast off all our works of darkness. We have no other choice but to come as the blessed gospel calls us to come. We cry to-day for the plain and simple gospel of the Lord Jesus Christ. Never mind our failures. Do not enlarge upon the mistakes that we have made. Condemn us not when we fall victims of the vices of civilization. We plead for the gospel. We see what wonderful things you can do, and hence we cry the more for your good help. Come over and help us.

CHAPTER XVI.

THE CAMP-FIRE AND ORATORIO.

Saturday Evening, July 10.

This now well-established and popular feature of the Convention programme drew a large audience to the Armory, despite the oratorio attraction at the Auditorium. Secretary Shaw originated the informal and breezy camp-fire idea, and by his enthusiasm and wit always kept the logs blazing. He found an able and apt successor as chief fireman this year in Dr. James L. Hill, who has an inexhaustible fund of illustrations and overflowing spirits. He kept the company in the best of cheer; and, if there were any tears, they were the result of laughter, not grief. "What do the initials Y. P. S. C. E. stand for?" asked some one of him, he said. "What do they stand for?" was his reply; "why, because they are so full of animation that they can't lie down." He advised his speakers, of whom he had many and of various sorts, to stick to their texts, but not stick to them too long, since there was a long programme. The audience was quick, and the sallies of the leader evoked immediate response.

The musical leader, Mr. Foster, opened the exercises by teaching the people how to sing a hymn to his taste; and the music after that was furnished by the chorus in costume, which rendered some national anthems, European and Oriental, with plaintive effect; and by the Hawaiian quartette, who sung two native songs while some Hawaiian views were thrown upon the screen. Encores greeted the singers.

The first to bring a log for the fire was Rev. Edward Marsden, of Alaska, who, according to Dr. Hill's introduction, is skilled at everything, a talented musician, and builder of his own missionary boats. Mr. Marsden recited John 3:16 in his native tongue, and sung "Rock of Ages" in the Indian language. An irresistible encore brought "Jesus, lover of my soul," the Indian's favorite hymn. Mr. Marsden is an Indian Endeavorer of a fine manly type, and started the fire into a blaze.

He was followed by Rev. W. T. Johnson, a negro preacher, who sung one of the old-time slave songs," I'm a rollin' through an unfriendly world," and had to sing another, "He is King of Kings," before the audience would be satisfied. Dr. Hill said

93

it was a remarkable fact that the negro melodies could not be set to musical notation, because this music was wrung out of the heart.

Next a Finn was introduced, Rev. Resto Lappala, from Ohio, an Endeavorer delegate and a real Finn, not one of the Swedish-Finnish family. He represented the only Finnish society in this country, a society founded by himself. There are forty Endeavor societies in Finland, he said. He spoke of the many Finnish children in America, and the opportunity to organize Endeavor societies among them.

Rev. S. Guy Inman, missionary in Mexico, displayed a beautiful Mexican flag, which called forth applause. He said Mexico was so near that we overlooked her, but she is destined to become one of the mighty nations. When we speak of America, we mean only ourselves and Canada, and forget Mexico; but Mexico, more courteous and fair, always speaks of the three North American nations—Canada, the United States, and Mexico. He had the audience say, "Viva Mexico," and gave in Spanish the hymn, "Wonderful words of life."

Dr. W. F. Wilson told the remarkable story of the conversion of an old lady of Hamilton, Ontario, who is one hundred and seven years old. She was converted with the help of Dr. Wilson's Junior Endeavorers; and, when she joined the church, a Junior of seven years joined with her, a whole century between them.

Dr. Hill said this Convention had struck a key-note, that of brotherhood, fellowship, such as we have never had before. He called on Mr. Coleman to speak of this new fellowship, as one who exemplifies its spirit. Mr. Coleman briefly and forcibly responded. He said that the fellowship we Christians of different denominations and races have in this Convention should teach us of the wider fellowship that we must have in a democracy if we are to fulfil our citizenship obligations. We must work with and for all, love God and man. The audience gave hearty approval.

Palestine was next heard from through Rev. A. Edward Kelsey, delegate to the Convention from Jerusalem. He told of the three Endeavor societies in his own Friends' Mission, and sang some of their songs in Arabic. These too were greeted with great applause. He said he was training his students to do foreign work, and they are at it in Egypt.

Then Dr. Hill called Dr. Clark, who had come in to enjoy the service and rest a bit, to the platform to compare St. Paul Convention with the past conventions. Dr. Clark said this would be difficult, because it was too early yet to estimate the St. Paul Convention aright. But some things are clear already. One thing that impressed him was the joyous note.

This would be known as a joyous and a singing convention. He recalled incidents of the earliest Conventions when it was thought wonderful that any delegate should come a hundred miles to be present. The chief thing that marked the St. Paul Convention was, in his judgment, the seal of interdenominational fellowship and brotherhood, for it marks the beginning of a new era among young people's societies. Another thing marking this Convention is the splendid singing, not only in the Convention, but on the streets throughout the city. Neither had he ever seen the equal of the singing parade Friday night. It was simply superb, and had captured the citizens of St. Paul.

"The Standard Oil Company has invaded China," said A. L. Warnshuis of China; "and it is the mightiest factor in the commercial development of the Oriental empire, which is just awakening to its opportunities, and is reaching out and grasping everything the West has to make its own. It is only two years ago that China adopted a flag, and at the present time, while we are sitting here, China is holding an election to the first Parliament, which will soon assemble in Pekin. But no less important than the commercial development of the Eastern empire is its religious development, which rests in the hands of Christians of all lands."

T. Makino, of Kyoto, Japan, told briefly of the work of the Endeavor Society in the Sunrise Kingdom. The Minneapolis societies, under the leadership of C. W. Mountain, sang hymns in Chinese, Japanese, and Spanish. The chorus was dressed in costumes of the different nations.

Closing the camp-fire, Dr. H. B. Grose, of New York, threw slides and moving pictures on the canvas, representing scenes from foreign countries. These included a view of the Mengo Cathedral, with the king and congregation entering the church; a preaching-scene in a village in northern India, illustrating the missionary at work; a fascinating kindergarten band in Japan; and several others of equal interest and profit.

THE ORATORIO OF "ELIJAH."

The production of Mendelssohn's "Elijah" brought to the Auditorium one of the largest audiences that has yet attended any of the meetings. Fully five thousand people remained throughout the rendering of the oratorio, and many who were anxious to attend the camp-fire at the Armory stayed long enough to hear the first part.

All the galleries, with the exception of the two or three upper rows, were packed; and the balconies were crowded to their full capacity. In the parquet not a seat was to be found, and the boxes were all well occupied.

The oratorio itself was said by many competent critics to be the finest rendering of that or any other oratorio ever given in the Twin Cities. The choir was the recipient of glowing praise. No choir ever heard in the Northwest, it is said, could compare with it in the splendid voices it contained or in the way it carried out its part of the difficult performance without a hitch.

The part of Elijah was sung by Mr. Harry Phillips, and with his splendid barytone he put all the stress and vehemence into his voice that the prophet must have used in his dire predictions and lamentations.

Austin Williams, tenor, who sang the other male part in the production, was in fine voice, and in every way equal to Phillips in the realism of his harmonious appeals. Miss Clara Williams and Mrs. Alma Johnson Porteous were all that could be asked, and time and again brought the house down with their beautiful rendering of the solos.

Mr. George H. Fairclough, who conducted the performance, deserves a special word of praise for the finished production he so ably managed. Without the slightest hitch or jar of any kind, he led orchestra, choir, and soloists through the intricate mazes of emotion in the great oratorio.

THE PATRIOTIC SERVICE ON THE CAPITOL STEPS.

CHAPTER XVII.

THE MEN'S MASS-MEETING.

The Auditorium, Sunday Afternoon, July 11.

There were numbers of men who said afterwards that the Sunday afternoon men's meeting was the most impressive of the whole St. Paul Convention. And every one who was present could easily see how such a feeling should prevail, for there were few, if any, who went away from that meeting without the knowledge that their religion was a more vital part of their being and their Christ a stronger personal presence than he had ever been before. The meeting was marked by its deep spiritual power, which moved men now to applause, now to silence, now to weeping. Here men were not ashamed of their tears, for in their earnestness and devotion the speakers and audience were deeply moved.

The large Auditorium was not filled, but it contained a goodly crowd of earnest men, about fifteen hundred, eager for some messages which would satisfy. The very first verse of the first song was a prayer, and was enthusiastically sung, under Prof. Excell's leadership, "There shall be showers of blessing." Mr. William Phillips Hall was the presiding officer, and as usual he had the meeting perfectly under his control. Between the several opening songs Rev. Charles Stelzle, D.D., of New York City, offered prayer, and Mr. William Shaw read the Scripture, the lesson being "The Prodigal Son." After these inspiring opening exercises the chairman introduced Rev. James A. Francis, of Boston, a great favorite in these men's meetings, and a capable and inspiring speaker. One man said, "I expected something good from Mr. Francis, and I got it." The address was an appeal to the soundest reasoning, the clearest judgment, and the deepest, truest emotion of the hearers. He said:

I have but one proposition: Jesus is God's answer to all of man's deepest questions. As I went, some time ago, through the halls of the British Museum, I saw a curious-looking black stone, about three and a half feet long and two and a half feet wide. I learned that it was called the Rosetta Stone. As a stone for building now it would be worthless, but it could not be purchased for any price. The conundrum of Egypt was for ages found in the inscriptions, which men called hieroglyphics, on its pyramids and temples. So the world was in darkness, in this regard, for ages. Only one hundred and ten years ago some of Napoleon's men unearthed this stone at the Rosetta mouth of the Nile. It bore three inscriptions. The one at the bottom was in Greek, which any scholar could read; the one in the middle was in Egyptian script, which likewise was no puzzle; the one at the top was in these strange Egyptian hieroglyphics. Scholars studied for years until they found that this Rosetta Stone was the key which unlocked the story of Egypt's history. What the Rosetta Stone is to the puzzle of Egypt, Jesus Christ is to the riddle of the universe. Christ says: "I am the answer to all questions. I am all the light that this world ever needs."

I want to put now five great questions of the soul, to find out what answer Jesus makes to them. If he is the answer to all our questions, he can answer these five, and, if he can answer these five, he can answer any and all. The five questions are these:

1. What is God really like?
2. What is the real meaning of a man?
3. What is man's relationship to God?
4. What is man's relation to the other men?
5. What is beyond the grave?

Jesus can answer satisfactorily all these questions.

1. The real character of God. Some say: "Turn to nature to find out God. See the fields, the flowers, the heavens; and you see God." But nature tells us not the deepest things about God. It only tells us that God is there. This is Jesus' answer to the question: "He that hath seen me hath seen the Father." Jesus Christ is God uncovered. Jesus Christ is God translated into the language of human life. Now, when I want to know God, I study Jesus Christ.

2. The real meaning of man. What am I? Only a mere mass of flesh, six feet or less in height, 175 pounds or less in weight, yet bigger than all the stars of heaven. Sometimes man degrades himself. Sometimes he rises so high that he seems to be a vest-pocket edition of God himself. What is a man? Jesus says, "I am the Son of man." Jesus answers this question also. He is God's standard man. The thousands of yardsticks in this and other cities are all fashioned after a metal bar in the city of Washington, which measures exactly one yard. Jesus Christ is God's standard man for this world and for eternity. And, more, Jesus Christ is not only God's standard of what a man ought to be, but God's eternal prophecy and promise of what every man will be, who turns to him. "It doth not yet appear what we shall be, but we know that we shall be like him." This is the largest promise that Jesus Christ contracts to take in his mighty arms of love and power every soul who trusts. Jesus Christ thus becomes the explanation of the human race, and the question is answered.

3. Man's relation to God. God's regard for man is greater than any of its manifestations. The cross of Christ is the advertisement at one point in time of God's eternal regard for man. Jesus thus made possible the greatest connection between man and God. He is the connecting link between a sinful man and a holy God. What is left for me? To come

"Just as I am, without one plea,
But that thy blood was shed for me,
And that thou bidst me come to thee,
O Lamb of God, I come."

4. Man's relation to other men. Jesus' answer is this: "Love one another as I have loved you." Let every man take the same kind of interest in his fellows as Christ takes in us, and work it out in every sphere.

Unless men care for one another, all the bands of coercion you put around them cause more and more friction.

5. What beyond the grave? Years ago in Boston there was a strange funeral service in a hotel. It was a little girl who had died, the only comfort of her father. Only three persons were present at the funeral service, the minister, the hotel-keeper, and the father. Only two went out to the cemetery, the minister and the father. Silently they went to the grave, and there the father took a little key out of his pocket, unlocked the little coffin, and took the last look at the silent form. Then he locked the coffin, and it was lowered into the grave. The key he gave to the caretaker of the cemetery. On the way back in the carriage there was silence for a while. Then the minister said: "Well, you have laid her away, haven't you?" "Yes," said the father. "And the key you gave to the caretaker?" "Yes." "Did you ever hear these words: 'I am he that liveth, and I was dead, and behold I am alive forevermore, and I have the keys of death and the grave'?" "No; who said them?" "They are the words of Jesus, spoken after his ascension to the throne of God, through his servant, John."

Jesus says: "I am on the other side of the grave." The grave cannot frighten me if Jesus holds the key.

Now, if Jesus Christ is the eternal revelation of God, if he is God's standard of the human, if he connects man to God, if he becomes the embodiment of man's regard for his fellow, and if Jesus is on the other side of the grave, where does a man stand when he leaves Jesus Christ out of his life?

As a fitting climax to this great address the audience sang "All hail the power of Jesus' name." The men had hardly been able to realize the first address when another rich treat was presented. Mr. Hall introduced the "lumber-jack sky-pilot" of the north woods, Rev. Frank E. Higgins. It was a simple story he told; yet every word was filled with the power of God, and the whole address was a strong call of God to the salvation of men. The speaker told how fourteen years ago he was led providentially into some of the lumber-camps of northern Minnesota, and had found the great need of the men for God. It was through the words of a dying logger whom he had comforted that the decision came to give up the church, and take up actively the work in the lumber-camps. "There are twenty thousand men every winter in these logging-camps, ostracized and isolated from every good influence and help. Conditions are even worse now than formerly, for all along the railroads there have sprung up towns with saloons and gambling-places and brothels."

Mr. Higgins's stories of how hard, rough men were won to Christ by the message of his lips were inspiring and touching beyond measure. Many handkerchiefs were in evidence as he told of dying men who "made the grade" in safety, and left this earth rejoicing. The earnestness of his spirit and the great love of Christ manifest in his character will be long remembered.

As a token of what the message meant to the hearers, this may be told. Mr. Higgins said that if he had two hundred dollars he could put an additional missionary for a year among those needy men of the forest. Did the audience respond? The hats were passed under Mr. Shaw's direction, and the announcement made that two hundred had been raised, with one dollar more promised. And Mr. Higgins received with every dollar the prayer that God might bless the work.

Of course the meeting would not have been complete without some words from Mr. Hall. And he did not disappoint. In an earnest manner he told of some personal experiences that made men wonder why they ever doubted God's care and power. He, too, moved the vast audience with his deep spiritual message which made men think of themselves and of God. And then, when he gave the invitation for men to give themselves over to God, the response was gratifying. Scarcely a man in the house but stood up for Christ, many for the first time. And how the men did surge to the front to grasp the hands of the speaker, as a seal to their appreciation of what God had done for them!

Thus closed the men's mass-meeting, with prayers and tears, and happiness on every side, every man stronger than when he entered the room. To God be the glory for such a meeting!

CHAPTER XVIII.

THE WOMEN'S MEETING.

Central Presbyterian Church, Sunday Afternoon, July 11.

The Central Presbyterian Church was filled on Sunday afternoon, when earnest and enthusiastic women met to consider "Woman's Special Part in Christian Endeavor Work." With Mrs. Francis E. Clark presiding the audience showed that no musical leader was necessary, for the hearty singing of the opening of the first hymn proved that all were united by the common aim of "Christ for the world."

Miss Florence E. Lanham, of Indianapolis, Ind., the first speaker, emphasized the ideal of Christ seen in the individual. Ah, if this could only be realized, there would be no Sunday baseball or theatres. The children in the schools would be drawn to the Saviour by the winsomeness of his character exemplified in the teacher. The business man, the family in the home, the church circle, would have to accept the Christ if we in all our daily walk lifted him up, not Christ in me, the hope of glory, but Christ given out through me, the hope of all those who know him not.

Mrs. Clark in her usual interesting and forceful way then spoke of the purpose of the Junior societies. "When my own boys were younger, I used to take them to the Junior society. I even took my youngest, though he mas but a four-year-old, for I hoped he would absorb the atmosphere. It did not disturb me in the least when on the way home he would sing at the top of his voice, "Only an armchair proudly I stand, ready to follow at the King's command." I thought when he grew to be older he would know the difference between an armchair and an armor-bearer. I have felt that the intense interest he has felt in Christian Endeavor and church-work began in those Junior meetings when he sang 'Only an armchair.'

"We try to tell the boys and girls just what it is to be a Christian; and then we try to train them up to be working Christians; to teach them Bible-study and daily prayer, and to do such work in the church as children may do. Through this many of them have learned to do active and earnest work in the church.

"I have found that two Juniors have come as delegates
101

to this Convention and they are going to tell you one thing which they have learned to do in their society in Iowa. There are about fifty members in their society, and they are just samples."

She then introduced Mrs. E. S. Condon, who said in part as follows: "The best thing we can see in Iowa in Christian Endeavor work is in the Junior work. In Iowa we have twelve districts. We have been trying, among others, this method. These boys have taken the book of Matthew. Other societies have taken other books of the Bible. They study it by chapters. The Juniors take their Bibles, and then the Junior superintendent reads a verse in any of these chapters, and the children have to find it."

Then followed one of the most interesting features of the service. The two boys stepped to the platform with their Bibles. Some one in the audience would read a verse at random from the book of Matthew, and the boys would find it in their Bibles, the first one finding it reading it aloud. So quickly could they find the verses that at one time, before the lady had finished reading the verse, both boys were on their feet interrupting her.

Mrs. Charles Hutchison then spoke on "The Mother's Part in Christian Endeavor Work." She emphasized in a tender, sympathetic manner the need of a more active interest in the affairs of the children. Mothers could use more personal influence in bringing the young people into Christian Endeavor work and active church work. Keep the family pew sacred, and hold the children there instead of letting them slip into a back seat with a chum. "I want to beg of the mothers who are here this afternoon to be sure that boys or girls never go out from your home without carrying with them the remerbrance of a praying mother. Let the children know we are praying for them."

"Our Christian Endeavor Work in Missions" was taken up in a practical way by Miss M. Josephine Petrie, as she answered the challenge, "Where in church or state are the good fruits of your twenty-five years' endeavor and your four million members?" by showing that, although we must confess we were tardy in starting, our young people's societies have accomplished wonderful things in the way of practical work in missionary fields. She cited as an example a Christian Endeavor hospital in Porto Rico where hundreds of men and women have been won to the knowledge of the Saviour through the personal message of Christian nurses, who in many cases are native girls drawn to our Lord during their course of training in this same hospital. One old Spanish woman said, while the tears coursed down her cheeks: "Why didn't you come to me before? Think of the people I might have told if I had only known."

Mrs. Clark then gave a "thought or two about the religious training of the children and foreign Christian Endeavor," and beautiful thoughts they were.

"Why should it not be the understood thing that children should have a religious training as well as a secular training?

"I knew a boy who was not always regular at the Junior Endeavor meeting; and his mother said she didn't want to make him go, but she almost had to whip him off to dancing school every week. We often emphasize non-essentials so strongly that we lose sight of the highest and best.

"Organize a Mothers' Christian Endeavor society whose principal object shall be to raise the standard of Christian living in the home and to train the children in Christian living.

"Just a word about foreign Endeavor, some of the fruits of Christian Endeavor I have seen in my journeys. A woman in China wishing to help the boys in the streets formed a society, using nothing but colored tassels as badges. By degrees she led them to care for the things of the Kingdom until within two years a missionary told me, 'Why, you can always tell those little Christian Endeavor boys, for they behave better than any other children on the street.' "

Mrs. Clark then pictured in charming fashion a Christian Endeavor convention she had attended in China, and told tenderly the story of a lad who, at the time of the Boxer uprising, stood so firmly for the Christ whom he had been taught to love that death of father, mother, friends, imprisonment in the home of a leader who saved his life because of his courage, even the denial of any outward semblance of worship of the Lord who had protected him, could not shake his faith; and to-day he is in one of the schools of China preparing to be a missionary.

CHAPTER XIX.

BOYS' AND GIRLS' MEETING.

House of Hope Presbyterian Church, Sunday Afternoon, July 11.

Picture for yourself a large, square Sunday-school room filled to its utmost with bright-eyed Juniors and an equal proportion of seniors, and you will have the rally for boys and girls held Sunday afternoon. From first to last it proved one of the best meetings of the Convention. Mr. Foster stirred up every one at the beginning with his singing, and after that was over each of the five speakers seemed "mutually to surpass one another" in the way they held the attention of the audience. There is space here only to give a brief sketch of what was said by but one, Rev. William Carey, missionary to India.

The way in which Dr. Clark introduced Mr. Carey whetted our appetites for all that followed. He said that years ago he had travelled in India with a missionary of considerable prominence. The place to which he and his friend were going was a long way up a river, and several changes had to be made. First the party took a house-boat, going as far as there was water enough to float it. Then they took a canoe, and then they had to go on foot. It was two o'clock in the morning when they finally reached their destination at a small native village; and the only rest they then secured was on a little pile of straw thrown on the floor of a native hut. Next day they had the Christian Endeavor convention for which they had made the trip.

Such was the strangeness of the experience that Dr. Clark said that he never forgot it; and, as for the missionary with whom he travelled, he it was whom we were going to have the pleasure of hearing in our meeting. Such an introduction made us all listen with unusual care as Mr. Carey spoke, and we were by no means disappointed. As we followed the speaker's thought, we were led to take a journey clear over to Bengal; there we saw two or three hundred dark-skinned boys and girls gathered for a meeting similar to our own. They were all bare-legged and barefooted. The girls wore large rings in their noses, and did their hair up in a strange manner, while the dress of the boys was equally curious.

104

A GLIMPSE OF THE PROCESSION TO THE CAPITOL.

ANOTHER VIEW OF THE PARADE TO THE CAPITOL.

Mr. Carey told us that these were the little people whom he was accustomed to meet every Sunday when at home. Space will not allow a longer description here of the scene he pictured, but the vision he brought to some of us will never disappear. The address closed with the thought expressed in the epistle of John, "Little children, I write unto you because your sins are forgiven."

After the speaking was over Dr. Clark closed the service with a few moments of quiet meditation and prayer.

CHAPTER XX.

CIVIC REFORMS.

The Auditorium, Sunday Evening, July 11.

One of the "greatest of the great" fitly describes the session devoted to civic reform at the Auditorium. Great in its speakers, great in its theme, great in its spirit, it was a fitting climax to a crowning day.

In spite of the rain, Christian Endeavor reigned supreme in the hearts and minds of the great audience.

Dr. Howard B. Grose, an honored trustee of the United Society, presided with his inimitable charm. "Everything in New York, where I live, is done strenuously; it rains hard; the water comes from reluctant heavens," said Dr. Grose; "but I never saw it rain so easily as it does here in St. Paul."

Professor Excell led a most inspiring and worshipful service of song.

Dr. Clark was the first speaker, taking for his theme "Christian Endeavor and its Relation to Reforms." His address was a revelation of the vital and far-reaching influence of Christian Endeavor in reforms in many parts of the world. It was a strong, stimulating, comprehensive presentation that left a profound impression upon his hearers.

From various standpoints we might view this important subject. We might marshal a vast array of facts to show how Endeavorers have lined up in a thousand cities and towns throughout the world to resist evil in high places and low places; how they have engaged in local, State, and national contests for purer politics, for a holier Sabbath, for the destruction of the saloon, for the abolition of graft, for justice between man and man, and for peace throughout the world.

We might go into particulars to tell you how in one city our societies have brought about the enforcement of the laws against baseball, in another have put the indecent picture slot-machines out of business, in another have compelled the authorities to pull down the lewd posters and billboards, and in a score of others have combined with other good citizens to vote a corrupt ring out of office and to put good men into office.

All this has been done without a suspicion of playing politics or of being used for partisan purposes. Indeed, in spite of tremendous pressure at times, and at the cost of much vituperation and abuse from politicians who wanted to use the Society to pull their particular chestnuts out of the fire, the Society has steadily refused to ally itself with any

106

party, but has told its members in all parties to vote for good men and good measures, and then to see to it, to the best of their ability, that the good laws were executed.

To this end, members of the Society have co-operated with Good-Citizenship Associations, the Anti-Saloon League, the Woman's Christian Temperance Union, and other temperance workers, with Sabbath Protective Leagues and committees, and with local reform organizations where the members have been convinced that they are wisely managed and are pure in their motives.

I might tell you how our societies have extended their sympathies beyond the vast domain of America, and have prayed for and co-operated with those who have had the peace of the world at heart, and how they flooded the Peace Commissioners at the Hague with letters and telegrams of sympathy and support, which, we are told, greatly cheered the hearts of those who were laboring, in the midst of many difficulties, to beat the spears of the nations into pruning-hooks and their swords into ploughshares.

But I have time to ask if, in all these years, any one in this audience can point to a single instance where, in any large way, the Endeavorers have been arrayed upon the wrong side of any great moral question. Have they ever aided the forces of intemperance or of impurity or of graft or of political corruption? Have they not stood during all these eight and twenty years, not only as passive resisters of the wrong, but as active advocates and promoters of the right, in the great moral issues of the day? Have they not always welcomed to their platforms such men and women as Frances E. Willard and Francis J. Heney, the man who makes the grafters of San Francisco to tremble, and Charles E. Hughes, the noble and fearless governor of New York, and Governor Glenn of North Carolina, and Governor Marshall of Indiana, and the peerless governor of this great commonwealth, and the great orator of Nebraska, who have thrilled our hearts at this Convention, speaking not as politicians, not as statesmen merely, but as Christian reformers who have the welfare, not of one party, but of the whole country at heart.

The answer is very simple. Because ours is first and last and all the time a religious society, and because the roots of every great reform run down into the soil of religion. We have promised in our pledge to strive to do whatever Christ, the Master, in whom we trust for strength, would like to have us do.

Every Endeavorer knows in his inmost heart that the Master would like to have him resist intemperance and impurity and dishonesty in high places and low, and injustice between employer and employed and between employed and employer as well; so he cannot be true to his covenant pledge or to the fundamental principles of his society unless he takes the side of right.

Moreover, the line is usually drawn so broadly and clearly between true and false reform that the Endeavorer has no question where he ought to stand. In addition to his own innate sense of right and wrong, and the promptings of his conscience, the Endeavor movement has been given unequalled opportunities, through its meetings, its local-union gatherings, and its great conventions, to educate the mind and conscience of its young people.

It has been estimated by those in the position best to know, that there have been, during these twenty-eight years, forty-five millions of Christian Endeavor prayer meetings held, with an aggregate attendance of a billion and a quarter of young people. In all of these the purpose has been to press home upon the conscience some truth of the gospel, and often some truth that relates to the duty of man to man upon which all true reforms are based. In the course of these years literally millions of strictly temperance meetings have been held, and millions more that relate to some other phase of reform. It cannot be that these have not had their influence.

It has also been estimated that during the last quarter of a century fully 90,000 Christian Endeavor union meetings and conventions have been held, numbering in attendance from 100 to upward of 50,000, and aggregating tens of millions of auditors. At almost all of these larger gatherings some form of good citizenship has had a place upon the programme, as it has had a conspicuous place upon the programme of this Convention, and good citizenship spells "reform," wherever reform is needed. It cannot be that these meetings, whose enormous numbers make one's head reel when we try to comprehend them, have not affected the life of this nation and of the world. The facts fully bear out our theories.

I have recently travelled through the South, attending conventions in Tennessee, Alabama, Georgia, Florida, and North Carolina, Texas, and Oklahoma, and for fully 3,000 miles of the journey I was in dry territory. Since the world began I do not believe that it has been possible for a man to travel so far and so long where liquor was absolutely barred by law. And this is only an indication of the sweeping progress of the present-day spirit of reform.

But time forbids me to multiply illustrations of the reform spirit of Christian Endeavor, though they might be drawn "from Indus to the Pole." It only remains for us to consider briefly how this spirit may be increased and our efforts made more effective. In three words I would say this can be done,—information, agitation, action; more information, more agitation, more sane and efficient action.

The action in favor of wise reforms must be taken by us as individual Endeavorers or by our societies or unions; the agitation is furnished by earnest but level-headed men in our conventions and union meetings; the information is fortunately at our command at all times.

I would commend to you especially the Patriots' League, a Christian Endeavor organization of which former President Roosevelt, Governor Charles E. Hughes, and other eminent men are members, and our own George W. Coleman, a reformer of the first order, is superintendent. This league, through the Christian Endeavor publications, will furnish abundant information and numberless suggestions for carrying on the reform propaganda.

But with all this information, agitation, and energetic action, fellow Endeavorers, let us never forget the source of all our power. It is the same for the mightiest reform as for the humblest prayer meeting— it is the power of the Spirit of the living God. In his name and in his name alone can we go forth to conquer, for he has said that one of these days "the earth shall be filled with the knowledge of the glory of the Lord, as the waters cover the sea."

Dr. J. T. McCrory, of Pittsburg, former president of the Pennsylvania State Union, and a splendid type of Christian patriotism, made a ringing address upon the annihilation of the saloon. It was an overwhelming indictment of the saloon, and an intense appeal for Christian service.

I like this statement of the subject, "The annihilation of the saloon." It aims at the right thing. It goes to the root of the matter. When anything is annihilated, it is done for; it is gone, destroyed root and branch; and that is what ought to happen and what will happen to the saloon. The saloon must go. Why? Because it ought to go. And He who stands for the oughtness of the moral universe has decreed that it shall go. He came to the world to bring that to pass. He came to destroy the works of the devil, and the saloon is the work of the devil.

But now let us not overlook or blink the fact in our enthusiasm that this is a tremendous undertaking—to annihilate the saloon. The saloon will die, but it will die hard. It will rally to its aid every evil resource, earthly, sensual, devilish. It has its grip by means of appetite on millions and millions of men and women, and will not be easily shaken off. It has its ramifications running through all lines of enterprise. It is intrenched, grim and confident, in the politics of the land. The Christian patriotism that inspires the glorious expectation of the enthronement of King Jesus over the affairs of this nation will consume with the hot blast of its righteous indignation, and wither with the consuming curse of an outraged, long-delayed, and fiery justice this giant iniquity, this enemy of God and humanity. Yes, the saloon is doomed to annihilation.

But now the proposition you have put to me is, "How unite the forces to this end?" Nothing short of a union of all the forces opposed to the saloon will be sufficient to accomplish this result.

And that raises the question as to what are the forces against the saloon. And, when one comes to consider these, he is utterly amazed that this iniquity, mighty as it is, is able to stand out for one hour against these practically omnipotent forces. What are they? We may divide them into two distinct classes; viz.: First, the forces that aim directly at the annihilation of the saloon; and, second, the forces that are working indirectly toward the same end.

In the forefront of the host whose specific purpose is the annihilation of the liquor traffic let us put this glorious "White Ribbon" army, the Woman's Christian Temperance Union. And this is not done for the sake of courtesy, but for the sake of accuracy; for, while not the oldest of the organized workers, yet, when we consider its origin, begotten as it was from above in the energy of the Holy Spirit and marshalled forward in faith and prayer on lines of activity that touch vitally every point of warfare against this iniquity, to it belongs the place of leadership.

And then we have all these fraternal organizations, Good Templars, Sons of Temperance, Loyal Temperance Legions, total-abstinence societies, both Protestant and Catholic, with the mighty hosts of the Anti-Saloon League and the "Old Guard," the Prohibition party.

To all these I should like to add the Christian church of America. Then there are some tremendous allies working indirectly toward the same end, which must not be overlooked. All these great railroad and traction-car corporations and other organizations, employing hundreds of thousands of men and shutting the door of opportunity against saloon patrons; the public school with its twenty million boys and girls being instructed and safeguarded against the drink; the medical profession, more and more falling into line, warning the world against that deadliest enemy, alcohol; business, opening its shrewd eyes to the fact that its goods are left on the counter and its bills remain unpaid where the saloon flourishes and the publican grows rich.

With all these forces it would seem—would it not?—that the liquor traffic is doomed to speedy and complete destruction; and yet it flourishes, yes, and seems to grow in power and insolence and destructiveness with every passing year. Why, the world is standing aghast at the fearful, appalling ravages of this ferocious, malevolent, hydra-headed monster.

It is the enemy of the American home, that most cherished institution under heaven, transforming every year more than a million American firesides into abodes of such abandoned wretchedness and hopeless despair as should make the devils pity and the angels weep. It is the modern

Beelzebub, the god of filth, the "monstrum horrendum" of twentieth-century civilization, seizing our noble sons and beautiful daughters, and dragging them through the gambling-hell and the brothel, tens of thousands of them every year, and through blood and shame and heartbreak, leaving them to rot along the shores of time. The saloon—it is the heartless, modern Moloch, the destroyer of the little folk, driving more than two million American children with the cruel triple lash of homelessness, hunger, and ignorance down into the slums of a hopeless earthly hell every year.

And still the saloon lives; lives with the consent and by the suffrage of the American people. Lives and grows stronger, more defiant, and more destructive every year. And all this in the face of these opposing forces referred to, with latent power sufficient to crush it in an instant and stay its ravages forever. Then in the name of pity, in the name of heaven, why do we not use our power and annihilate it?

And here we are confronted with the solemn and tremendous fact that the only rational answer to that inquiry is our lack of unity against this hideous, murderous, malevolent, monstrous enemy of God and humanity. Surely then it is of infinite moment that we consider this question, how to unite these forces.

And now hear me, my friends. To come at once to the answer, I do not believe there is any place under heaven to get together from which to assault and annihilate the saloon but the broad, solid foundation of a profound moral conviction of the sin and crime of the legalized liquor traffic. The core of the matter is here,—that the business man, the physician, the teacher, if citizens, have for a consideration perpetrated the unspeakable stupidity and wickedness of providing for the doing of the very thing against which they warn as an appalling danger. They have organized a great trust and gone into partnership with it to lure to the destruction against which they have warned. Now we will get together, and get together effectively for the swift and certain annihilation of the saloon when we awake to the awful, shuddering, damning fact that as citizens of these great, free commonwealths and of this great free republic we are guilty before God of authorizing and promoting the greatest crime of the ages. And this hour will come. And, when it does come, it will bring along with it the greatest revival this world has ever seen. When the fact and the enormity of our guilt in this matter of the existence of the liquor traffic strikes home to our hearts, there will be such a stab of mortal agony and such a cry for mercy and pardon as the world has not experienced before. ·

Let us, then, work and pray and preach to bring about this awakening if we would annihilate the saloon. This is the real fighting line from which, with a mighty cheer in which the angels will join, the assault will be made that will sweep from the land this curse of drunkard-making. I have read that in a certain great battle one of Grant's corps-commanders, losing his position, wired his commander-in-chief how he could get back into the fight; and the lightning flashed back the sententious order, "Push to the front." Let us use and encourage every effort to harass and cripple and curtail the liquor traffic, but all the while let us be pushing to the front. Take the high ground of the sin and crime of the legalized saloon.

"The crisis presses on us; face to face with us it stands
With solemn lips of question, like the Sphinx in Egypt's sands.
This day we fashion destiny, our web of fate we spin;
This day for all hereafter choose we holiness or sin;
Even now from starry Gerizim or Ebal's cloudy crown
We call the dews of blessing or the bolts of cursing down.

"By all which the martyrs bore, their agony and shame;
By all the warning words of truth with which the prophets came;
By the future which awaits us; by all the hopes which cast
Their faint and trembling beams across the blackness of the past;
O my people, O my brothers, let us choose the righteous side."

Let us put Christ in the forefront of this conflict. Let us demand as citizens of a great Christian nation that our institutions harmonize with his will, and that the government shall not frame iniquity by law.

Let an awakened citizenship get into line on the high ground of the sin and crime of the legalized liquor traffic, and under the power and leadership of the omnipotent Christ we will annihilate the saloon and crown him Lord of all.

The last address of the evening was given by Dr. W. F. Wilson of Toronto, Canada. In his home land Dr. Wilson is known as "Move-on Wilson," and he lived up to this sobriquet most effectively. His theme was "America's Hope, the Evangelistic Church." It was a thrilling address, a most eloquent and masterful plea for an earnest, sane, comprehensive, victorious evangelism.

America is a magic word; it embraces my country and yours. America owns the future; as goes this continent, so swings the world. America spells liberty, opportunity, culture, prosperity, and religion. Its wealth, laws, and ideals inspire our race. We admire the Greeks who loved Athens, the Hebrews who loved Jerusalem, and as a Canadian I love the Union Jack, while you have your splendid Stars and Stripes.

Washington won your liberty; Lincoln preserved your unity; but Christ must save your manhood.

What is America's hope? Wealth, navies, armies, territory, and population? No, but the church, pure, practical, progressive, and evangelistic. The evangelism of the world is the supreme duty of Christianity.

The evangelistic church has a glorious mission, a living message, and splendid leadership. It is her duty not only to instil integrity, purity, and unselfishness, but to arouse the conscience, subdue the will, and turn the hearts of men towards Christ.

Then why not organize the church? Capital, labor, and commerce are all organized; why not the church? Not to do as little as we dare, but as much as we can. We have many kinds of churches—the sectarian church, near-sighted and narrow; the fashionable church, exclusive and cold; the intellectual, the institutional, and the critical church; but these will not do; rather, the evangelistic church will help to purify politics, destroy the saloon, preserve the Sabbath, and sweep away all evils until they shall find no safety beneath Old Glory's stainless stars.

We have many evangels of fidelity. How bravely Folk fought in Missouri, Hanley in Indiana, Heney in California, and Governor Hughes in New York! Must these civic heroes fight alone? No, the church cries, "Forward march;" shall we obey? We need the evangelistic spirit in our colleges and in our leaders in order that the church may maintain her place and follow on to conquer the world for Christ.

The evangelistic spirit is the basis of the church's growth. Self-preservation cries for evangelism. To organize an army there must be a patriotic spirit; to start a school, an intellectual desire; and to build a church there must be evangelistic spirit. Crowds, culture, and collections will not do, there must be power, fervor, and spiritual life.

The evangelistic spirit is the basis of personal growth, inspiration, and joyful experience. The evangelistic spirit inspires personal service that will bring practical results; caring for the helpless, the aged, the orphan, the hungry, and the diseased, but, above all, winning the sinful for Christ and his cause.

The great audience sang triumphantly "The way of the cross leads home;" the Mizpah benediction was pronounced; and one of the most inspiring and fruitful sessions of the great Convention was over.

THE INDIANAPOLIS DELEGATION.

THE TEXAS DELEGATION.

CHAPTER XXI.

THE SABBATH DAY.

Central Presbyterian Church, Sunday Evening, July 11.

The meeting in the Central Presbyterian Church on Sunday evening was an inspiring tribute to the spirit of Christian Endeavor, which flourishes everywhere most enthusiastically and in sunshine or rain. A thunder-shower of typical Minnesota proportions only served to bring into the lime-light the staying qualities in the spirit of the young people. The great auditorium of the church was crowded when the pastor, Rev. Harry Noble Wilson, D. D., very felicitously introduced the service. The official badge was much in evidence; in fact, the audience was almost exclusively made up of delegates. Everybody sang, sang as people sing who know what they want, know how to make the sacrifices to get what they want, and know when they are getting it. The addresses were enthusiastically received. The platform was beautifully draped with flags, a large picture of Dr. Clark being the centre of a well-conceived and most pleasingly executed plan of flag decorations.

Bishop Weekley, the first speaker of the evening, in no uncertain tone called the young people of the church to a more emphatic loyalty to the Sabbath. The bishop is a robust speaker, decisive of utterance, but with the rare twinkle of wit that sweetens the truth without in any wise weakening it. His message left a deep impression, not only upon the audience, but upon the Convention city as a whole.

Ours is a Christian nation. It is such because it was established by Christian men on Christian ideals. Its foundations were laid broad and deep in the belief that one day of rest out of every seven was in perfect accord with the Divine Word, and absolutely essential to man's best interests, whether mental or physical, spiritual or social. Therefore any attempt to destroy the sanctity of the Sabbath, or to divorce it as a day of rest and worship from our national life, is an effort to undermine and remove forever one of the chief corner-stones of our great republic.

It is a safe proposition that the future of this nation will be determined largely by our attitude toward this God-ordained institution. An eminent judge of the United States Supreme Court has said, "Where there is no Christian Sabbath, there is no Christian morality; and without this free government cannot long be sustained."

When the Pilgrims were exploring the New England coast, they came

113

to Clark's Island, where they spent Saturday drying their clothing and repairing their boat. They also made preparation for the coming Lord's day, and kept it holy. In their records we find this statement: "On the Sabbath day we rested." To obey God and keep his ordinance was their first and chief concern. It was an early consecration of the new world to a divine service, and contained a beautiful message to the toiling millions who were to live on these shores in the centuries to come.

"The Sabbath was made for man," is the declaration of the wisest and best of all teachers. That is to say, it was made to serve his highest interests by multiplying his religious and social enjoyments. No man can truly keep the Sabbath without being a Christian; for the Sabbath means worship, and worship implies the exercise of faith, the cultivation of benevolent impulses, devout meditation, and prayer. Nothing else is worship, and nothing else is keeping the Sabbath.

Those who seek to spend the day in wanton revelry, or in money-getting, are the infidels of the country; and, if they predominated (as, thank God, they do not) and their selfish desires were gratified, the nation would soon be under the control of influences absolutely unchristian and un-American.

It is argued by many that the Sabbath was all right for the Hebrews and Puritans, but that we cannot keep it, and need not do so if we could. This is the rankest heresy. If a day of rest was required by a peasant nation like the early Jews, and by our forefathers in the wilderness, we need it much more to-day because of the ceaseless mental and physical strain under which we live.

Spending the day in feasting, in unnecessary travel, in discussing business affairs, in frequenting ice-cream parlors, or buying groceries for the Sabbath's rations, is needless, and merits condemnation.

"Remember the Sabbath day to keep it holy" is the injunction of Jehovah himself. This means more than the mere keeping of the day when it comes; we are to "remember" it beforehand and prepare for its observance. Enough manna must be gathered on Saturday to supply the needs of Sunday. Thoughtfully arranging beforehand for the keeping of the day is a just and praiseworthy recognition of God and of our obligations to him.

We have two especially dangerous elements in the midst of us. One is composed of those who out of greed and a downright disregard for the welfare of others seek to carry on their business affairs seven days in the week. They take no rest themselves, and refuse it to those in their employ. The other class consists of such as spend the holy Sabbath in pleasure-seeking. This may mean theatre-going, or dancing, or gluttonous revelry; no matter. They want pleasure, such as a morbid moral nature craves; and that they must have, regardless of the cost to themselves and others. This is a vicious element because it seeks to strip the Lord's day of its true meaning, and to destroy all reverence for holy things.

The corrupt, debauching influence of these two classes must be held in check and utterly destroyed. The battle is on in earnest. Faith and courage and devotion are at a premium, and were never needed more than at this moment.

Among the church's agencies I know of none more potential in achieving the results for which we pray than the great Christian Endeavor army. It should thrust itself anew into this field with a mighty purpose of soul to save the nation from the awful blight of degeneracy which must inevitably fall upon those who ignore the divine law of rest and worship.

Archdeacon J. B. Richardson with a tenderness of spirit that met an immediate response from his audience brought the message, "Fellowship for Service." It was a fruitful call for a closer allegiance to Christ and a more potent, an immediate, fellowship among all Christians for larger service. This subject seems appropriate for consideration toward the close of this happy Convention. We have been hearing and doing a great deal in the matter of fellowship, and we have given due attention to service. This evening we may well put these together and note their bearing upon each other. One of the speakers last week mentioned three ships in which he took pleasure in travelling; viz., friendship, citizenship, and fellowship; but the best of the three was fellowship. Fellowship, not in the ordinary, but in the Christian Endeavor sense, is a most comprehensive term. Notwithstanding the social difference among its members—and these are very marked in some quarters—there is a real oneness enjoyed by all. National differences may tend to sunder them, but the greetings which came to this Convention on Thursday evening from all quarters of the globe testified to the unity of Christian Endeavor everywhere. The same fellowship exists, notwithstanding the denominational differences, and there is more real unity among the churches in Christian Endeavor to-day than ever before. But we must have something more than fellowship, something more than sentiment. Our fellowship is for service. We are saved to serve, and our Christian life after conversion is given to us for service.

The disciples once, confronted with the vast multitude at the Sea of Galilee, a hungry mass of humanity, felt unable to give any relief; and they suggested to their Master to "send them away." His reply was most suggestive, "They need not depart; give ye them to eat."

The church is face to face to-day with the question, How shall we deal with the masses? We dare not evade or escape them. Our Lord calls us to serve in their behalf, and never before as in the present did the church seem to rise to a sense of the high responsibilities in this regard. She is not now content with Sunday services and week-day meetings, and Sunday-school teaching, with singing hymns, saying prayers, and reciting creeds. She is engaged in great social reforms, going down among the wretched and degraded, and lifting them up to a better life. She is occupied with mighty and world-wide missionary enterprises. She is organizing her young men and women in the ranks of Christian Endeavor in service for Christ and the church.

The attendants at this great Convention will return to their homes with fresh inspiration for fellowship in service.

The closing address of the evening was delivered by Rev. T. P. Stevenson, D. D., LL.D., of Philadelphia. "The March of the Nations toward the Kingdom of Christ" was a trium-

phant shout from the militant church, voiced by the eloquent
tongue of one of her widely honored sons. It was a call to
universal "peace on earth, good will to men." The great
audience were again brought face to face with the fact of the
the mission of the Kingdom, the bringing in of all nations.
Dr. Stevenson said:

The kingdom of Christ is an actual present fact. Because he died
to save the world the Father has committed the government of the world
into his hands. It is also a progressive fact. Therefore we pray, "Thy
kingdom come."

There are some sixty independent nations in the world. What is
the relation of these moral agents to the kingdom of Christ? My theme
implies they are all to be subject to Christ, and affirms that even now
they are marching toward it. Probably no nation or government to-day
draws the motives of its public life from the will of Jesus Christ. But
he as the Lord of providence is guiding them by ways they know not,
and bringing them all nearer to his kingdom. Secretary John Hay spoke
of the events that led up to the Spanish-American war as "the imposition
of invisible hands" on our nation. These "invisible hands" are upon all
nations.

1. The control of the world is passing into the hands of the nom-
inally Christian nations. When Martin Luther nailed his theses to the
church door in Wittenberg a little less than four hundred years ago,
only seven per cent of the habitable area of the globe was under the
control of Christian government, while ninety-three per cent was under
pagan or Mohammedan rule. To-day this situation has been almost
exactly reversed. Eighty-two per cent of the land surface of the globe
is under the sway of the Christian powers, and only eighteen per cent
under Mohammedan or pagan government. This computation, moreover, does not include Africa, so much of which has recently been parti-
tioned among European nations. We are not forgetful of the crimes
that have been committed by so-called Christian nations in the extension
of their territory, but they have carried order and liberty and justice
and an open door for the gospel into all the lands over which they have
spread their flags.

2. The Christian governments of the world are becoming more Christian. The proof of this statement is found in the fact that four hundred
years ago there were no Protestant governments. These arose with the
Reformation. Compare England and Germany and the United States
with Spain and Italy and Austria, and judge whether Protestant governments are an improvement over governments which bow to the Vatican.
Two hundred and fifty years ago the king of England claimed absolute
supremacy over both church and state. Thanks to the Covenanters and
Puritans, who laid down their lives in resisting this claim, civil and
religious liberty is enjoyed through all Christendom. For more than one
hundred and fifty years England ruled India through the East India Company, a company always hostile to missions. For sixty years India has
been governed directly by the crown, and her governors-general, including
such men as Sir John Lawrence, have been the friends of missions and
equally friends of India. The abolition of slavery, the temperance
reformation, the elevation of woman, the restraint of cruelty, are steps
of progress which reveal the influence of Christ and of Christianity upon
the nations. This is no ephemeral or transient work. It has been going
on for centuries. He who has drawn the nations and governments of
the world thus far toward his kingdom will draw them all the way, until
the kingdoms of this earth become the kingdom of our Lord and of
his Christ.

CHAPTER XXII.

REFORMS: INTERNATIONAL PEACE.

People's Church, Sunday Evening, July 11.

Notwithstanding the storm there was a good gathering of young people in the People's Church. The service was opened by the junior pastor, Rev. Samuel G. Smith, D. D. The opening hymn was sung with a true appreciation, and the prayer was direct and appropriate. The first speaker, Rev. F. D. Power, D. D., was strong in his exposure and denunciation of the evils of war. He said:

When a small boy I dug up, and used as playthings, bullets, cannon-balls, and old weapons on the historic field where Washington and Lafayette closed the Revolution in their victory over Cornwallis. Later, a lad, I heard the thunder of the guns in the first battle of the Civil War at Big Bethel, and in the first conflict of ironclads at the mouth of the James, and saw with delight the marching and countermarching of scores of thousands of troops gay with banners and buttons, gold braid and feathers, all the millinery of the military, the sunburst colonels and roll of drums and glint of bayonets—all the glitter of glorious war. It was a brave sight. Then came the devastation of the land, the burning of homes, then the return of the cripples from the field and the wrecks from the prisons; and many I remember never came back; and there were widowed women and fatherless children, and the stern struggle with poverty, an Eden made desert, and the fountains of human tenderness and kindness poisoned with a bitter hate.

1. What I know of war leads me to brand it as inhuman. Mankind is *mankinned.* We who say "our Father" should never dream of butchering our brothers. The work of throwing the resources of nations and mighty forces of nature into engines of torture and destruction to be used against creatures of our own flesh and blood belongs to the malignity of demons, not to the spirit of man. The time has passed when one murder makes a villain, millions a hero. It is with a nation as with an individual. A nation is not an abstraction. It is not a vague mass. It is made up of individuals, husbands and wives, parents and children, who love one another. It consists of affectionate women and sweet children and noble men, children of a common Father, redeemed by a common Saviour, heirs of a common inheritance. It is an aggregation of homes and interests and institutions. To butcher by wholesale in organized war is only national, concentrated, more deliberately planned murder even than individual assassination. Pickett, after the magnificent charge at Gettysburg, with tears streaming down his face salutes Lee, and, pointing to the blood-soaked valley, says, "My noble brigade has been swept away!"

"You and your soldiers have covered yourselves with glory" answered Lee.

117

"Not all the glory in the world, General," said Pickett, "can atone for the widows and orphans this day has made."

Humanity has its claims. Universal sympathy of man for man is an older sentiment than Christianity. War is inhuman. It is beastly. It is the path of Cain. It is the child of hell. It is hell.

2. We would war against war because it is unchristian. He on whom the revelation of Christ has not yet dawned is one on whom the idea of humanity has yet to dawn. Christ imparts a new meaning to that word. His gospel was to be the gospel of peace. His word to nations is, "Put up thy sword." Disarm. Of him it was foretold, "He shall judge among the nations, and rebuke, that is, arbitrate for, many people; and they shall beat their swords into ploughshares, and their spears into pruning-hooks; nation shall not lift up sword against nation, neither shall they learn war any more."

How far are so-called Christian nations fulfilling this prophecy when busy building Dreadnoughts and assembling great guns? "I have been laboring among a people who once delighted in war," said a missionary, "but since Christianity has prevailed here war has ceased altogether, and they are astonished how they ever engaged in all those deeds of savage cruelty which threatened the extinction of their race; but now the Prince of peace reigns."

War is never a part of the gospel. It is always bad. Standing where the crowned Sufferer stands, it is hateful and hideous. Is our Christianity, then, a failure since the great modern nations are Christian, or is our modern Christianity different from the old original Christianity of the Christ? Have the ideals of Jesus ceased to be the ideals of his professed disciples, and the crime and curse and cost of this thing lost their meaning in the light of the teaching and practice of Jesus? No; men have simply departed from the programme of Jesus.

3. We declare war against war, again, because it is irrational. If man carried away by anger loses his senses, the same is true of nations. If war has its pageantry, its chivalry, its enthusiasms, it has also its hideousness, its demoniac woe, its universal lust of death and vulgar slaughter, its wild unreason. From every point of view war is utterly without reason.

Here is its cost. Eight billions to maintain the army and navy on the Union side alone during our civil war; 350,000 lives on the Union side, 150,000 on the Confederate, sacrificed; and, as war demands the best, of the 2,200,000 enlisted men in the Union army, 412,000 under eighteen, and half the whole enlistment twenty-two years of age and under. I stood on one spot where within a few miles 85,000 men who wore the blue or the gray bit the dust. And oh, the weeping of the women, the cry of the children, the horrors of the field! To-day, practically two-thirds of our total national revenue is going for past wars and preparation for future wars.

We are shocked when we read how Turkish soldiers in Asia Minor sack and burn schools. We should think a man who spends five times as much for guns as for his children's schooling was a lunatic. Yet France spends five times as much on her army as on the intellectual training of her youth; Germany gives to educational purposes one-third as much as she devotes to military purposes; Russia gives nine dollars for powder and shot where she gives two to education; and Italy spends nine times for war what she does for the schooling of her girls and boys. What is this but armies robbing the schools? A single Dreadnought would build ten Tuskegees.

4. War forever against war because it is unnecessary. Armies and navies, they say, are a necessity; they make for peace. Would not a fleet of merchant ships flying the stars and stripes, and bearing our bounties to suffering lands, be better promoters of peace? Would not the

millions spent on our recent show of force have done infinitely more good
in fighting tuberculosis, or building good roads? Could not every war
of modern times have been settled by arbitration, as a hundred international difficulties have been disposed of within a score of years? "If
statesmen were more accustomed to calculation, wars would be less frequent," said Benjamin Franklin. Canada, he declared, might have been
purchased from France for a tenth part of the money England spent in
the conquest of it; our Revolution could have been settled without conflict. "I have been apt to think," he affirms, "there never has been, nor
ever will be, any such thing as a good war or a bad peace."

Three signs of promise:

First, settlement by pacific means of all difficulties arising from international differences, without peril to the national honor and vital interests of any nation, may be met by the plenipotentiaries of the third Hague
conference. This alone should realize the parliament of man, the federation of the world.

Second, the sober thought of mankind. There is nothing like what
Garfield used to call "the reserved sovereignty of the people." The greatest revolutionizing force in the world to-day is thought; and people are
thinking in the shop, on the farm, in the factory, in the bank, in the home.
War is a game which, were their subjects wise, kings would not play at;
and, when the people say, "Thus far and no farther," we shall reach the
limit. When the people say, "We want no more battle-ships," there will
be no more battle-ships. When the people say, "Out upon this barbarism,"
it will out.

Third, the air-ship. I read when a child Bulwer's "Coming Race,"
predicting that the death-knell of war would be sounded in the upper air.
I saw the child with a marvellous force, vril, slaying whole armies miles
away. I dreamed with Tennyson of "pilots of the purple twilight," "ar-
gosies with magic sails," "airy navies battling in the blue." Who shall
say the fulfilment of the prophecy is not here? The air-ship fitted with
deadly explosives soaring over cities, fortresses, and battle-ships can put
all of them out of action in a day. Frontiers, fortresses, and fleets, all
must yield to the conqueror of the air. War becomes impossible. "Blessed
are the peace-makers."

The Rev. R. G. Bannen, president of the Pennsylvania
State Union, told why Rev. S. S. Waltz, D.D., of Louisville,
Ky., had been obliged to leave the city before giving his address. He had left a synopsis of it, however, which we give
herewith.

The kingdom of Christ, though he be the Prince of peace, is to
be won by fierce and fearless conflict. The conflict grows not a whit
the less desperate as we approach the final victory. On every great
battle-field there is a point where the conflict reached high tide. It
was just before the victory. So it is on the field of earth where God's
people are contending for his kingdom. The conflict has reached high
tide. Never was Satan more desperate. Never was God's host more
determined. The fierceness of the battle but indicates the supreme
conflict that precedes the victory.

Every foe of right is met by a force that is more than conqueror.
The passion for wealth that is consuming the honor and the piety of
many is met by such a spirit of making money for Christ and con-
secrating it to his service as has never been equalled in human history.
The Bible, assailed everywhere by unfriendly criticism, has in this generation made its most marvellous headway in circulation and in the
affections of the people. While many are drifting away from the old

landmarks of religion, never has the Protestant Church of America been so evangelical as to-day. Though there is a fierce conflict between congested capital and organized labor, between the classes and the masses, never before has capital done so much to improve the condition of labor, and never have riches done so much to relieve poverty. Though gambling is rife in places high and low, holding sway in wheat-pits and stock-markets, in pool-rooms and in parlors, I am wont to believe that never before has it been so hunted and hard pressed as to-day.

These are the conditions as they must appear to any candid observer as he scans the lines of battle arrayed in the world conflict. What effect shall the summons of these facts have upon God's people? With what spirit shall they meet the challenge that everywhere confronts them? With what sort of power must we be endued to meet successfully the allied forces of evil, and to help to bring victory to the kingdom of Jesus Christ? I briefly mention three things:

First. There must be the call to the heroic. Sentimentalism in Christian service will not meet the conditions. The chivalry of sacrifice, and not the love of ease, must thrill the Christian soldier of to-day. The giants of difficulty and the hosts of Satan that confront God's people to-day are but a challenge to courage. A spirit other than this is unworthy a people redeemed at such a cost, led by such a peerless conqueror, and called to such a kingdom as that of Jesus Christ.

Second. Power for service requires hopefulness. God does not use discouraged people for large service in his kingdom. Everything connected with God's cause is an inspiration to a triumphant hope. Victory, and not defeat, has ever crowned the conflict of the sacramental army. Even its seeming defeats have turned out to be more than victories. This great convention will have served a high and holy purpose if it sends people home inspired with hope. It is well, when your buoyancy flags and you feel almost as if you were fighting a lonely and losing battle, to get a view of the mighty hosts to which you belong, engaged in the same cause for which you are contending. We belong to a mighty army, marching to a certain victory. Above us and around us are the invisible but innumerable hosts of God, who fight with us and for us.

Third. Power for service in the kingdom of Christ requires holiness. Only do not interpret holiness to mean such a stilted, separated attitude to the world as will prevent you from being in loving, helpful touch with it. Holiness means such a wholeness of manhood and womanhood as will bring and keep you in closest sympathetic touch with human beings like yourself. Whether at the marriage feast or the grave of buried love; whether in the home of the busy business man or the quiet family circle of Bethany, Christ was the same natural, great-hearted, sympathetic, manly man, commanding the reverent respect of all. This is the holiness that is power. Such power comes in but one way. It is the result of personal and continual fellowship with Christ. This is the sort of holiness for which I pray, and which I covet for you and for myself. It is the holiness that equips for service. It gives to each of us the armor Paul commended to those who would do valiant service in Christ's kingdom, "the corselet of faith and love." It meets Isaiah's conception of the disposition needed by God's people in those troublous times, by which they might overcome his enemies and build his kingdom—tireless work and ceaseless prayer. "Take ye no rest, and give him no rest, till he make Jerusalem a praise in the earth." The holiness we need is that which is ever forgetful of self and continually exalts him, who, if he be lifted up, will draw all men unto himself. This, and this alone, is power in the kingdom of Christ.

Dr. Bannen said the secret of power for service in the Kingdom is the power of God. We have too often forgotten

THE ILLINOIS DELEGATION.

THE OHIO DELEGATION IN THE PARADE TO THE CAPITOL.

that with him all things are possible. Is anything too hard for God? The spies that brought back the evil report forgot that God had promised that he would give Israel possession of the land. This is my Father's world; the Lord is king; let the heavens sing. God rules; let the earth be glad.

Dean Herbert L. Willett, D. D., of Chicago University, was exceedingly clear, masterly, and most instructive in his address, and was followed with keenest interest by all the young people. His subject was "Education in the Kingdom." He said Jesus was on the mountain the teacher with authority. He was always a teacher. His followers were called disciples, learners. Christianity has even been connected with education. Paul was a teacher; Luther, Knox, Wesley were teachers. Huss was in the same line. Education has ever been one of the most notable instruments in the kingdom.

His second thought was on the place of education in life. It is the Golden Fleece; all want it; youth and parents crave it; childhood is the great point at which to begin to lay the foundation of all true education, intellectual and spiritual. It gives courage, fearlessness. There is a want of the Bible in the public schools and also of home instruction and training. His third thought was as to the crown of education. It is the search for the best in this life. The Holy Grail is its object. To be educated means qualification for the highest and noblest ministries here and hereafter. Christian Endeavorers stand for this. Know God in Christ as revealed in the Bible.

CHAPTER XXIII.

THE LAYMEN'S MEETING.

House of Hope Presbyterian Church, Sunday Evening, July 12.

In spite of a heavy downpour that continued throughout most of the evening a generous company of earnest listeners gathered to hear the laymen discuss "The Christian Layman in Civic Reform, in Social Reform, and in Church and Missionary Work." With the exception of Dr. Swearingen, pastor of the House of Hope Presbyterian Church, in which the meeting was held, who conducted the devotional exercises, all those that participated in the programme were laymen.

Mr. Trafford N. Jayne, president of the Minnesota Union, in presiding called attention to the fact that the development of the laymen had resulted in obliterating to some extent the sharp line of demarcation between the clergy and the laity. Mr. John P. Hartman, of Seattle, presented in a very earnest way the great privileges and responsibilities of the laymen in civic affairs in such a country as ours and in such a day and generation as this in which we live. He said:

In the centuries long agone civilization attained its highest form in the valley of the Euphrates, if we can trust the conclusions of the savants. Among the people there contention arose. One sect desired to let things alone as they were, but gradually evolving a little better condition on the stereotyped lines laid down. These were the ultra-conservatives. The other contingent was progressive,' and had a burning desire to make each succeeding day better than the one before, and produce results for the betterment of mankind in every respect as the days should go. These were the liberals. The conservative turned his back on his brother, and laid his course towards the Orient. The liberal turned his face to the westward, and sought new fields. Each has gone his course since. The liberal peopled the western part of Asia, thence went to Europe and northern Africa, and in 1492, and probably at an earlier day, on to the Americas.

In North America we see probably the highest type of the progressive class. In China and Japan we witness the greatest achievements of the conservatives. Now they are meeting upon the great central plains, mountain districts, and western coast of America. The struggle is still on. The desire for supremacy still exists in the heart and breast of each. The one civilization has builded churches, homes, hospitals, schools, and all those agencies of state, home, and society which have made the best and highest form of civil and religious government. The other still worships the ancestor to a certain extent, and is content to look to the past for guidance, with little hope for the future.

Not which people, but which principle, shall succeed, is the question that presents itself to every American citizen, in fact to every man of the world, no matter from what nation he may spring or to what power he may owe allegiance. The struggle, therefore, has been transferred from the valley of the Euphrates to the valley of the Mississippi and the great region stretching to the Pacific coast. Properly is it transferred there, because in this vast region the world is destined to see the highest type of civilization that ever has been or ever will be produced, because the conditions there exist to make it.

Another reason why the struggle is on in this remarkable region is that its production of the things which humankind must have is unlimited. The annual agricultural crop exceeds seven billions of dollars a year, a sum greater than that of the value of the crops of the remainder of the world. This can be increased many-fold, a stake well worthy the best mettle of the two forces. The mountain regions have produced as much gold, when we include Alaska, as all the other gold-producing sections of the world. The timber has no equal anywhere else in the world, and the fisheries are sufficient when properly cared for to produce a product that will feed twenty-five per cent of the world. This great production of wealth, if managed by righteous men, means the perfecting of the highest form of government where individual rights shall be held the most sacred, or, by unrighteous men, the building up of a plutocratic government and force which must finally destroy the great civilization. Men, therefore, of courage and conviction must be at the helm and control the affairs. These men must be those whose hearts and souls are right, whose aims are high, whose desires are not for personal gain, but for gain that will mean the best for all.

Most is expected to-day of the Christian man, and the world has the right to expect that of him. He sets a standard, or at least by the mere profession is assumed to set a standard; and, if that is not high, failure must come. Therefore the Christian man of our country—and that is the great majority—who does not thrust himself into the civic affairs of the day, and there make his voice and vote felt, falls short of the mission which called him into being. To meet, therefore, the problem which is now thrusting itself upon us in the Orient, we must not shut our gates, we must not build a wall, we must not say that he who lives on the other side of the Pacific Ocean, and so many millions strong, is not worthy of the confidence and protection of this country. Rather, we must so amalgamate him when he does come that his existence must be for a higher type of freedom, that his understanding for government and right shall be more optimistic, that he must think more and act more for the living present.

Men, therefore, of highest patriotism, strongest virtue, and purest principle must, shall, and will dominate the public affairs of this great district in which the drama for supremacy shall be fought. No man who desires to see the world grow better dares absent himself from the caucus, the primary, the convention, and the fulfilling of public duty in holding office and assisting those who do hold the public office. It is far more honorable to be a councilman, and make a mistake, and be criticised, than to sit back and idly criticise him who has made a mistake.

The great Endeavor movement has brought consecrated men and money into public life. While it is not necessary to recall the instances, they are all over the United States and England, and the South Seas, manifesting themselves in noble purposes in all countries. This principle, this power, this influence, will and shall solve the problem confronting us. Then, in that day, and when these powers and influences have grown to their full fruition, the world shall see here the greatest, the highest, the purest, and the most lofty of all the civilized peoples, where justice, right, and equity shall control in all things.

Mr. George W. Coleman, publisher of "The Christian Endeavor World," laid emphasis upon the indivisibility of social, civic, and church life in its appeal to the layman, and then proceeded to show that after individuals have yielded their hearts to the Master there still remains the work of Christianizing the body politic and the body social. Men may be devoted Christians, and still sustain unchristian relations to one another in the body social, just as they did, for example, in the days of slavery. The master might be an earnest Christian man and the slave also a simple follower of the Master, and yet the relationship of master and slave was not Christian.

The new times in which we are living require the adaptation of the gospel to the new competitions that surround us. The condition of our churches in the down-town districts raises the question whether we are interpreting the gospel message in its fulness, in that the work of the churches in so many cases does not appeal at all to the swarming multitudes, and the church is thus driven to move out into the suburbs to serve its old-time constituency, having failed of a message to the denser population in the old environment. Evidences are multiplying on every hand that there is a growing hunger and thirst for the application of the gospel to the social side of human nature where the zest for the individualistic interpretation of the Master's message is no longer keen. The lines of the old Hebrew prophet, together with innumerable New Testament teachings, make it perfectly plain that God's message to men as members of society is quite as important as his message to the individual heart. We are members all one of another, and no man liveth unto himself; and God's kingdom must come in the body politic and the body social just as surely as it is coming in the hearts of men.

We cannot teach the equality of man before God and the equality of man before the law without providing also equal economic opportunity. In this great country of ours, through the social crisis that is upon us and which De Tocqueville foretold a hundred years ago, democracy is on trial for its life, and the issue will be determined by our faithfulness in preaching and applying the whole gospel of our Lord and Master Jesus Christ.

General Secretary Shaw brought the meeting to a close with a ringing speech showing the part the layman is taking in church and missionary work. He made it most concrete and full of life by presenting a portrait gallery of young men who have made a mark in the world of Christian service and who all received their training in Christian Endeavor.

Mr. Shaw's connection with Christian Endeavor from the beginning has given him an intimate acquaintance with all the Christian Endeavor leaders.

He gave a most interesting review of the church and missionary activities of ten representative laymen who have been trained in Christian Endeavor. They included Mr. John P. Hartman, Mr. K. C. Ewing, and Mr. W. H. Lewis, of Seattle, Wash., three of the most successful men in that city and leaders in every good work. They represent the Presbyterian, Baptist, and Congregational churches, but stand together for the spread of the Kingdom.

Mr. William E. Sweet, of Denver, was cited as an example of Christian Endeavor's contribution to Young Men's Christian Association work. It was largely through Mr. Sweet's generous gift and personal service that the magnificent new building was secured.

Mr. William T. Ellis, of Philadelphia, began his successful journalistic career as the editor of a little Christian Endeavor paper published in the interest of a city union. He is now one of the most widely read and influential writers in the country on religious and missionary themes.

The Laymen's Missionary Movement was born in the heart of John B. Sleman, of Washington, D. C.; and he was trained for just such service in Christian Endeavor.

The Chicago Brotherhood was the beginning of the great Presbyterian Brotherhood movement, and Andrew Stevenson was its founder. In conversation with a friend on this subject, he said, "All the credit for this movement belongs to Christian Endeavor, for it was the training received in my Christian Endeavor work that led to the Brotherhood movement."

Mr. M. A. Hudson, the founder of the Baraca Sunday-school movement, simply applied the Christian Endeavor principles to men's Sunday-school classes after he had served through all the grades of Christian Endeavor work as private and officer.

And, lastly,—and these are only samples of a multitude of similar successful workers,—Mr. Shaw referred with great feeling to his old-time colleague, John Willis Baer, who came from the presidency of the Rochester, Minn., local union to the general secretaryship of the United Society, then into the secretaryship of the Presbyterian Board of Home Missions, at the call of his church, and now is president of Occidental College, Los Angeles, Cal., 'one of the growing and most successful educational institutions in the West

CHAPTER XXIV.

THE EVANGELISTIC CONFERENCE.

Central Presbyterian Church, Monday Afternoon, July 12.

We were led in most soul-stirring songs and earnest prayer; then, entering upon the great subject, we were led by Rev. J. P. Rice, D. D., pastor of the Portland Avenue Church of Christ, Minneapolis, Minn., on the subject, "The Church as the Evangelistic Force."

Our Lord intended his church to be evangelistic. In the most solemn and authoritative manner he commissioned his disciples to be evangelists, and to make evangelists of all who should become disciples. "The New Testament religion," says Mr. Brierley, "is from beginning to end a lay religion." "The vital religious movements ever since that time," says he, "have been essentially laymen's movements." Very early in the history of the church, when its members were scattered abroad, they "went about preaching the word." Churches began to spring up in the wake of these zealous refugees, and it was not long until the gospel message had been heard in all the leading cities of the Roman Empire.

The New Testament plainly recognizes a division of labor, but the various ministries are all in order to the "building up of the body of Christ to the work of ministering." Every one who is living in union with Christ is an evangelist. The world is waiting to hear the testimony of the non-professional man. Vast multitudes of people care not one whit for what the ministers say, but listen with eagerness to the words that may be spoken by upright and intelligent men of affairs. Every church has such men in its membership, and women too, who could lend themselves to a programme of evangelism that is greatly needed both in the city and the country. There is a church in England that has enrolled more than five hundred personal workers, and not a Sunday has passed in twenty-five years without conversions in that church.

There are methods in evangelism. The big revival with an eloquent preacher, whose message is simple, direct, and persuasive; who is assisted by a big chorus of gospel singers and numerous personal workers, is one method, but it is not the only one. The first expression of evangelistic zeal on the part of the disciples was their desire to tell others that they had found the Messiah. Andrew "findeth first his own brother," and "he brought him to Jesus." It is ever thus. It is almost an axiom that those who are saved must be won, and in the last analysis the winning must be done by some one near and dear. Personal evangelism is not the light and trifling thing that some seem to think it is. It is not rushing up to a stranger and impulsively importuning him or her to be a Christian. That is often the essence of unwisdom. Soul-winning takes time and patience and rigid self-discipline. It means personal service of the highest and divinest sort. It is the strong giving themselves for the weak, the free helping to break the chains that bind the enslaved, the enlightened shedding the light of the Sun of righteousness into the hearts that have been darkened by sin, the hopeful imparting courage to the hopeless; it is dying daily that others might live. The church must become such a force in every community. God is calling his people to the performance of tasks that they might have never conceived to be their tasks. He is opening the gateways to new fields and bidding us enter and gather the harvests that are already over-ripe. Fundamentally the work is evangelism. The preacher is but one member of the church, and he is helpless save as the multitude of the redeemed shall rally under his leadership with money, time, personal effort, and unstinted self-devotion. The church as a whole is the evangelizing force through whose efforts the kingdom of God shall be made to appear.

The second address was given by Rev. Thomas Ashburn, pastor of the Cumberland Presbyterian Church, of Knoxville, Christian Endeavor Society as a Training-school for Evangelism."

The Christian Endeavor Society is the church training-school.
No work of the church is more important than her work of evangelizing.
The Christian Endeavor Society trains her members in soul-saving.
1. By having her members read their Bibles every day. The Bible is the sword of the Spirit, and he who conquers for Christ must be familiar with its teachings and applications.
2. Then the Christian Endeavorer is pledged to pray daily, which keeps him in touch with God, where the Holy Spirit can fill and fit him for winning the lost.
3. The young man or woman is prepared for this work by living daily the Christian life, which every one in taking the pledge promises to do. They are to do throughout their whole life only the things Jesus would have them do. This Christian living gives force to their messages of love to the lost as nothing else could do. For in this practical age the world wishes to see samples of our work.
4. The social feature of the Christian Endeavor Society does much in training her members for evangelism. To approach the wayward in friendship's tactful manner is necessary in order to win. Social to save is one prominent feature of Christian Endeavor.
5. Also, by training her members to give one-tenth of their income to the support of the gospel. It takes money as well as prayers and work to do successfully evangelistic work.
6. The Christian Endeavor Society trains her members for evangelism by doing the thing. No training for any work equals the doing of the thing for which one is being trained.
The Christian Endeavor Society does this by taking in associate members who are not Christians, then by various helpful influences leading them to decide to give their lives to Christ for service.
Then by going out into neglected districts in bands of workers and giving the gospel to those who have it not. In this way not only is much good being done both in the cities and in the country, but a large number in this way are being trained for professional evangelists.
Again, by bringing and holding the young under the preached word of the pastor and the evangelist in their own church many are doing much toward winning a lost world.
As the young people thus go out and engage in evangelistic work in their various ways, they not only do much directly in evangelizing their community; but in addition thereto they are training themselves for a lifetime service in this Christly work.

The third address was by Rev. D. A. Poling, field secre-
tary of the Ohio Christian Endeavor union, on the subject,
"The Personal Workers' Training-Class in the Society or
Union."

The idea of a personal workers' class is to bring young
people to realize the great privilege. The class should not
be larger than seven. The class should be recruited by personal solicitation, not by public announcement. Count nothing too dear to give up for Christ. When you reach this,
you will be successful. The supreme need is the close fellowship with the Master.

The fourth address was given by Rev. U. F. Swengel, D. D.,
pastor of Grace United Evangelical Church, of Lewiston,
Penn., on the subject, "Evangelistic Methods that Succeed."

Evangelism is one of the great watchwords of Christian Endeavor.
This is quite natural because Christian Endeavor was born in and of a
revival.

The very term "evangelism" suggests the best of all methods, namely,
"zeal in spreading the gospel." To evangelize is to instruct in the gospel. To do such important work, which affects and secures the eternal
welfare of our fellow men, requires a study in methods. Almost any
method is better than a haphazard manner. Yet with the best and most
approved methods there must not be an iron-jacket or inflexible enforcement of a rule. The Holy Spirit must have the right of way to
direct, to amend, or to annul and supplant our carefully thought-out
methods.

A study of Old Testament methods as used by those whom the Spirit
honored by special mention reveals God's way of dealing with men to
bring about their salvation. That some of them did not accomplish all
that God wanted only argues the hardness of men's hearts, and proves
the fact that man is a free moral agent, allowed to choose for himself
to his own hurt even when messages come to him directly from God.

The plan adopted by the man after God's own heart to influence people
religiously by religious song and enthusiastic singers has always proved
to be a mighty force in touching the hearts of men with religious sentiment and life. The plaintive, pathetic appeals of song have frequently
reached hardened hearts that had steeled themselves against the words
of the preacher. Mr. Moody had his Sankey, and Mr. Torrey had his
Alexander, who supplemented them grandly in their great revival work.

Evangelistic service must not always be done in an obscure corner.
Publicity for the sake of souls and for the Master's sake is not only per-
missible but perfectly justifiable. Tracts, placards, bulletin-boards, and the
secular newspapers, judiciously pressed into service, quietly and effectually
carry invitations into many unthought-of nooks and corners and to many
unknown persons whom you cannot reach in any other manner.

The young people are moving in larger or smaller companies. Men
can do in companies or in masses what they cannot do singly. Some one
has said that bees build their mathematically accurate cells by working in
swarms. The Christian church has learned from bees working in swarms,
from birds going in flocks, from animals going in herds, that there are
advantages in concerted movements in spiritual as well as in natural life.
Many a good plan has been abortive because of the loneliness of its
projector, when an association of two or more might have created and
maintained enthusiasm and success. Our Master sent out his evangelistic

A VIEW IN COMO PARK.

MISSISSIPPI RIVER AND VALLEY.

forerunners in companies of two. Co-operation is a great watchword for the accomplishment of things. We are living in days when trusts in commerce, in manufacture, in agriculture, in labor, in everything, are apparently essential.

It is important to be ready for God's time and authority to move forward. Moses failed at first because neither he nor the people were ready for the forward movement, but forty years of preparation made the greatest difference.

Jonah was not ready when God first bade him go to Nineveh, and suffered great loss because of it. But when he, a lone evangelist, ready at last to accept his mission, for forty days preached the word of God, he led a proud king and his idolatrous people to their knees and to salvation.

Peter and his coadjutors, made ready by the Spirit of God for work, endued with promised power, won three thousand in a single day. The same apostle was as ready to go into a single household and preach the gospel to the family Cornelius, the Roman, had gathered about him.

Christian Endeavor, with its great inspirational and evangelistic campaigns, its local societies and committees and its individual workers, has won many thousands for Christ and the church. It is well equipped to harness every willing worker among young people, and to train him for the most advanced and the most thorough work in the great soul-winning conquest. While it enlists small groups and kindles the enthusiasm of masses, it lays hold on the individual for personal work. It begins with the individual by placing him in a covenant relation with God. It first insists on dependence on God for strength; without that, man's weakness will frustrate every effort at evangelistic work. With that there is nothing we can do with more positive assurance that we are pleasing him than bringing souls to him for salvation. The occasion, a zeal tempered with knowledge, and the guidance of the Holy Spirit must determine how it is to be done.

I spoke a while ago about preparation for the work of soul-winning. Did you read that story of a great revival in which in two weeks' time eleven hundred souls were saved? The secret of power was the fact that nine weeks had been spent by the rvivalist in preaching to the churches until professed Christians were so chastened for lack of interest in the salvation of their fellow men that they sincerely consecrated themselves to the work, and that was the reason why two weeks brought so great a harvest of souls. Shall we not dwell on this theme until our hearts are aglow with a burning zeal for souls?

CHAPTER XXV.

"THY KINGDOM COME," IN ALL THE WORLD.

The Auditorium, Monday Morning, July 12.

Though it is Monday morning, and the great strain is telling on the young people, yet here they are in large numbers to follow a strong programme. The subject is "Christian Endeavor Work as an Agent in Bringing in the Kingdom of Christ." What are we doing in the wide, wide world? Are we making good our profession? Listen to our declaration. Mr. Foster swings his magic right arm, and a great wave of song sweeps the assembly.

> "Christ for the world we sing;
> The world to Christ we bring,
> With loving zeal."

Is that our purpose? Shall we do it? Will it be done in this generation? Hear that song filling this great building.

> "Ambassador to be of realms beyond the sea,
> I'm here on business for my King."

If Christian Endeavor gets that into the marrow and muscle of its being, then the Kingdom will come, as even now we are repeating, "Our Father which art in heaven, thy kingdom come, thy will be done in earth as it is in heaven."

Dr. Clark prays for world-wide evangelism, and again we sing "All hail the power of Jesus' name."

"A soldier of the Old Guard" was the introduction of Rev. Albert A. Fulton, D. D., of Canton, China. "With but twenty-five minutes in which to speak, I can make no introduction or conclusion, but plunge into my subject. I want to show you Christian Endeavor work in China.

"Millions in China are worshipping idols—a fearful delusion. There are four hundred millions in China, and you cannot change them by railroads and telegraphs. You must give them the gospel. See how Christian Endeavor has worked here.

"We go into the cities, villages, etc., get a shop, clean it

130

out, put in a Christian worker, and establish a Christian centre. Here is where Christian Endeavor is doing a vast work, establishing chapels and training native helpers. For one hundred and fifty dollars we can establish such a preaching-hall or chapel, and this will become a great light amid the darkness of heathenism.

"Christian Endeavor can put such centres of light into thousands of towns and villages; and now is the hour, for China is wide open. You have sung, 'Where He leads me, I will follow.' Now put the song into deeds.

"For one hundred dollars you can support a native Chinese preacher. For forty dollars you can support a woman worker.

"Now, Christian Endeavorers, will you make an effort to help put thousands of these light centres into China?"

Hundreds of Christian Endeavorers rose to their feet, pledging themselves to do all they can through their church boards to light these lights all over China.

Prayer is offered by Mr. Karl Lehmann. "O God, roll upon us the burden of the world. Give us the vision to see, the strength to follow."

The programme now turns to "Cheering Messages from the World-wide Field."

Rev. S. Guy Inman, missionary to Mexico, brings the cheering word that the Christian church is studying the South Latin lands as mission fields.

He tells the awful condition of Mexico in the paganized Roman Christianity. The facts he gave were startling. He said:

The question is sometimes asked, Why send foreign missionaries to Mexico, a Christian country? Is Mexico a Christian country? Dr. Abbott, in speaking of the way the Roman Church won the native Indians says: "Christianity, instead of fulfilling its mission of converting and sanctifying, was itself converted. Paganism was baptized; Christianity was paganized. Three centuries and a half of undisputed sway of Romanism has changed the situation so little that whatever reason may be given for mission work in any other country on the globe may be given also for the preaching of the gospel in Mexico."

Do the mothers of India dedicate their daughters to lives of shame as dancing girls in the Hindu temples? In Mexico many a peon mother considers it an honor for her daughter to be ruined by the parish priest. Is a young man in China cast out of his house because he becomes a Christian? Then in Mexico a whole village turns against a family who accepts Christ.

These relics of the Dark Ages existing yet among the lower classes, but driving the educated into atheism, have brought about in a country that is rapidly becoming one of the world's great nations, conditions that make such experts as John R. Mott declare that Mexico is the most difficult mission field in the world.

There is no difficulty, however, in finding things that cheer. One of these is the way our young converts become personal workers. I know a sixteen-year-old Christian Endeavorer who works twelve hours a day in a coal-mine, and gets up half an hour earlier every morning to copy a chapter out of his Bible to take with him to read to his companions at the noon lunch period.

A drunken shoemaker, after he was converted, gave one or two days every week to visiting a neighboring town with his pastor to establish work there, saying, "Why should I not give this time to my Master when before he saved me I used to spend entire weeks in drunken sprees?"

Educational work has always been a prominent part of the programme of our mission in Mexico. While Romanism was working on the platform expressed by the Pope, that "it is false and pernicious doctrine that public schools should be opened to all children and free from ecclesiastical authority," the Evangelicals since they entered the country in 1865 have been the leaders in the work of direct instruction, as well as furnishing the government with some of her best men for organizing her public-school system. We still need to enlarge our influence in the public schools. Where we do not furnish the teachers, they are most likely to be agnostic in their influence, as the government schools are usually hotbeds of atheism.

Here at our very door, with our nearest neighbor, is taking place one of the world's greatest conflicts. At present all is confusion. Often brother fights brother, and kindred forces turn fiercely upon one another. The fanaticism of Rome, the degradation of the peon, the agnosticism of the educated, and the forces of evangelical Christianity struggle mightily for supremacy.

Young people, I bring you a call to help King Jesus win the victory.

Rev. T. Makino, of Kyoto, Japan, brings Japan's greeting and cheer. "The time is gone for separations—all together for Jesus." He spoke of the foolish talk regarding war between this country and Japan. "You love your country; we love ours." He then held up a beautiful flag given to him by the Sunrise Christian Endeavor Union of Cleveland, Ohio. The banner is of two flags, those of Japan and America, held together by Christian Endeavor. "This, said he, "will be cherished in Japan as an inspiration to all."

Dr. Julian C. Caldwell, of Nashville, Tenn., brought greetings from the negro Christian Endeavor societies of America. A great voice, beautifully modulated, a message from a thousand societies, couched in poetic language, honoring the flag, honoring Jesus, extending greetings to all, such was Dr. Caldwell's speech. Paper cannot translate the spirit of his ringing address.

"Blest be the tie that binds our hearts in Christian love" was sung with a will, and General Secretary Shaw spoke of Christian Endeavor extension, and pleaded for the new Christian Endeavor building. The present crowded hired quarters at Boston are so inadequate that it is a shame to all the world.

"It is no credit to you to let that work live in a starved, pinched condition. We shall be recreant to Him if we fail properly to equip that building at Boston as a national headquarters."

He told of contributions from the Marshall Islands, the Fiji Islands, the Caroline Islands, and pleaded for a great offering from American societies.

CHAPTER XXVI.

"THY KINGDOM COME," HERE AND EVERYWHERE.

The Auditorium, Monday Afternoon, July 12.

The Monday afternoon meeting at the Auditorium was well attended. In the absence of Bishop Fallows, Dr. Clark presided, while Prof. Excell drew from the audience the genuine Christian Endeavor singing which has so marked all the Convention. Rev. George B. Stewart, president of Auburn Theological Seminary, spoke on "Training the Church to Meet our Opportunity at Home."

"Charity should begin at home, but it ought not to end there. The place where we actually live to-day is missionary ground. Do you live in a great city? What city has not a foreign population that presents the most vital of missionary problems? How about the country church that you come from? Does it reach out into the outlying districts? Many of our beautiful valleys, alas, are fast becoming heathen.

"Are you giving to your frontier missionary the support he needs, not of money alone, but your prayers and sympathy? He sorely needs it.

"Train the young people in the principles of giving, and they will give more as they get more."

Dr. Stewart then gave striking illustrations of what young Christian Endeavorers have accomplished when they have set about in earnest in the country districts to do real missionary work. In an incredibly short time instead of no Christian Endeavor societies there were four, instead of no children coming from the outlying districts, four wagon-loads, more than a hundred children, drove miles every Sunday morning to study about the word of God.

There is too much rivalry among the churches. Each church works too much for itself instead of for the community. Let us get the spirit of Christ. Let us remember that it is a long pull and a strong pull and a pull all together. In this way the question will be solved; and, when we have solved the home-missionary problem, we shall have gone a long way to solve the foreign problem as well.

Dr. John P. Jones, of Pasumalai, India, gave a stirring address upon "How We Are Meeting our Responsibility Abroad."

In this twentieth century God has brought the whole world to our very doors. The nearer they have been brought to us, the greater is our obligation. The Christian church has only just entered upon its consciousness of a world-wide mission and opportunity. This is the dawn of a new era for Christianity as its sympathies encircle the world.

Yet thus far only one-quarter of the members of our churches and two-thirds of the churches themselves are giving or doing anything for the conversion of the world. The Protestant churches of all countries have only twenty thousand missionaries, and America only 6,611, laboring in mission fields to-day.

All Protestant Christendom contributed the last year only $23,000,000 for foreign-missionary enterprise; and of this America's share was ten millions. This is not one-tenth the amount paid by our people for tobacco alone. It will hardly build two Dreadnoughts. Thus Protestant Christians spend for the conversion of the world the smallest fraction of what it invests in war engines and wastes in drink or smoke. Are we not still "playing at missions"?

Nevertheless, with these small resources our missionaries are doing much that is inspiring. In foreign missions there are four and a quarter million converts to be found at present, one-twentieth of the heathen world. Last year 165,000 souls were brought into the kingdom of Christ in these missions, a congregation of 450 souls every day in the whole year! In these fields there are five thousand ordained native ministers and one hundred thousand native workers of all classes, a splendid force of men and women for the upbuilding of the kingdom of our Lord.

God has opened all lands to the gospel and the missionary. Deep foundations have been built for a world-wide kingdom, and the superstructure is beginning to rise with rapidity.

The missionary of to-day knows better the people for whom he labors than did his predecessors. He enters more thoroughly into the temperament, sentiments, and view-point of the East, and seeks more to understand his faith than did the fathers.

The missionary adapts his message to the Oriental mind, and reduces the gospel to its fundamental truths, and especially exalts our Lord, and makes his life and death the supreme, and as far as possible the only, gospel to be promulgated in those lands of the East.

Missionaries are to-day cultivating more than ever before the spirit of Christian union. They are more than ever sensible of the limitations that our sectarian divisions place upon them; and they eagerly desire a release from a divided Christianity and to reveal to the heathen world the unity of the faith and the glorious fellowship and oneness of all that bear the name of Christ.

We are witnessing also a new baptism of outgoing activity and a self-denying altruism in the native church of the foreign missions. The infant native church is entering upon its great responsibility and rejoicing in its new-found opportunity to bring the peoples of those lands to Jesus. They are establishing missionary societies, and are already sending forth their representatives to conquer their own lands for Christ. This is pre-eminently true of the church of India. Many home-missionary societies and one Indian national missionary society are entering upon their heritage, and are seriously undertaking the work of bringing the millions of India to Jesus. This also is the special feature of the life and activities of Christian Endeavorers in that land, and that is one reason why our Endeavor movement is so valuable in India.

Moreover, the leaven of our faith is working mightily in those lands. Even the heathen religions are sloughing off many of their hideous features in the presence of the growing dawn of Christian light in those lands.

Thus we have a thousand reasons for putting on new courage and

hope in the ultimate and speedy conquest of the world by the Spirit of
our Lord, as he is riding victoriously in the great non-Christian lands of
the world.

We need, as a Christian people in this land, to enter more into the
mighty prayer of faith that the Holy Spirit may soon bring the millions
of those countries into the life and the joys of his kingdom. We need
a new consecration of our money and a new dedication of ourselves in
the glorious service of this world-wide enterprise with our heavenly Master.

Rev. W. T. Johnson, D. D., of Richmond, Va., gave an
eloquent plea for men and women of consecration who will
by their presence and work transform our communities, carry
on our Christian Endeavor work, and devote a generous por-
tion of their means that others not in their immediate vicinity
may know of the Christ who is doing so much for them.

A delightful surprise came when Rev. William Carey,
great-grandson of the William Carey whose memory we so
honor, was introduced to the audience. He brought the invitation of three hundred and thirty thousand Christian Endeavorers in India to attend the World's Convention to be
held at Agra in November.

"Christian Endeavor is the 'Pay Streak' of the church
of the future. Men are wanted especially to-day for a man's
work. That 'a' suggests that men have been wanted for
something not worthy of their manhood, and there is a call
to men in our ranks to-day to come and take up tasks that
are worth doing with all the energy and power of which we
are capable.

"What is a man? 'A' man, not 'the' man. Relationship
to all the future; that is the essential thought in the idea of
a man."

He pictured vividly the sin in man, how it hampers growth
and works, and how only through Christ is it taken away.
Without him we cannot live or think or work. O, let us
love the Saviour, the man without whom there is no manhood
in any office possible, the man whose power and love alone
can uplift this fallen world.

"Men are wanted; men endowed with the beauty of Christ,
imbued with his power; men filled with his love. We are
in the city of St. Paul. Think of that man. A man who,
when the Master touched him, went into the city like a little
child. How it melted him to see what he had done and against
whom he had fought! Love came to him, and it came in all
the fulness of power. The great joy in his life was to proclaim to all the world around what a dear Saviour he had
won. The world became one through him.

"We want to love with the world in our heart. It is our
business to write Christ's name on all the world. God help

us to do men's work, that we may win the world for him. Pant after the fulness and the blessing of the world for Christ. Think of the world when you pray, when you work; and do all with the spirit of Him who died to redeem the world. When a man gives his heart to God, God makes it worth while. God took this obscure village minister in a little country place in England, and gave him a task to do which the world wonders at to-day, and which has given him a name that can never die. God did all that, not a man. Four duties of a man are, first, mastering himself; second, protecting the home; third, supporting the state; fourth, benefiting mankind. I should like to leave with you something from my great-grandfather. 'Surely it is worth while to lay ourselves out with all our might in promoting the cause and kingdom of Christ.'"

CHAPTER XXVII.

THE NOON-DAY EVANGELISTIC MEETINGS.

The Metropolitan Opera House.

Every day, with the exception of the Lord's day, during the Convention a splendid company of people gathered at the Metropolitan Opera House to attend the noon-day evangelistic services held there under the auspices of the Convention.

The opening service was made especially noteworthy by the presence and fine address of Hon. William Jennings Bryan, of Lincoln, Neb. Those who had heard Mr. Bryan's matchless lecture on "The Prince of Peace," were delighted to hear again portions of that remarkable deliverance, while those who had never been so favored were profoundly impressed by the splendid address in advocacy of the King and his kingdom by our beloved and greatly gifted brother. The address is printed in full elsewhere in this report.

On the remaining days that princely preacher and pastor, Rev. James A. Francis, discoursed with rare eloquence and convincing reasoning of the great love and unescapable claims of the Prince of peace upon the hearts and lives of men.

Of all the present-day truly great expositors of the Word of God, none excel, if any equal, Mr. Francis, as with heaven-born skill and great love for his fellows he unfolds the teachings and exemplifies the spirit of the Master.

Both Old and New Testament scenes are drawn with marvellous fidelity to their originals, and with heart-moving power.

Unfortunately a notion was current in the city that only delegates were admitted to the evangelistic meetings. The result was that the audience was nearly all Christian Endeavorers. Mr. William Phillips Hall, of New York, who so richly deserves the title of "master of assemblies," was the leader.

The themes were, "The Road to Ideal Character," "The Christian's Errand," and "A Portrait of Jesus." Each session was closed with a few tender, discriminating words by the leader. Mr. Hall knows how, as few men do, to seize the chief impression of a service and then fasten it like a nail in a sure place.

Under the general direction of Prof. E. O. Excell the

138

music at the noon meetings was most ably conducted and greatly enjoyed. The presence and service in sacred song of our Hawaiian brethren was highly appreciated, and was blessed of God to many hearts.

Perhaps more than ever before on similar occasions was the attendance most largely made up of Christian people, but many lives have been spiritually strengthened, and some souls have been led out into the light and liberty of the love of God, for all of which blessings we desire to record our devout thanksgiving to our blessed Lord.

CHAPTER XXVIII.

THE QUIET HOUR.

Central Presbyterian Church.

Among the most important, inspiring, and helpful of all the Convention services must be placed the Quiet-Hour service conducted each morning in the Central Presbyterian Church by that inimitable devotional leader, Rev. Floyd W. Tomkins, S. T. D., of Philadelphia, Penn. The singing, led by Mr. Percy S. Foster, was devotional yet inspiring, and the selections admirably fitted into the thoughts of the leader in every service. With so many other attractions on the programme, of a more imposing and spectacular character, it was indeed refreshing to see the young people gather in the early morning hour in so large numbers for the Quiet-Hour service, thus evincing a keen interest in the deeper things of the Spirit.

The first service was attended by about two hundred Endeavorers. The interest deepened, and the attendance increased from day to day until the body of the large audience-room was well crowded, and even the galleries were finally brought into requisition. One very noticeable feature of the attendance was the large number of young people, a large proportion of whom were young men. As an indication of the interest in these meetings and of the benefit derived from them, a young lady was heard to say that she had to rise at half-past five and travel all the way from Harriet to attend these Quiet-Hour meetings, and she had not missed one of them; and the first thing she was going to do on her return home was to "start a meeting of the Comrades of the Quiet Hour."

Dr. Tomkins's quiet manner, devotional spirit, simple language, clear thought, practical common sense, his interpretation of the Christian life in the commonest things, his familiarity with the "throne of grace," seemed to lead every one into the immediate presence of God, into the holiest of all. Space will not permit an extended report. A brief outline of the first meeting will suffice to convey some faint idea of the character of each of the series.

Promptly at the hour appointed Mr. Foster opened the song service with "Nearer, my God, to thee," which was the key-note for all the services. This was followed with "My Jesus, I love thee" and "Holy Spirit, faithful guide." "Let us all close our eyes," said Dr. Tomkins. A moment's silence. "Just think. I am with God, away from the world with its noise and din and battle, alone with God. He is waiting for my coming, bids me welcome, loves me with an everlasting love." These quiet comments at brief intervals while all heads are bowed and eyes closed seem to lead out and to voice the desires and heart-yearnings of all. Then followed a verse of "Holy, holy, holy."

"This is the very centre of this Convention," said the leader, "just as the 'Quiet Hour' is the centre of the Christian life. It is important that we come into the presence of God. Do not come here to hear a man. Do not think about me at all—just think about God, of that 'love that will not let me go.'" This introduced the subject of the first Quiet Hour, "Think of God." The thought was based on the verse in John, "This is life eternal, to know thee, the only true God."

"Our Lord seemed to want us to know God more than anything else. Why? Because Jesus, being God, knows God; and this is life eternal, to know God. It is sad indeed for a child who has never known father or mother. But it is still sadder to have known them, and then to have known separation or alienation from them. Yet how the father loves and longs for his child! The story of the prodigal son should really be called the story of the father. Jesus' purpose in that parable is to show us the Father.

"How may we know God? By loving and obeying God. Sin keeps me from knowing God. Loving obedience reveals him to me. Have you intellectual difficulties about God? If we will to do his will, we shall know.

"What is God? God is our Father. Let us think of him as our Father, as my Father.

"1. He made me, made me in his own image. His Son took our nature, our human body, and in it lived, suffered, died, rose, and took that human body into heaven. So the body is divine or God-made.

"2. By re-creation he is my Father. He makes us anew. My little girl was dressed in white in anticipation of company. She spilled the ink of my desk all over her lovely dress and hands. In shame she hid herself. Mother found her, and with the love and tenderness of a mother's heart stripped her of her ink-stained garments, put on another white dress, kissed away her tears, and presented her to the visitors clean and white and radiant. That is just what our Father does for us.

"3. Our Father helps us. Think of his kindness, pity. God does not give us hard tasks, and then watch over us to see whether we do them, like a boss, but treats us as a father, pities and excuses our mistakes and failures, and helps us perform our tasks.

"4. He gives us such wonderful comfort. 'As one whom his mother comforteth, so will I comfort you, and ye shall be comforted.' 'Come unto me, and I will give you rest.'

"5. Think of the way in which he reveals to us things, things in the Bible, as we live near to him. We cannot understand either the Bible or our own lives unless we live near to God as his children. 'The secret of the Lord is with them that fear him, and he will show them his way.'

"6. Think, too, that he needs us, wants us! How wonderful that the great God wants me! Needs me! Wants me to tell my cares, my love for him. And we want him. Think, then, of him as your Father. Think of him thus all through the days; live in the thought of him always as Father."

"Jesus, lover of my soul" was sung softly; a brief prayer, and the Aaronic benediction; and this first Quiet-Hour service closed promptly on time, and all hearts truly felt that they had been sitting with Christ in heavenly places.

On Friday morning the theme was "God Speaking to Us." This he does in nature, providence, experience, revelation, especially the last-named. The Bible is always fresh, new, because inspired, a lamp that never goes out, a light that never grows dim. Do not be disturbed about what men are saying about the Bible.. It is God's word from Genesis to Revelation; God will take care of his own word, and every word of it can be relied upon.

1. Have a Bible of your own. Use it; mark it; turn down the corners if you want to; put into it pictures and newspaper clippings that illustrate it. Go to it for comfort, light, guidance, help.

2. Handle it reverently. Ask the Holy Spirit to give you a personal message.

3. Take a little at a time, a single verse; put it into your mind and heart, and think over it; let it saturate your mind. Learn a verse each day by heart. Three hundred and sixty-five verses a year; how rich a treasure!

4. Go to it in sorrow and in joy.

5. Jesus is the centre of the Bible, the key to the Holy Book.

6. Use it as food for your soul.

7. Think of its vast resources. Fitted to all needs, sorrows, doubts, troubles, sins. For all circumstances, peoples, ages. Promise God to love the Bible, to read it more, to follow his words, obey his precepts.

The third hour was devoted to "Our speaking to God."

"If ye abide in me, ye shall ask what ye will." Prayer was defined as abiding in Christ, communion, fellowship with God. Such prayer never fails. We were exhorted to pray not for ourselves first but for others—the courtesies of prayer; to think of the reality of prayer, not "a reaction of the emotions upon ourselves," as the critics say; and to experience the relief of prayer. Pray for little things as well as big ones, over the smallest details of your daily tasks, even the loss of important papers.

> "Who sweeps a room as for Thy laws,
> Makes that and the action fine."

"I can do all things through Christ" is literally true. Pray for your enemies; forget the injury they did you in the desire for their good. Remember also the assurance that God hears and answers. Believe that in the face of all seeming contradictions.

A strong plea was here made for family prayers, the re-erection of the family altar and the invocation upon the family meal as one of the most effective means of restoring harmony and happiness in home life. Pray over your work, home, church, Christian Endeavor. God hears and answers.

At the final service of the Quiet Hour the leader directed our thought to "Service." The three preceding themes naturally led up to this.

1. Thinking of God.
2. Listening to God.
3. Speaking to God.
4. Service for God. The story of Peter's confession of love to the Master and of the Master's command to feed his sheep and lambs was read, and the theme of acceptable and efficient service was developed. We are saved to serve. Love is essential to true service. It is not so much the service as the spirit in which it is rendered which makes it acceptable to God. Love to God is the first commandment, and it is the basis of all our work for God. We must love not the thing we do, the service itself, but God, and then we cannot help doing the thing he wants us to do, whether pleasing to our tastes or not. God calls us to do it, asks us, wants us do this for him. What an honor! What a privilege! What a joy! Because he calls me to do it he will empower me to perform the task, and I shall not know what weariness means, what discouragement is. I shall not know defeat or failure. There will be no "blue Monday" or any other day "blue"! Love will prevent and cure "that tired feeling." Hard work never killed anybody, even if the doctors do say so. It is worry, not work, that kills. Those who serve God

from love of him will work without worry. They shall be quiet and calm in soul when in "labors more abundant" for God. "Labor is rest, and pain is sweet" under such motives and inspirations of service. O, the blessedness of this service! By and by the Kingdom will come, and the thought that you have done something to bring it—that will be your crowning reward.

"I'll go where you want me to go, dear Lord" was sung, the benediction pronounced; and these refreshing hours closed. But those in attendance felt that they had been on the mount of vision, had caught new views of God, of communion with him, of duty, and of service; and, like the disciples when they returned from the mount of transfiguration, were inspired, strengthened, requalified and recommissioned for service and sacrifice, and the opportunity was already awaiting their descent from the mount of God.

MR. BRYAN AND THE NEBRASKA DELEGATION.

THE WISCONSIN DELEGATION.

CHAPTER XXIX.

SCHOOL OF METHODS.

Christian Endeavor Methods.

Three sessions of a Christian Endeavor School of Methods were held in the Memorial English Evangelical Lutheran Church, Thursday, Friday, and Saturday mornings of the Convention.

The first was in charge of Rev. Willis L. Gelston, of Philadelphia; the second, in charge of Mr. Clyde E. Van der Maaten, of Louisville, Ky.; the third, in charge of Mr. W. Roy Breg, of Dallas, Tex.

The practical methods of work that were brought out at these different conferences will be of inestimable value in the work of the societies during the coming years.

At the first conference the chief subject discussed was in line with Dr. Clark's proposition, "A million new members for Christian Endeavor by 1911." Among the suggestions for increasing membership of our societies were, an attendance contest, an inter-society contest, pitting two societies in the same town, or two in the same county, against each other; dividing the societies into groups of six, and spurring each one to increase their membership to ten; making all committees co-operate in a general campaign, the lookout committee looking up strangers, the social committee inviting them to the meetings, the prayer-meeting committee giving them a welcome; starting the lookout committee on a special campaign, securing lists of possibilities from pastors and Sunday-school secretaries, and a better use of Christian Endeavor literature.

At the second day's session the general topic was "Christian Endeavor a Training-School for Service through Committee Work," and the following suggestions were made to the different committees:

Lookout Committee. Write letters and post-cards; telephone; announce the meetings in your church services; have notices put in the daily papers; appoint a committee to visit members in their homes; divide up the city and take a religious census; organize personal workers' classes; hold recep-

145

tions for new members of the church; use a card system, writing the names and addresses on one side of the card, and upon the other the principal points brought out in your conversation with the prospective member; then, when you call next time, begin the conversation where you left off.

Missionary Committee. Divide the committee up into six sections as follows: prayer, meetings, literature, systematic giving, mission-study, correspondence with the boards and missionaries; use the budget plan to raise money; follow the questions and answers given in "The Christian Endeavor World" and published by the United Society.

Music Committee. Co-operate with the prayer-meeting committee; exchange song-books with other societies so as to have something new; have special music.

Information Committee. At every meeting report the most important happenings of Christian Endeavor during the week; report various conventions; and pray for the success of their work.

Prayer-Meeting Committee. Keep out of ruts by having the leaders fully prepared; meet with the leader and help arrange programme; do not make cripples of leaders who have never led before, but help them; have a committee ready to fill in pauses; occasionally have leaderless meetings, chain meetings, where one takes part and calls on the next; telegram meetings, getting telegraph-blanks and writing a message upon them pertaining to the subject; machine meetings, taking a certain machine and letting the young people select the part of the machine they would rather be and tell why.

Social Committee. Have good socials once a month; arrange something new; occasionally combine them with the business meeting or mission-study class; greet people at the church services; have socials to save.

Flower Committee. Secure flowers for the pulpit every Sunday; then send them to the sick together with a Scripture verse.

Good-Literature Committee. Place literature in stations and other public buildings; see that members are well acquainted with all the United Society publications.

Denominational Committee. Correspond with your own board; secure literature and keep informed regarding the board's doings; organize classes for the study of denominational history and doctrines.

The third day's session was devoted to the "Best Ways of Developing Witnesses for Christ." Among the first of these was the Quiet Hour. A number of those present told how the Quiet Hour had developed their Christian lives. It was shown that the societies having the most Quiet Hour Comrades are the most consecrated societies. It was reported how one church and society had been made strong by praying definitely in the Quiet Hour for an increase in membership and for money to build a manse. They had prayed for fifty members, and had received fifty-five. They had asked for $500 and had received $1600; many valuable suggestions were given regarding the importance of the Quiet Hour for Juniors; how to get people to take an original part in the prayer meeting was thoroughly discussed, and it was suggested that a prayer service should be held immediately preceding the regular prayer meeting; give the timid members something special to do. The Tenth Legion was also thoroughly discussed, and many agreed to become members.

The meeting closed with a half-hour of moving pictures on "The Moslem World," strikingly described by Dr. Grose. He showed many pictures taken from the varied lands of Mohammed. It was perhaps the most interesting of the three illustrated lectures that Dr. Grose gave during the Convention.

Missionary Methods.

The Thursday and Friday morning sessions of the missionary conference were conducted by Rev. John M. Moore, secretary of the Forward Movement of the Baptist Missionary Boards of Boston, while the Saturday morning session was in charge of Rev. A. L. Warnshuis, missionary of the Reformed Church at Amoy, China.

At the Thursday morning session the subject discussed was "The Field and the Information." A rapid survey of the world's field was made, and it was shown that the difference between home and foreign missions is that home missions are largely a strengthening and intensifying of Christianity where it already exists, while foreign missions aim at extending the frontiers of the Kingdom. Missionary committees should not do all of the work, but should work through the regular organizations, to the end that all may realize that it is the duty of the whole church and the whole duty of the church to give the whole gospel to the whole world as soon as possible. Every society should supplement the missionary meeting with a mission-study class for the sake of the more personal, fundamental intensive work that can be done in a small group. Study classes should be made up of people whose ages and attainments are nearly the same. The group should be small, six or ten being the ideal number. To form a mission-study class, get into touch with the educational secretary of your own missionary board. Personal work is the one sure method of securing members for a study class.

"How to Make the Missionary Meeting More Effective" was the subject discussed at the Saturday morning session. It was stated that one sure way of killing a missionary meeting is to have the members read clippings taken from papers and preface the reading with the statement, "The leader has asked me to read this." Participants in meetings should make their part their own. The meeting should be under the supervision of the missionary committee. A definite aim should determine the plan of each meeting. Make the missionary topics specific by applying them to your own denominational work. The committee should always be on the lookout for missionary material; keep a complete file of missionary periodicals, and systematically file all missionary clippings and leaflets so as always to have abundant material for use in all kinds of missionary meetings. Preparations for missionary meetings should include the prayers, which should be definite and in line with the meeting. Intercessory prayers are needed more than men or money. Maps and charts and curios and stereopticons should be used whenever possible. Plan every detail, and pray always.

"Missionary Literature, and How to Circulate It" was one topic Monday morning.

The call for the titles of missionary books that had been read in 1909 by those present brought out a long and varied list, and among these the most prominent were the new study-class text-books and books in the libraries that accompany these books. No better books than these can be recommended, and those that have yet to read their first missionary book need not look farther than these libraries. Periodicals and leaflet literature were fully referred to as important parts of the available supply of missionary literature with which the missionary committee should be intimately acquainted. To circulate this literature, these suggestions were made: Talk them up; read in a meeting parts of some book, and leave off at some interesting point; refer participants in missionary meetings to books and magazines. Leaflet literature, carefully selected, should be used in connection with the monthly meeting.

"Generous, Proportionate Giving by the Individual: How Can We Promote It?" was asked.

Study the Bible to learn its principles of Christian stewardship. Enroll the members in the Tenth Legion, or in a league of proportionate givers. Have a meeting once a year on giving; use Tenth-Legion ballots; enlist the support of a missionary substitute, or underwrite the support of a parish; use pledges and envelopes; distribute the best literature on stewardship.

"Systematic Collection and Distribution by the Society: How Can We Secure It?" was discussed. One of the essentials is a good, live treasurer, who will do his work for the sake of helping to inculcate right principles of giving. The total amount of money given by young people's societies is not of first importance, but they should be trained to give systematically and in proportion to their income. The field is the world, and the gifts should be divided between work at home and that abroad; and, when denominational authorities have prepared schedules showing the proportionate needs of the various boards, that schedule may well be adopted by the society as the basis for the distribution of their gifts. In other cases the gifts for foreign missions should at least equal the total amount given to all home objects. The money should be collected not less frequently than once a month, and then it should not be hoarded; but it should be forwarded as fast as it is collected, so that it may be used at once by the boards, and so help the boards to get away from the annually recurring necessity of borrowing money from the banks during the early months of the year.

To promote missionary work of every kind, it is of first importance that the lives of all of us should be guided by the central, controlling aim of doing our utmost to give all the world an adequate opportunity to know Jesus Christ and to accept him as their Saviour.

The Junior Workers' Conference.

The first Junior workers' conference was conducted by Mrs. E. L. Condon, Junior superintendent of the Iowa Christian Endeavor Union. The subject was "The Child in the Home." Among the many valuable suggestions given were the following: The value of mothers' meetings was clearly shown. Once in six months a meeting may well be held to which mothers should bring their babies. Let the mothers suggest what they would like to have the Junior superintendents do; let the Juniors give a social once a year to their parents, at which time the superintendent may well explain what the Juniors are trying to accomplish. Once a year at the morning church service let the Juniors present the work that they have done. Be sure to have an interesting and interested Junior superintendent. Have Decision Day at least once a year. Try to have the children as respectful to their parents as they are to their superintendent. A good suggestion to give a child to take home from the meeting is "Can I help you in some way to-day, papa or mamma?"

As definite work for the Juniors at home or abroad the following were suggested: Map work, lessons on the blackboard, making scrap-books, comfort powders for prisoners, work for the sunshine committee. It was stated that three-fourths of the homes are reached by Junior work that are not reached in any other way.

The Junior workers' conference Saturday morning was one conducted by Miss Agnes Suman, Junior superinten- dent of the District of Columbia Christian Endeavor Union.

Mrs. Francis E. Clark was present with a plea for the or- ganization of a mothers' society in connection with the Junior Christian Endeavor society. This suggestion was heartily accepted and fully discussed. It was proposed by one of the Junior workers that this be called the "Parents' Society" in order to include the fathers of the Juniors.

Mrs. Hutchison, of Toledo, Ohio, spoke of the round robin and of the International Junior and Intermediate Union. A discussion of the subject, "The Church's Duty toward the Junior Society" followed. Mrs. Francis E. Clark suggested that, when a superintendent of a Junior society re- signs, the church should feel it as much its duty to provide a new superintendent as it would in case of the resignation of the Sunday-school superintendent. Give the children the best leader you can get.

The following are some good suggestions presented:

A Junior superintendent should have from six to nine as- sistants under her or him, as the case may be, they being se- lected by the Junior superintendent rather than by the Chris- tian Endeavor society. It was mentioned that very often the most uninterested and inactive members of the society are placed on the Junior committee. The Junior superintendent, preferably a consecrated person suggested by the pastor, should be appointed by the official board of the church.

When a new pastor comes to a church, a representative from each society should greet him at the pastor's reception with an announcement of this kind:

"We, the Junior (or Intermediate) society, greet you as our pastor, and we ask that you co-operate with us to make our society the very best possible." This will show the pastor that you expect him to take a personal interest in your so- ciety.

On the subject of "Children and Church-Membership" the following thoughts were brought out:

There should be a church roll for Junior members.

A child whose parents are members of the church is an associate member of the church from birth; and, when he reaches the age of accountability, he is expected to become an active member of the church.

Before talking to the child about church-membership, first see the mother, and find out whether she thinks the child is ready to join the church. Ask the mother whether she has talked to the child on this subject. The Junior superintendent should call a special meeting of those children that are intending to become church-members. After they have come into the church do not neglect them, but have a few of these meetings to explain your doctrines, and to help them lead a Christian life. Be sure to impress on them that they should always attend the communion service.

Mrs. Clark announced a beautiful book that all Juniors' mothers should read, entitled "The Diary of an Adopted Mother." The story is probably a true one of a childless home where the lady decided to adopt a child, but she would not legally adopt him until he had adopted her. One day the child exclaimed, "O, I wish you were my mother!" after which the lady legally adopted the child.

It was suggested that a child should have the credit of being able to decide for himself what is right and what is wrong.

The meeting closed with all singing, "Open the door for the children," followed by the Mizpah benediction.

Floating Endeavor Conference.

Secretary Shaw was the leader of the conference on Floating Endeavor. Those who live far from the seaboard hardly realize the importance of a work like this, or what part they can have in it. At many of the seaboard towns in this country as well as abroad Endeavorers are doing splendid work among the sailors, and hundreds of members are to be found on the high seas. It was suggested that inland societies might help this good work by making comfort bags for the sailors, by gathering magazines and forwarding them to seaport societies, and by constant prayer. Evangelistic work is being done among the ships in many harbors, and one way to help is to send books or money to print them to these places.

Conferences on the Ministry of Healing.

These conferences were conducted by Right Rev. Samuel Fallows, D.D., LL.D. Bishop Fallows made a brief address each day to a large number of ministers and others. The bishop held that the so-called Emmanuel Movement as carried on by him is not in any sense Christian Science. He believed in the great fundamental truths of Christianity, in the reality of sin and sickness. In early post-apostolic times the Christian minister was also the physician. Bishop Fallows always requires a physician's diagnosis, and very often that of prominent neurologists in addition. He never uses hypnotism. The purely scientific features of treatment are persuasion, suggestion, and auto-suggestion. The distinctly religious features accompanying these are the appeal to the Bible always at hand, faith in God and in Christ the healer, personal and intercessory prayer. Bishop Fallows strongly affirmed it was the duty and the privilege of the Christian minister to bring to bear directly upon the ailing one all the potent forces that a true Christianity places at his disposal. He should blend in his week-day services instruction in practical Christian right living which the new psychology presents. He urges as the necessary adjuncts to mental and moral recovery the principles advocated by Horace Fletcher, of thorough mastication, of food proper in quality and quantity, of deep breathing, of appropriate and varied exercises, and the like.

In urging the adoption of the methods presented Bishop Fallows claimed that the minister in no sense whatever is an intruder into the physician's domain. He is simply asserting the right that inherently belongs to him. It is his solemn and imperative duty to "minister to minds diseased." The programme of Christianity is for the ministers of reconciliation to bind up the broken-hearted, to proclaim deliverance to the captives and the opening of the prison to them that are bound. Man is not the creator of God. He apprehends God more and more by right conceptions of his character. "Christ in you the hope of glory;" "It is not I that live, but Christ that liveth in me;" be "filled with all the fulness of God," these are the ever old, and yet ever new thoughts the Christian minister is to proclaim.

The Intermediate Workers' Conference.

Mr. C. C. Brown, Chicago's noble Intermediate superintendent, led on Monday morning the very best conference yet held by Intermediate workers, best in attendance—the large room was packed, best in enthusiasm, best in participation. The audience voted to keep right on when the time for adjournment drew near; and, when Mr. Brown announced a song, they cried "No! No!" and continued the discussions without a break. The only intermission they would allow was that they consented to rise, turn around once, and then sit down again.

From a crowded note-book we select only a few from the hundreds of practical hints that were given. For disorderly children, temporary expulsion; seat them beside the superintendent; give them something to do; go to them and have a frank talk. No one can care properly for more than fifteen or twenty children. If you have a larger number, divide the society and place an assistant superintendent over each fifteen. For your assistant superintendents go to the Young People's society, but do not take its best workers; take those that are not doing anything. One of the best Intermediate workers present said that before he was captured for that work he sat in the back seats of the older society, and threw spitballs. One society was reported that has four assistant superintendents, the Junior superintendent of the same church having six assistants.

Juniors are interested in the wonderful world in which they live; Intermediates in the wonderful I; success with them is largely a matter of psychology. Have a double limit of membership. Some children are far more advanced than others of the same age. You may graduate them into the Intermediate society when they reach the age of eleven or twelve. or when they reach a certain grade, say the seventh, in the grammar school.

To start a society, get a few members; give each some membership application cards; and, as these are filled, string them on ribbons and hang them up in the meeting-room as an inspiration to the ingathering of more members. Be sure to have the Intermediate leader make the opening prayer at the meeting. One society got so large that it had to have two or three lookout and social committees. One social committee would care for the programme of the monthly social and the other for the refreshments. When some one expressed the fear that several assistant superintendents would cause constraint in the society, it was answered that no one should work in the society whom the children do not love to have with them at all times.

The Pastors' Conference.

The pastors' conference was held in Christ Episcopal Church, Monday morning, July 12.

The meeting was in charge of Rev. Samuel H. Woodrow, D.D.. pastor of the First Congregational Church, Washington, D. C. The topic considered was, "What do you want the Christian Endeavor Society to Be and Do?" The discussion was opened by Rev. J. G. Huber, D. D., of Dayton, who said:

Christian Endeavor possesses unique functions that render it indispensable in the activities of the local church.

1. It grips young people in the perilous age. It lays its

hands on them in the intractable adolescent stage, when they are leaving the Sunday-school and taking back seats in the church services; when they are standing at the foot of life's hill in the first flush of conscious manhood and womanhood; when with radiant faces, lifted eyes, and throbbing hearts they are seeking a way for their feet; when they are trying to poise themselves in the midst of mysteries and temptations that are new and appalling in their significance; and when the great choices of life are irrevocably determined. At that critical hour Christian Endeavor is to be to them an inspiration and a restraint, a school of prayer and discipline, offering happy and holy friendships and opening beautiful doors for communion with God.

2. Christian Endeavor gives religious training and moulds character in a unique and effective manner. In our present church economy there are three factors of religious training: the home, the church, and the Christian college. In many cases the home is unspiritual, and fails in proper direction, incentive, and ideals. A very few have the privilege of attending a Christian college. Only the church is left, and, if it fails, multitudes of young people must enter life unequipped spiritually. Christian Endeavor is the training agency of the church. It offers the opportunity and creates the atmosphere and initiative for doing things, and intelligent doing results in training. No other department in the church at present meets so successfully this imperative need.

3. Christian Endeavor has rare educational value. There is a vast range and variety of topics for a single year, covering missions, stewardship, temperance, citizenship, Bible characters and books, and all the practical themes of a Christian life. Besides, Christian Endeavor proposes studies in the Bible, missions, and other lines that are, most helpful.

4. Then there are the practical ministries of Christian Endeavor. These are so varied, and are carried forward in numberless and far-apart churches, all so quietly and modestly that we may not be aware of what is really being done. If the best things done by one hundred different societies represented at this Convention were flashed on the screen, the coldest heart would be swept with waves of gratitude and joy. Every pastor should be far-sighted and fertile in programmes, suggesting to his young people such tasks as will command their energies and lead them to realize their highest possibilities.

5. Christian Endeavor is the recruiting-station of the church, providing it with workers, missionaries, and ministers. Here are massed the most promising young people, and

the pastor meeting them at close range should cultivate them for future Christian service.

In the meetings are discussed the needs of the field, the methods and motives of Christian work; and the voice of God has a chance to be heard. In these days of a depleted ministry earnest prayer should go up to God that multitudes of efficient young men may choose this high calling as their life-work.

In the enthusiastic conference that followed not a moment was wasted. It was reported that under the tactful oversight of some pastors societies so co-operated with the midweek prayer service as to transform it entirely.

Joint meetings of Christian Endeavor and the church during the summer months were mentioned as giving excellent satisfaction.

One society had trouble getting hold of young men, but won them through prayer. Organized Sunday-school classes induced older members to graduate from Christian Endeavor, and so made room for younger ones.

Nothing objectionable is in the pledge, it was said, but much to help young people to get on the right side and lead a life that squares with their profession.

Christian Endeavor helps to make efficient Sunday-school officers and teachers.

A Sabbath in good works and worship well spent means a week of strong growth and happy content.

A rapid-fire series of two-minute speeches was engaged in by a large number of pastors. The question was raised about enforcing the pledge in relation to the midweek prayer meeting. Many Endeavorers do not attend this meeting, and it seems harmful to have them neglect a part of their pledge. It was said that this clause should be removed or enforced. To this it was replied that, if a minister has a church of one thousand members, fifty of whom attend the prayer meeting, and out of an Endeavor society of one hundred five attend, he must not complain of the society so long as nine hundred members of the church go where they please. The minister must get into touch with the young people. Several ministers, on the other hand, strongly emphasized the fact that the society had been an immense help and blessing.

Dr. Woodrow pointed out that one must not judge the society from its relation to the prayer meeting alone, but in its relation to all the church's activities. One minister told of changing the Christian Endeavor prayer meeting to a week evening, with the result that the Sunday-night attendance was doubled. Others claimed that Sunday night was the only possible night for them, one minister saying that seventy-five per cent of his young people attended both Sunday school and church service. The combined service of young people's meeting and the church evening service was favorably mentioned. One minister had success in reaching the young men through the organized Bible class, but little success in interesting them in the Christian Endeavor society. In some cases it is felt that the Bible class is taking the place of the society. The problem is, to find the proper relation between the two. Dr. Huber told of a society that chose a young man for president out of that group of young fellows whom the society could not reach, and this solved the problem.

In a large society where a few people monopolize the time it is well to divide the society into sections, so that all may have a chance. To the query as to whether the presence of older people in the society hinders the young people from coming in, it was replied that tact and kindness obviate the difficulty. Another good suggestion was to organize young men or boys by themselves, and then later get them to come to the Christian Endeavor society in a body. Dr. J. Stanley Durkee, Boston, said that he made the society the centre of his work; the various classes in the church are composed of and called by the names of the Christian Endeavor committees.

Dr. Woodrow closed with a brief discussion of the pledge and its value for the young people.

The Field Secretaries' Conference.

Sentence prayers by the field workers were followed by the business session, Rev. C. H. Hubbell presiding.

The nominating committee, consisting of Clyde E. Van der Maaten of Louisville, Ky., and Rev. William R. Hall, of Michigan, was appointed to prepare a ballot for election of officers.

Mr. Karl Lehmann, secretary and treasurer, reported that five budgets had been sent out to the field workers, and that the year closes with all bills paid and fifty cents in the treasury.

The conference was thrown open for discussion.

What are you using in printed matter? was asked.

Manitoba reported that they have sent out printed budgets forming about a sixteen-page pamphlet. The first one was to let their people know that they had decided to have a field secretary, and to give a report of the Seattle Convention; the other one contained a great deal more information about their field secretary's work and how successful it had been.

They have sent out circulars once in a while to pastors regarding the coming of the field secretary, and also circulars in regard to this St. Paul Convention.

Minnesota sent out a circular stating who the field secretary is, what he does, and how to get him. Another gives some testimonials, explaining fitness for the work, what may be expected of him, and what they are expected to do. Also window cards and questions for question-box work. The rest is done by the State paper.

How much of the finances is your field worker supposed to raise? was another question.

Pennsylvania's field secretary does not raise any; their finance committee attends to this.

Minnesota's field secretary raises the travelling expenses, usually by offerings.

Indiana's field secretary is expected to raise the travelling expenses.

Ohio's field secretary raises about half of the State's finances.

Pennsylvania gets contributions from individuals and countries to the extent of $2,500; they spend about $2,300 annually. They have a committee of three men who keep in touch with every county in the State in regard to this work, and get their contributions. However, the county must first be organized.

Do you raise money at your State conventions?

Ohio is trying to get away from the idea of presenting finances at their State convention because of the fact that a large number of the members are yet in school, and there are those that will pledge when they really can not afford it, and it is wished that nothing should interfere with the enthusiasm of the convention.

Rev. C. H. Hubbell, formerly field secretary of Ohio, says: "Don't hesitate to present the matter of finances for Christian Endeavor. He who does present it is not a mercenary, but he is a missionary. We ought not to feel hampered along these lines. It is an opportunity, not an obligation."

In how many States is the State secretary the field secretary? In Pennsylvania, Indiana, and Ohio.

How many States have a State headquarters office? Ohio, Pennsylvania, and Colorado.

One reason suggested why the field secretary should be the State secretary was that the field secretary should have the work of the State, especially the corresponding end, in order to keep in close touch with the societies.

Reasons why these offices should not be combined are: The officer has not time.

It is possible to line up two extra workers, a corresponding and a recording secretary, in the State.

Which are you emphasizing, rallies or conferences?

Conferences.

Why?

That is where you get the best results. For inspiration and enthusiasm.

Whom do you invite to the conferences?

Everybody.

Whom especially?

Officers and committee workers.

A few words of greeting were given by Dr. Clark and Mr. Shaw.

It was voted that Dr. Clark be made an honorary member of the association.

The nominating committee reported the following nominations:

For president of the International Field Workers' Union, Walter D. Howell, Minnesota.

Vice-president, A. J. Shartle, Pennsylvania.

Secretary-treasurer, Karl Lehmann, Colorado.

Counsellor, Mr. William Shaw, Boston, Mass.

Membership Committee: C. E. Van der Maaten, H. Gordon Lilley, Miss Florence E. Lanham.

It was voted that the secretary-treasurer be instructed to collect the dues of fifty cents a member for the two years.

The States represented were Texas, Minnesota, New Jersey, Iowa, Pennsylvania, Wisconsin, Arkansas, Oklahoma, Illinois, West Virginia, Washington, Indiana, Colorado, Ontario, Quebec, and Manitoba.

The meeting adjourned with a prayer by the new president, Mr. Walter D. Howell.

Conference of Pastors and Church Workers.

"The Church, the Laboring Man, the Immigrant," was the subject. It was indicative of the growing interest among ministers with reference to modern social conditions to find so many of them present at this conference. Dr. Stelzle opened the discussion with the statement that the immigrant is coming to us in such numbers because for many years the church has been asking God for an open door to the foreigner. God has opened the door, but it swings both ways. Not only may we go to the foreigner, but the foreigner is coming to us.

The problem of the immigrant is most intense in the city. Fifty per cent of the immigrants in this country live in the 160 cities having a population of 25,000 or more. During the past fifteen years about nine millions have come to this country, but two-thirds settled in the four States of New York, Pennsylvania, Massachusetts, and New Jersey, although Illinois ranks high in the States of "privilege." However, there is scarcely a State or even a town that may not have a part in redeeming the foreigners.

The trade-union is the organized expression of the working man. It means more than the mere securing of bigger wages and shorter hours. It has a moral and ethical value that few can realize. It is closely related to the church in that it too stands for the care of the human body, the culture of the human mind, and the development of the human soul. There is so much religion in this movement that frequently working men in the trade-union have requested that their organizations be converted into churches which should have working men as ministers and officers. Socialism must be reckoned with. There are twenty-five million socialists to-day throughout the world, and the number is still growing. Nine million have cast their ballots for socialist candidates. They conduct more open-air meetings than are conducted by all of the churches combined, including the Salvation Army. Socialism also has become a religion to thousands of those who have embraced it.

These are some of the questions with which we are confronted, and concerning which we must as a church become interested.

Rapid-fire questions were asked, the speaker being frequently interrupted during the progress of his remarks. Following are some of the practical plans suggested by Dr. Stelzle in reply to questions: The careful study of one's field, so that the minister may know accurately just who lives in his community. The investigation of the social centres that working men patronize, especially the saloon and the labor union. It was suggested that ministers' associations and central labor unions exchange fraternal delegates. This plan, Dr. Stelzle said, is now in operation in about one hundred and twenty-five cities, and nearly two hundred ministers are regularly visiting central labor bodies as fraternal delegates. The advantages of the institutional church were discussed. The fundamental principles of the problems and the methods of work were presented, the aim of the conference being to present these that they might be applied to any field.

Christian-Citizenship Conference.

If there ever existed any doubt in the mind of any one as to whether or not the young people of the various local societies of Christian Endeavor have been giving any thought to our civic and social affairs, that doubt must have been completely dispelled in the mind of any such person, if any there were, in attendance at the conference on Christian citizenship held on Monday morning.

Mr. W. H. Thomas, superintendent of the Christian-citizenship department of the North Dakota Christian Endeavor Union and secretary of the Bar Association of North Dakota, was the leader.

After the usual preliminaries the young people went into conference, and took hold of the situation like old hands at the business; and it did not take long to develop the fact that the existence of the saloon and the liquor traffic seem to hold first place on the boards. The question as to how to secure better enforcement of law was well considered by them, and one of the things that they seemed to emphasize very much was the absolute necessity that good citizens everywhere support men with principle rather than support the party under all circumstances. This sentiment simply shows the way the wind is blowing, as the conference represented practically every State in the Union.

At the request of Mr. George W. Coleman, superintendent of the Christian Endeavor Patriots' League, Mr. Thomas delineated, just as an example of what young people who give their loyalty to Jesus Christ can do, the magnificent, glorious, and successful fight that young people of Denver, Col., made in behalf of the Hon. Ben Lindsey against the combined efforts of Democrats and Republicans. They succeeding in electing Judge Lindsey as an independent candidate by a majority of more than thirteen thousand. He gave instances of personal sacrifice and devotion on the part of the young people, who under the wise leadership of Mr. Harry G. Fischer, himself a very young man, succeeded in bringing about such magnificent results.

There were at the last election two hundred and eleven voting-precincts in the city of Denver, and there was placed at each one of the precincts either a young man or a young woman (women being allowed to vote in Colorado) whose business it was to see to it that all persons about whom there was any question as to their right to vote were challenged.

Several times during Mr. Thomas's relation of this magnificent work and the personal devotion on the part of the

A FLORAL DISPLAY IN COMO PARK.

"THE GATES AJAR" AT COMO PARK.

young people of Denver, he was applauded lustily by the very attentive listeners.

Also as an indication that the young people mean business the following resolution was presented by the leader, and it was unanimously adopted:

"Whereas we, the attendants on the conference on Christian citizenship held in connection with the International Convention of Christian Endeavor in convention assembled on July 12, 1909, at St. Paul, Minn., believe that the greatest need of the American young people to-day, next to spiritual awakening, is an awakening along social and civic lines, and,

"Whereas we believe that by education, agitation, and reorganization the young people will not only be enlightened regarding civic and social affairs, and thereby accomplish large results in the battle against social and civic corruption, but will attain to and become a powerful influence for good in the nation; and,

"Whereas we heartily indorse the work done by the Christian Citizenship Union of Denver, Col., together with other similar organizations, as one of progress and helpfulness to young people in maintaining a place in the activities of the world along such lines, therefore,

"Be it resolved, That we recommend to and urge the United Society of Christian Endeavor to establish in conjunction with the Patriots' League a national department of Christian citizenship, with the recommendation that each State or Province establish a similar department, said department to be organized along the lines of the Denver Christian Union, or such other as may be deemed advisable according to the different local conditions in said State or Province."

At the close Mr. George W. Coleman, of Boston, Mass., gave the young people some very valuable, timely, and important pointers as to what can be done along these lines, and emphasized particularly the necessity that the young people throughout the United States take up the matter, with the respective Congressmen and Senators, of enacting legislation that will prohibit the existence of the saloon in the District of Columbia.

The Esperanto Conference.

A number of Endeavorers interested in Esperanto, the new international language, assembled Thursday morning to hear Rev. R. P. Anderson, associate editor of "The Christian Endeavor World," lecture on "The Universal Language a Prelude to Universal Brotherhood." Mr. Anderson pointed out that two currents are easily distinguishable among the nations to-day: first, one that makes for increased international relations among the peoples of the earth; and, second, one that seeks to revive the patriotic sentiment, as seen in movements for the reinstalment of old national tongues. He pointed out that Esperanto is the key to the situation. It does not seek to oust any national language; on the contrary, encourages such tongues; but it seeks to introduce a common language that all nations may use in international communication.

The great need for such a medium of international communication was clearly pointed out; and its value for commerce and science. Mr. Anderson gave examples of the language and explained some of its fundamental principles. Considerable interest was awakened, as the questions asked showed; and the result will doubtless be additions to the ranks of Esperantists.

CHAPTER XXX.

THE DENOMINATIONAL RALLIES.

African Methodist Episcopal and the African Methodist Episcopal Zion Church.

The denominational rally of the African Methodist Episcopal Church and the African Methodist Episcopal Zion Church was held at St. James A. M. E. Church, Rev. Horace Graves, pastor.

Music was furnished by the choir. Rev. J. C. Caldwell, D.D., general secretary of the Allen Christian Endeavor League, presided. Rev. J. W. Jackson, of Chicago, offered prayer.

Addresses were delivered by Miss E. Marie Carter, of New Orleans, La., on "Personal Work, the Demand of the Hour," and on "Interdenominational Fellowship" by Rev. W. D. Carter, D. D., of St. Paul, Minn.

A symposium, "How can we do More and Better Work for God and the Church This Year?" was led by Rev. C. S. Whitted, D. D., of New Haven, Conn.

The following thoughts were suggested by different speakers:

1. More consecration.
2. More Bible-study.
3. More systematic giving.
4. A greater enthusiasm for the cause of missions.
5. Loyalty to our church.

The rally was a source of great inspiration and helpfulness to all who attended.

The Brethren Rally.

Messages were received by the leader from several. Dr. C. F. Yoder, trustee of the United Society of Christian Endeavor, who with his family was to sail on July 10 as a missionary to South America, sent a message that centred around the following truths:

1. You young people are called to evangelize the world as the chief business of your life.
2. The young people of this generation must evangelize this generation.

3. The young people of the Brethren Church should prepare for soul-winning.

Rev. G. E. Drushal, of Lost Creek, Ky., Brethren Christian Endeavor missionary among the mountain whites, and superintendent of the Riverside Brethren Institute at the the above place in Breathitt County, sent an inspiring message. In four years he has received more than one hundred members into the church, and built up a school of eighty or more students, founded several new Sunday-schools, built a church, and is erecting a dormitory at the present time. He writes: "Here are wonderful opportunities. Prayer, workers, and money are needed. May the Brethren Endeavorers enter in and possess the land."

The message of Rev. G. C. Carpenter, general secretary of the Brethren Young People's Society of Christian Endeavor, should stir to new endeavors all the societies of the church. "Let us," he said, "push forward the Master's work in these three ways:

"1. By living the Christ-life.

"2. By winning souls at home.

"3. By full obedience to the Great Commission.

"The good Jew, on Saturday night before the passover, after putting away all leaven, said, 'And now if any leaven abides in this home, it is here against my will.' Let us say, 'And now, if any sin abides in my life, it is there against my will.' Then, and only then, can Jesus use us and shine forth through us upon a lost world."

The Baptist Rally.

There was a goodly gathering of young people from all sections of the country at the Baptist rally, including many members of the Baptist Young People's Union, and the spirit of fellowship and unity prevailing throughout the session made an impression that will not soon be forgotten by those who were privileged to be there.

Mr. George W. Coleman, publisher of "The Christian Endeavor World," who presided, introduced his pastor, Dr. James A. Francis, of the Clarendon Street Church, Boston, to lead the devotional exercises.

Rev. Avery A. Shaw, of the First Church, Winnepeg, Man., brought greetings from Canada, showing us that the same problems are pressing upon the Christian religion in that far-off metropolis of the north that stir our hearts and test our courage here in every populous centre in the States.

Dr. W. T. Johnson, of the First Baptist Church (colored) of Richmond, Va., gave an inspiring message covering the progress and development of the colored Baptist Endeavorers and pointed out the advantage that would accrue to all their young people's work if there could be a union of forces between the Baptist Young People's Union and the Christian Endeavorers.

Mr. Percy S. Foster, of Washington, D. C., the brilliant and beloved Convention music-leader whom Baptists are proud to own, made a charming little talk, dealing with the faults and failings and the peace and power of the musical expression of religious principles and sentiments. He aptly characterized his address as "Crystallized Hallelujahs."

President E. W. Van Aken, of Parker College, Winnebago, Minn., in making a diagnosis of the situation of the Free Baptists expressed his gratification in the approaching union of the denomination with the main Baptist body, and wished that it might be hastened.

General Secretary George T. Webb, D. D., of the Baptist Young People's Union of Philadelphia, was very happy in his outline of the part Christian Endeavor has played in Baptist denominational progress.

Mr. H. N. Lathrop, treasurer of the United Society, a young business man whose large services to Christian Endeavor are all voluntary and unpaid, presented in crisp business style a statement of the recent doings of the Baptists of the North, who through their new central organization have provided Baptist business for busy Baptists in a way that has inspired Baptist laymen from one end of the country to the other.

Dr. Howard B. Grose, editorial secretary of the American Baptist Home Mission Society, took as his topic "The Get-Together Method in Missions," and after a splendid development of his theme gave a practical exhibition of it by presenting the following remarkable resolution:

"Resolved, That it is the sense of the Baptist young people assembled in conference at the twenty-fourth International Convention of Christian Endeavor in St. Paul, Minn., July, 1909, that it would be to the advantage of our denominational life to take such steps as are necessary to bring about a close organic union among Baptist young people, who are now organized as Baptist Young People's Unions and Christian Endeavor societies. We believe that this end could be easily and naturally secured if the Baptist Christian Endeavor societies would add the words 'Baptist Young People's Union' to their name, and all Baptist Young People's Unions add 'Christian Endeavor' to their name, giving the common name of 'Baptist Young People's Union of Christian Endeavor' to all our Baptist young people's organizations; thereby opening the way for a united **Baptist** movement that will fully safeguard our denominational interests, and at the same time give us the added impetus of the world-wide movement that brings together the Christian forces of all denominations. We therefore express our cordial approval of such a course, and devoutly hope that this end may be achieved.

"Resolved, That this matter on our part be placed in the hands of a committee of three that shall carefully consider the details and confer with the Baptist Young People's Union and any other organizations that might be affected by such a change."

After an inspiring appeal by Rev. John M. Moore, general secretary of the Baptist Forward Movement, to make the advance in Christian missions more like a mighty army as we have it in our songs, and less like the hesitating, scattered advance of a company of indifferent and half-hearted church-members, the resolutions presented by Dr. Grose were taken up, and after a full and free discussion by leaders of both Christian Endeavor and the Baptist Young People's Union, were on the motion of Dr. McLaurin, of Chicago, unanimously adopted. Mr. George W. Coleman, Dr. Wayland Hoyt, and Dr. Howard B. Grose were appointed as the committee to carry out the instructions of the resolutions.

Rally of the Disciples of Christ.

High water should not interfere with a rally of Disciples, but it did keep Rev. Claude E. Hill, of Mobile, Ala., their national superintendent of young people's work, away from the meeting, and cost us his leadership and address at the rally.

Guy M. Withers, of Kansas City, president elect of the International Intermediate and Junior Union, led in his stead. The singing was exceptionally enthusiastic.

Rev. A. D. Harmon, pastor of the entertaining church, welcomed the visitors, and told something of the history of the Disciples in the Twin Cities since the organization of his church under the American Christian Missionary Society. Dr. W. F. Richardson, pastor of the First Christian Church of Kansas City, Mo., followed with a splendid address on "Christian Endeavor and Our Country," not excelled by any patriotic speech among the many of the Convention.

Rev. S. Guy Inman, of Porfirio, Mexico, spoke intensely of "Christian Endeavor and Our Missions," urging mission-study and prayer, and giving money and men. He is a great man with an impelling message.

Rev. R. P. Anderson, associate editor of "The Christian Endeavor World," spoke on "Christian Endeavor and Our World-wide Fellowship" in his usual happy, forceful way. Referring to the denominational separation, he told of the Irish priest who was asked, "What is the difference between cherubim and seraphim?" With a warning finger uplifted he said, "S-s-sh, there was once a difference, 'tis thrue, but it has all been settled now."

Dr. F. D. Power, of Washington, D. C., made a masterly presentation of "Christian Endeavor and Our Plea"; and Dr. J. H. Garrison, of St. Louis, Mo., spoke briefly on "The Centennial Convention, Pittsburg, October, 1909." In closing, the leader asked four things to be put down in notebooks and worked out in the four months before the Pittsburg meeting.

1. Start a home-mission study-class, and report to the home-mission secretary.

2. Start a foreign-mission study-class, and report to the foreign secretary.

3. Organize or re-organize a Christian Endeavor society, and report to national superintendent Claude E. Hill.

4. Organize a Junior society and report to him.

A verse of "Blest be the tie that binds our hearts," and one of "All hail the power of Jesus' name," and the Mizpah benediction closed the best rally ever held by the Disciple Endeavorers.

The Congregational Rally.

The Congregational rally was a surprise and a treat. It was a surprise because of its cosmopolitan character, its magnitude and power. It was a treat because it fairly throbbed with energy and enthusiasm, suggestive of battles fought and great victories yet to be won. The gathering was called to meet in the spacious basement of the People's Church, but long before the hour for beginning the room was overcrowded. It was then decided to march four abreast into the main auditorium of this grand and beautiful church. In this necessary change a kindly Providence had guided, as to the delegates was given thereby the privilege of quietly viewing the splendid artistic productions of the building.

Dr. W. T. McElveen, of Evanston, Ill., was to have presided, but on account of illness in his family was prevented from coming. At the opening a resolution of sympathy and greeting was ordered to be forwarded to Dr. McElveen.

Devotional exercises were conducted by Rev. J. Spencer Voorhees, of Adams, Mass., who spoke briefly of the joys of a great consecration: viz., the privilege of getting better acquainted with one another and that of getting better acquainted with the Master.

Washington Gladden's hymn, "O Master, let me walk with thee," gave the audience a chance to express its consecration and enthusiasm.

Dr. Francis E. Clark, president of the United Society, having been discovered in the audience, was escorted to the platform by Dr. Curtis, pastor of the People's Church.

Then began the exchange of greetings from many nations. Rev. E. H. Tippett, of Hamilton, Canada, spoke for Canadian Congregationalists. After reciting many humorous incidents illustrative of ignorance of the situation and extent of Canada, Mr. Tippett revealed clearly that interest in Christian Endeavor work among Congregationalists in Canada was on the increase and hopeful for the future. He closed his address by expressing the hope that the sister nations, the United States and Canada, might give to the world a never-ending example of national fraternity in the promotion of civilization. The Hawaiian quartette took the gathering by storm, giving their greetings in the native language by song.

Japan was next heard from in the person of Rev. T. Makino, who said that the Congregational was the only self-supporting church in Japan.

Rev. J. P. Jones, D. D., of Madura, India, gave the message from that far country. He spoke largely of the unifying work which Christian Endeavor has done in India and is doing in all lands. He is himself a splendid specimen of the kind of citizen that Congregationalism under Christ breeds for the kingdom of God.

Dr. Clark made a short, telling, and practical address. Two points were prominent; go back to your home churches determined to create a friendly and fruitful Christian Endeavor atmosphere; then think of, and pray for, the World's Christian Endeavor Convention in Agra, India, November, 1909, and go if possible; but by all means send a proxy, a native Indian. A practical plea resulted in this meeting's sending three hundred and thirty-three and one-third delegates, at an expense of thirty cents each.

"How to Relate the Christian Endeavor Society to the Denominational Work" was ably presented in three short addresses. Rev. Jesse Hill, of Portland, Me., said, "Know the need in the fields we are working in; know our own plan to meet that need; and then support that work." Dr. S. H. Woodrow, of Washington, D. C., pointed out that the Christian Endeavor society was founded on supreme faith in the Lord Jesus Christ and loyal obedience to him. It starts at the heart of life. It is a training-school for practical efficiency. Arouse the spiritual life, and the missionary problem is solved.

Dr. Charles R. Brown, of Oakland, Cal., introduced a keen Pacific coast denominational breeze. He said in part: "We gain nothing by minimizing our characteristics. We stand for pure democracy; the people, under God, rule. We educate our rulers. We stand not only for the right, but also for the obligation, to think. We believe in intelligent missionary zeal. We stand for the thorough and wise application of Christian principles to the solution of the problems of social life. Know and practise these things, and thereby help solve the missionary problem."

Friends' Rally.

The rally was presided over by Rev. A. Edward Kelsey, who is just entering upon his duties as pastor of the Minneapolis Meeting.

After singing "All hail the power of Jesus' name" Mr. Foxworthy, of Plainview, Neb., was called upon to conduct the devotional exercises.

Mary E. L. White, president of the Minneapolis Friends' Christian Endeavor, gave the address of welcome, which was responded to most cordially by Thomas Jones, of Fairmont, Ind.

The visiting delegates were asked to join in singing the Minnesota State Endeavor song and also the Minneapolis Convention song, which they did with enthusiasm.

The roll-call of Yearly Meetings showed seven out of fourteen represented, as follows: New England Yearly Meeting, 2; Indiana, 4; Western, 2; Iowa, 40; Kansas, 1; Nebraska, 1; California, 1; total, 51.

Rev. A. Edward Kelsey's talk on "Young People and the Foreign Mission Field" was full of helpful suggestions. He believes the young Friends of the present day are not doing so much as they might do for the advancement of the missionary work of the church, that they are not giving as they ought to give, and that these conditions exist mainly on account of lack of organization. He expressed a desire that we might have, as other denominations have, a young people's secretary of the Board of Foreign Missions, who could be in touch with each and every Yearly Meeting and keep them informed of the foreign-missionary work.

Right in line with this thought was a suggestion made by William J. Sayers, of Winchester, Ind., and emphasized by Lillian E. Hayes, of Dunreith, Ind., that a summer training-school be established where young people might be trained for missionary work, and it was suggested that the several Yearly Meetings take action at once to this end.

At the close of the rally a social hour was spent, during which time a substantial lunch was served by the ladies of the missionary society, and the delegates had an opportunity of getting acquainted and exchanging names and addresses in souvenir booklets provided for that purpose by the Minneapolis society.

The Lutheran Rally.

The Lutheran rally was the most significant meeting of its kind ever held in the history of the movement, having representatives from so many branches of the church and from so many nationalities.

Rev. R. G. Bannen, D. D., of Williamsport, Penn., presided. The pastor of the (council) church in which the rally met conducted the opening service, and then cordially welcomed the company as friends, and wished them God's blessing.

Rev. J. S. Strand, pastor of the Norwegian Trinity Lutheran Church of Minneapolis (the old mother church), spoke in behalf of the Norwegians. After bringing greetings, he said among other things: "I have observed many organizations of various names, and notice some of them have failed. I asked myself the reason, and found it is because they are not spiritual enough. To the Word and the Holy Spirit was not given the place they ought to have. Christian Endeavor may not be faultless, but it is good. There is no life in the society until kindled with power from on high, and the day of God's power is here. There are two words in the English language that have greatly impressed me. One is 'surrender,' the other is 'consecration.' In these two words is bound up the secret of a useful and happy life, and from this great Convention may there be those who will say, 'Father, glorify thyself in me.' "

Rev. S. S. Waltz, D. D., of Louisville. Ky., was the speaker of the day. His subject was "Knowing and Loving Our Own." "I organized the first Endeavor society in Kentucky, and through all these years it has been my loyal and loving servant. The society that is not loyal to its own church should change its name, for it is not Christian Endeavor. This movement comes to our hearts because it puts Christ first; and, when he is honored, he comes in blessing on the society, and makes it a mighty power in the congregation and the denomination.

"Christian Endeavor honors everything we hold dear. It

honors the Christ; it honors the church; it honors the
Word, and has nothing in it we cannot heartily accept. There
is coming a glorious day of fellowship and power in our great
church."

Then followed brief and informal greetings from the
young people present from almost every part of our land,
from New England to Texas. Rev. A. Oftedol, a Norwegian
pastor, said, "I cannot tell you what Christian Endeavor has
done for me and for my church."

Prof. John M. Lenker, D. D , spoke with much emphasis on
the importance of the prayer life in the coming of the Kingdom. We need to ask, like those of old, "Lord, teach us to
pray"; and as a church we need to-day to be delivered from
the bondage of confusion.

The meeting was a real "love-feast," and closed with the
benediction.

The Methodist Rally.

The rally of the Methodist Episcopal Church, Methodist
Episcopal, South, and the Methodists of Canada, was held in
the fine Central Park Methodist Episcopal Church. William
Phillips Hall, of New York, trustee of the United Society of
Christian Endeavor, presided. Prof. E. O. Excell, that eminent Methodist composer and conductor, and musical editor
of the new Christian Endeavor hymn - book, "Jubilant
Praise," conducted the song service with great acceptability.
and Rev. Dr. W. F. Wilson, of Toronto, Canada, delivered
a most inspiring and helpful address. Mr. William Phillips
Hall spoke of the great need and importance of the evangelistic emphasis and work in our young people's societies, and
many of those present gave most interesting and instructive
testimonies to the spiritual and evangelistic efficiency and
results of the work in their respective societies, both in the
United States and in Canada. The Vancouver delegates
spoke of the splendid work accomplished by their societies
in the moral purification of the city, especially in respect to
the enforcement of the law of Sunday-observance. The principal thought of the rally seemed to be of the evangelistic
opportunity, duty, and work of the societies, and the need
of a general forward movement along these lines. The rally
was encouraging and practically helpful, and will doubtless
result in great good.

The Moravian Rally.

The Moravians gathered at St. Paul enjoyed the hospitality of the Plymouth Congregational Church. The meeting was attended by thirty-nine Moravians, representing

seventeen societies. Rev. A. D. Thaeler, pastor of the Moravian Church of Bethlehem, Penn., presided. After a brief song service, using in English and German hymns dear to all Moravians, a personal but informal introduction of each delegate was held, introductions being self-made. Miss Emma Gade, formerly a nurse in the Panama Canal Zone, told how the first Christian Endeavor society was begun there; now there are six. Then Rev. H. B. Johnson described work among the Scandinavians of Wisconsin. He was followed by Rev. J. A. Heidenreich's testimony to the work which a country society can do, as evidenced by Zora, Minn.

Then came a conference of all present, with reference to forward movements. The Lantern-Slide Bureau was strongly advocated for the increase of missionary interest which it created. Then evangelism was discussed, and all present rejoiced in the appointment of a Moravian evangelist recently announced.

The Rev. Paul T. Schultz, a missionary in the West Indies, told of Christian Endeavor among the colored people; and finally a session of personal testimony and prayer was entered. Special intercession for the Alaska mission was called forth by the report just received of the probable loss of the Alaska mission schooner carrying supplies and a volunteer entering service.

The delightful fellowship of the Unity of the Brethren pervaded the two hours spent in the meeting.

The Mennonite Rally.

The meeting was opened by singing "Nearer, my God, to thee," after which the leader of the rally, Rev. S. M. Musselman, of Wayland, Io., led in the reading of the Scripture. The theme of the meeting was that of closer contact of the societies and the missionary efforts of our denomination, a deeper interest in the work at home, and closer union with the international organization.

Mr. H. P. Goertz, of Mountain Lake, Minn., spoke of the privilege of being a co-worker in the great field of missionary activity as well as in the general work "for Christ and the church." Such work as this cannot help making us forget our denominational distinctions in the greater work of united effort for Christ's kingdom.

Rev. P. A. Penner, of Champa, India, spoke especially of the advancement of Christ's kingdom in the foreign fields. He gave it as his testimony that there is hardly any privilege that is greater than to be a foreign missionary sent by God. The speaker emphasized the fact that even in India the personal life and influence mean so much in the work of transformation.

In the open parliament following the union with the international organization was emphasized, and the hearty support of the national society in raising the fund for the Christian Endeavor Memorial Building.

The Reformed Church in America and in the United States.

A very enthusiastic and representative audience of the two Reformed denominations gathered in the Bethlehem German Presbyterian Church. Rev. A. L. Warnshuis, Amoy, China, presided.

The spirit of this great Convention was manifest on every side in this denominational rally, especially by the splendid addresses and the hearty responses and singing.

The general theme was "Missions and Evangelism." Rev. G. Watermulder, of Winnebago, Neb., spoke of the great work among the Indians, and many encouraging illustrations were presented by the speaker, showing the steady progress that is being made in the interest of the red man. Mr. A. J. Shartle, of Reading, Penn., general secretary of the Pennsylvania Christian Endeavor Union, made an address on evangelism and the need of more personal work. He demonstrated in many ways how Christian Endeavor is helping to raise fallen humanity in the slums and prisons to a higher standard, and how Christian Endeavor, when practically applied, will meet the need in the larger work of the church.

The next speaker, Rev. A. L. Warnshuis, of Amoy, China, spoke on missions in the foreign field, and held his audience with rapt attention. Missions in the foreign field, he said, are the great need of to-day; and, when the church of Christ once begins to realize the great necessity of helping our brother beyond the sea, foreign missions will go forward as never before. His address was very inspiring.

The last speaker was Rev. E. J. Blekkink, D. D., of Holland, Mich. He summarized the work of the church, and gave many helpful suggestions to the Christian Endeavorers. The meeting closed with singing, after which a delightful social was held.

The Protestant Episcopal Rally.

The rally of the Protestant Episcopal and Anglican Church was held in the guild-room of Christ Church. Ven. Archdeacon Richardson, of London, Ont., presided. There was a good attendance, and marked results followed the meeting.

After devotional exercises the chairman reviewed the history of Christian Endeavor in its connection with the Episcopal church. He spoke of the Anglican Young People's Association, built on Christian Endeavor principles and having the same motto and aims, and its rapid growth and expansion throughout Canada. This Anglican Young People's Association is a direct development of Christian Endeavor, and shows promise of rapid and wide growth. The extension of Christian Endeavor in the Church in England was pointed out and its growing favor with English Churchmen.

Rev. Dr. Floyd W. Tomkins, of Philadelphia, Penn., spoke of the value of Christian Endeavor to his church, especially in connection with the worship, work, and devotional life of his congregation.

Rev. A. R. Hill, rector of All Saints' Church, Minneapolis, told of his personal interest in the movement and of his determination at the earliest opportunity to organize a society in his own church.

Right Rev. Dr. Fallows, who was present, urged the adoption of Christian Endeavor upon his brethren of the Episcopal Church, and promised rich blessings wherever it might be used. Rev. Sydney Smith, of St. Paul, Mr. A. N. Gilbertson, Mr. A. L. du Domaine, and several other ardent churchmen all added their testimony to the blessing of this glorious movement.

The result of the rally was to give a marked impetus to Christian Endeavor methods and principles among Episcopalians.

The United Evangelical Rally.

The pastors and people of the United Evangelical Church in attendance at the great Convention made Tabor United Evangelical Church their Mecca. Representatives were present from Pennsylvania, Ohio, Illinois, Iowa, Wisconsin, and Nebraska. Rev. U. F. Swengel, D. D., of Lewistown, Penn., had charge of the exercises. Rev. W. S. Harpster was musical conductor. Rev. J. Auracher, of Cedar Rapids, Io., read the Keystone League of Christian Endeavor chapter, 1 Cor. 13. Rev. F. D. Stauffacher, of the same place, offered prayer. Rev. B. F. Zuehl, the local pastor, spoke cordial words of welcome. "Blest be the tie that binds our hearts in Christian love" was sung in response. The chairman read a letter from Prof. D. M. Metzgar, D. D., of Dallas College, Oregon, containing greetings and thanks for contributions that made it possible to build a church in Dallas a few years ago.

Rev. Benjamin Hilliar, of York, Neb., discussed the Keystone League of Christian Endeavor and missions. Rev. D. C. Hauk, of Nerstrand, Minn., spoke of the Keystone League and church extension.

Rev. D. A. Poling, of Columbus, O., field secretary of the Ohio State Christian Endeavor Union, carefully considered the question, "The Keystone League of Christian Endeavor and Young Men."

Rev. J. G. Waltz, of Lisbon, Io., superintendent of Junior work in the United Evangelical Church, spoke earnestly on the important trust committed to him.

Rev. W. S. Harpster, of Columbus, O., president of the Ohio Christian Endeavor Union, interestingly discussed the Keystone League and the Sunday school.

During the exercises a delightful interruption occurred. The representatives of the United Brethren in Christ and of the Methodist Protestant Church, who had been assigned elsewhere for a joint rally, came marching and singing to the doors of the church to unite with the United Evangelicals in a united rally. As they entered, the audience arose and sung "Blest be the tie that binds."

Bishop W. M. Weekley, D. D., of Kansas City, was introduced, and spoke of organic union of the three denominations represented in the audience. Rev. C. H. Hubbell, D. D., secretary of the Methodist Protestant Sunday-school and Christian Endeavor work, of Adrian, Mich., and Rev. J. G. Huber, D. D., president of the United Brethren Christian Endeavor Union of the United Brethren in Christ, Dayton, O., and Rev. William Jonas, of St. Paul, presiding elder of the United Evangelical Church, all spoke enthusiastically of the desirability of organic union.

A committee consisting of Dr. J. G. Huber, Rev. D. A. Poling, and Dr. C. H. Hubbell was appointed to prepare resolutions expressive of the sentiment of the meeting. The report embodied the sense of the meeting so clearly that it was unanimously adopted. This was a veritable love-feast, and it is impossible to prophesy the result of this splendid joint rally.

CHAPTER XXXI.

THE ILLUSTRATED LECTURES.

Held in the Armory Each Day During the Convention.

The large drill-hall of the Armory, in which were the various exhibits of civic, moral, and religious progress, was decorated with the Christian Endeavor colors and with the flags of all nations. There were large displays for the cause of home missions, foreign missions, tuberculosis, and temperance, and also an excellent collection of curios and a Christian Endeavor museum in charge of Mr. M. B. Holley, of Traverse City, Mich.

The United Society of Christian Endeavor had a large booth, as well as one at the Auditorium, where several of the ladies from the Park Congregational Church, St. Paul, sold literature and Christian Endeavor helps of all descriptions, as well as pins and badges. These booths were in charge of Walter R. Mee, manager of the Chicago office.

On Thursday afternoon Mrs. Bessie Laythe Scovell, of Minneapolis, lectured on the Woman's Christian Temperance Union and its work, emphasizing the sentiment being created among children, and also calling the attention of Christian Endeavorers to the influence they may use in securing votes for prohibition.

On Thursday evening Rev. Howard B. Grose, D. D., editorial secretary of the Baptist Home Mission Union of New York, gave a most interesting lecture on "A World Survey of Missions," illustrated by the stereopticon and moving pictures. Japan, China, and India were touched upon as representing the foreign field, and views were shown illustrating the different forms and practices of worship of those countries. Their earnestness and devotion teach Christians some very forceful lessons, and should make them more zealous in efforts to claim those peoples "for Christ and the church." The home-missionary slides brought out the good that is being accomplished within the American borders for Orientals, Europeans, negroes, and Indians, and also emphasized the need for greater and more effective service in these fields.

Friday afternoon a large audience had the pleasure of

"THE CROSS" AT THE JUNIOR RALLY.

listening to Rev. T. Makino, editor of the "Kwas Sekai" ("Endeavor World"), Kyoto, who talked upon "Japan of To-day." The gracious personality so characteristic of the Japanese was especially pleasing in Mr. Makino, and won for him the sympathy of his audience. He spoke of the earnestness of the Japanese Christians, of the many lives which have been consecrated and sacrificed in service, and of the zeal and faith of these people, which, even though they number only eighty thousand, cannot but point to the way of the Kingdom in the Land of the Sunrise.

He spoke of the power of prayer and of the increased strength that would be given to the Japanese Christians for their work if our prayers were lifted with theirs.

One especial feature of the afternoon was the presentation of a beautiful banner by the Cleveland, O., Union to Mr. Makino, upon which were handsomely embroidered the Japanese and United States flags united by the Christian Endeavor monogram. The Cleveland Union has held since 1905 a banner embroidered in Kyoto, awarded by the United Society of Christian Endeavor for ten-per-cent increase in membership. They also support Mr. Sawaya, Christian Endeavor field secretary of Japan. These two facts have united the Union and Kyoto in very close bonds of fellowship.

Mr. Makino expressed the hope, entertained by all, that the giving and taking of these tokens of Christian fellowship may be a symbol of our lasting international peace and love.

Mr. George B. Graff, publishing manager of the United Society of Christian Endeavor, gave his new lecture, "Around the World with Christian Endeavor," on Friday evening. The lecture was illustrated by excellent views from all lands, which brought home to the audience the fact that Christian Endeavor means Christ everywhere.

Mr. Graff first told something of the beginnings and conventions of Christian Endeavor, and of the summer conferences at the seashore. The work in Canada, especially among the lumbermen, offers a very large field for Christian Endeavor, as does that also among the sailors on board the United States battleships.

Views were shown from Bermuda, Brazil, Hawaii, Japan, China, Australia, India, Africa, and the various countries of Europe. Appreciation of the splendid work that is being done by Christian Endeavor throughout the world was evidenced by frequent and enthusiastic applause.

Rev. H. B. Grose, D. D., also delivered a fine illustrated lecture on "The Mohammedan World." The views were exceptionally good, and showed the beautiful mosques of the various Mohammedan centres, as well as the large Uni-

178   TWENTY·FOURTH INTERNATIONAL CONVENTION

versity of Cairo, where there are seven thousand students
in attendance.

The divorce customs of Mohammedanism are perhaps its
greatest weakness, and should be a warning to the United
States. The divorce evil in our country, if allowed to continue, will doubtless prove the downfall of the nation.

The degradation of women and the neglect of children
are in marked contrast to the high regard in which women
and children are held among Christians.

At the same time, the Moslem in his knowledge of his holy
book, the Koran, and in his devotion to prayer far outclasses
the majority of those professing Christianity.

"Christian Endeavor among the American Indians" was
the subject of a very interesting address by Mr. G. W.
Watermulder, missionary to the Winnebago Indians.

The speaker referred to the lecture that preceded his
address, and expressed the wish that he too could throw
upon the screen pictures of the scenes among the Indians,
although they are not immigrants, their ancestors having
lived here long before Columbus reached our shores. Although they fought for their rights, they have been gradually drawn back until now they are herded like cattle in
our government reservations. Christian Endeavor's field of
activity is large and varied; yet little has been done for
the Indian, so that it would be easier, because of the great
need, to tell what has not been done. While there are
Christian Endeavor societies in some of the Indian schools,
they have not played an important part in helping the Indian. What is the cause of this? Is it because the Indians
lack appreciation of Christian Endeavor? Or, as many seem
to believe, is it because there are but few Indians? There
is a popular misconception as to the number of Indians.
The population among the Indians is on the increase. British America contains about 100,000; the United States about
250,000; Mexico, 400,000, and South America, 15,000,000.
The greatest field in the world to-day for evangelistic work
is among the Indians of North and South America.

The speaker spoke of a number of Indians that had attained positions of influence and responsibility, to demonstrate their capacity for the reception of higher life, mentioning particularly Rev. Mr. Marsden, of Alaska, who is
a full-blooded Indian, and also a boy taken from an Indian
reservation school, who is leader of the Bible class of the
junior class at Yale.

Twenty reservations in the United States are not reached
at all by mission workers, and few among the 27,000 Navajo
Indians have been reached by the gospel. The Indian is

our neighbor, and we should not pass him by in reaching the foreign field.

Between Omaha and Sioux City there are two tribes, known as the Winnebagoes and the Omahas, where you will find as great barbarism as you will see in Africa.

We should pray for these people, whose land we have taken, "May thy kingdom come for the American Indian."

One of our new Americans, Rev. Moses K. Nakuina, spoke in his earnest and interesting manner of the advance of Christian Endeavor in Hawaii.

He said that, although Hawaii is often referred to as the "Paradise of the Pacific," it is by no means a paradise, although they have summer there all the time. His invitation to the Endeavorers to hold their 1915 International Convention there was answered by applause. The first society of Christian Endeavor was organized in the Central Union Church twenty years ago, and for a long time had an up-hill struggle, owing to the fact that the churches there had the Young Men's Christian Association and did not want Christian Endeavor. Although Rev. M. Nakuina was converted only in 1900, he was elected president of the Hawaiian Territorial Union in 1901, which from 18 societies with 600 members has grown to 123 societies with 3,500 members. For a time the pastors opposed this movement, but their attitude is largely changed; and one pastor, who refused absolutely to have a society, now has five societies in his church, and has formed them into a union. The Endeavorers there are doing practical work and contributing toward the expenses of the American Board.

At the Seattle Convention the heart of the speaker was touched, and he decided to become a pastor, finally being ordained to preach. He declared he was praying that the same spirit might touch his three fellow delegates from Hawaii, two of whom are judges and the third a prominent layman.

CHAPTER XXXII.

THE CLOSING SESSION.

The Auditorium, Monday Evening, July 12.

At the great International Convention no one that can possibly be present misses the closing session. It is always a climax where the enthusiasm is focused. That accounts for the State "yells," which crackle like snappy peals of thunder from delegation to delegation in the different parts of the hall, and the State songs that swell from youthful throats.

Mr. Foster and Mr. Excell, those grand leaders of song that have conducted meeting after meeting for nearly a week with unfailing enthusiasm and power, are there; and the audience responds to their leadership with wonderful precision.

The service was opened by Dr. Clark, who led a short responsive devotional exercise, concluding with the Christian Endeavor fellowship song, "Blest be the tie that binds."

Dr. Swearingen, of St. Paul, led in prayer, and Dr. Clark prepared for the real business of the evening. He intimated that this was not a mere demonstration or a pageant, but a real purpose meeting, and urged that each one present make the purpose expressed by the State officers his own.

He then called upon some of the representatives of foreign nations to speak for their people.

Rev. Dr. Jones from India was presented to the meeting, and said: "Our purpose is to win India for Christ. For us Christian Endeavor means redemptive power."

Dr. Carey, the great-grandson of William Carey, the first missionary to India, sang an Endeavor song in Bengali, the sentiment of which he interpreted, "O Jesus, come into my heart; this wild heart will be stilled if thou comest in." The motto of the Indian Endeavorers is, "Christ for India and India for Christ." Rev. Dr. Jones, for thirty-five years a missionary to India, sang a favorite Endeavor hymn in the Tamil language, "The name of Jesus is sweeter than honey; therefore do thou flee unto him, O church of God."

After Dr. Clark had intimated that the offerings of American Endeavorers would enable one thousand Indian delegates to attend the Convention at Agra, Rev. Mr. Makino, of Kyoto, Japan, brought a greeting from his people: "Each one of the

Japanese Endeavorers, thirty-two hundred strong, will prove himself and herself a good soldier and take part in the coming campaign in winning one million souls for the Kingdom."

Rev. A. L. Warnshuis, Amoy, China, referred to China as the greatest Christian Endeavor field in the world, and said: "We have there one hundred millions of young people. China has been the land of ancestors, but to-day it is the land of young people. We go back, and we feel that these Chinese will go forth and win each man his brother, so that we shall not only have a new China, but a Christian China."

Dr. Clark cheered us by the good news that a message just received from China told of a great Christian Endeavor convention held at Nankin. It was also intimated that the bishop of the Methodist Church in China had given permission to the Epworth League to join the Christian Endeavor ranks and take part with Christian Endeavorers in the work of the evangelization of China.

Rev. S. Guy Inman, from Mexico, then mounted the platform, and said, "I wish to consecrate the Endeavorers of Mexico to take part in the work to which Dr. Clark has called us."

A never-to-be-forgotten feature of these meetings is the "march past" of the States. Representatives of each State, usually three or four, form in one of the corridors, and come up State by State to the platform, where they repeat their response, sing a verse of some song, and pass on. This, however, was a purpose meeting, and the responses of the States were for the most part an expression of some definite purpose for the year.

Canada was called first, and Rev. J. W. Litch responded by expressing his pleasure at being privileged to represent the great Dominion. Canada is weak in some things, he said, but others stand to her credit; she gave Christian Endeavor its founder and president. The motto is, "Canada for Christ." The Canadian delegates have just arranged for an "All-Canada" convention in 1912. It will be held at Winnipeg, Manitoba.

The Canadian delegates in the gallery joined then in singing "The maple leaf forever," while pennons and banners waved in rhythm with the music. This feature was repeated with splendid effect after each State's response.

Alabama was represented by Karl Lehmann and several others. Their greeting was, "Forgetting the things that are behind, and reaching forth unto the things that are before, I press on." "Alabama expects to make the State the Christian Endeavor centre of Dixie."

One man, a native Alaskan Indian. Rev. Mr. Marsden,

represented that vast Territory, and spoke for its scattered people this greeting: "Finally, brethren, pray for us, that the word of the Lord may have free course and be glorified."

The representative of Arkansas said: "We have done good Christian Endeavor work, and we hold the world's record for large gifts from small societies to the funds of the Christian Endeavor Builders' Union. Our greeting is, 'Study to show thyself approved unto God, a workman that needeth not to be ashamed.'"

One can only indicate the gist of the splendid responses and purposes made by the States. California said that more than five thousand Endeavorers met at their last State convention, and that it would be their purpose in the future to hold high the standard for Christian Endeavor work.

The Colorado delegation said: "We have been going some, and we are going some more. Colorado is going to do her share in all Christian Endeavor activity, in Quiet-Hour work, in the Tenth Legion, in personal work, and in the Builders' Union."

Connecticut was led by her State president, Mr. J. H. Mansfield. In a few choice words he indicated that the motto for the coming year is, "All for Christ and the church."

Percy S. Foster received an ovation—which he deserved on account of the splendid leadership of song that he and Mr. Excell furnished—as he headed the delegates from the District of Columbia. The purpose expressed was, "to fit all our Endeavorers as far as they can to carry out the work in a progressive spirit and attain the best results." Surely it was an inspiration that made Mr. Foster ask the audience to rise and sing "My country, 'tis of thee," which they did while every banner and pennon and flag was waved, bright spots of color among a sea of fluttering handkerchiefs.

Hawaii had four delegates present at an expense of $300 for each man, and each paid his own expenses. They, too, received an ovation as they stepped upon the platform with their beautiful Hawaiian yellow garlands hanging round their necks. "Hawaii," said Pastor Nakuina, "is the lone star of the Pacific. Her motto is, 'Loyalty to Christ and the church.' The one hundred and twenty-three societies of the Territory send this greeting: 'Grow in grace and in the knowledge of our Lord Jesus Christ, to whom be the glory now and for ever.'" Then followed a song, simple, soft, and sweet, by this quartette of Endeavorers, as they stood with their "wistaria" banner, made in Japan, with its beautiful design in clinging wild flowers.

S. C. Elder brought the greetings of Idaho. "In Idaho we are making good. We have secured a Sunday-closing law. We have a local-option law, and in September we hope to vote every county dry. Our purpose is to redeem thousands of young lives. 'I can do all things, through Christ, which strengtheneth me.' "

Mr. Ceperly spoke for Illinois. "Our desire is expressed in the watchword of every Endeavorer in Illinois, 'God willing, I will.' "

State President Orbison, who put in so eloquent a plea to get the next Convention to Indianapolis, took the stand for Indiana. 'Indiana will do its share to get the million members called for; she will be more aggressive in mission study and in personal work; and we expect to be a part of that movement that is to make Indiana a prohibition State."

Then came Iowa, headed by C. T. Ensign, the State president, with her splendid purpose, "Christ first." Iowa will take her part in the increase campaign. "Not by might, nor by power, but by my Spirit, saith the Lord of hosts."

Three young ladies stepped forward to represent Kansas. Miss Edith Adamson expressed the purpose, "Kansas for Christ," and said, "We will attempt to do the work that Dr. Clark has asked us to do."

"Our old Kentucky home" was the melody used for the song of the Kentucky delegation, headed by Rev. E. L. Wilson. The purpose of the State is to get the Baptist Young People's Union of Kentucky to join the Christian Endeavor ranks, and also to get the Epworth League to affiliate with us. A truly brotherly undertaking.

The pioneer State of Christian Endeavor, Maine, was represented by Rev. Clarence Emery. He said that Maine is more than the birthplace of Christian Endeavor; she has given, among others, Longfellow and Neal Dow to the nation. Then the delegates repeated John 3: 16 in unison.

Then came Massachusetts, whose president had to leave before the meeting. Dr. J. Stanley Durkee, of Boston, read Rev. Mr. Voorhees's message: "Knowing Him from whom their strength cometh, and daring to trust him; drawing their strength from him as freely as he desires to give; glad for the problems because of new strength gained in their solution; Massachusetts will not be the least among her sister States in the great campaign for one million new members in 1911."

Field Secretary Hall said that Michigan had started an express train by the Big Four: (1) An increase campaign; (2) Mission and Bible study; (3) A betterment campaign; and (4) The Builders' Union.

President Jayne, of Minnesota, our hosts and hostesses, rose to express the sentiments of his State. The great delegation of Minnesota Endeavorers greeted him and us with waving flags and handkerchiefs. "Minnesota will do her quota. She will meet the requirement asked, but 'not by might, nor by power,' but by the Spirit of the Lord."

When the St. Paul Endeavorers heard what was being done for the Builders' Union, they said, "We must be in it, and be in it now." So they got together a few of their societies and among them they subscribed for one hundred shares at five ·dollars each. This is only a beginning, an earnest of the great things they will do.

State Secretary Dollie Sullinger, Missouri, gave the watchword of her State, "One step in every direction." She pledged the hearty support of Missouri for the increase campaign and for all other Christian Endeavor work. The delegation repeated the beautiful motto, "More of Christ in me to save the soul nearest me."

Many were profoundly moved when Mrs. C. V. Franzmann and her daughter stepped forward to represent Montana, two generations of Endeavorers. "The motto for Montana is the same as it is all over the world, 'For Christ and the church.' "

President Salsbury, of the Nebraska union, said that his State was not so celebrated in Christian Endeavor work as in some other matters; yet she has accomplished something, for the Endeavorers have had a hand in making some cities dry.

At this point Mr. George W. Coleman stepped forward to read a letter from Nebraska's greatest citizen, William Jennings Bryan. It read as follows:

Lincoln, Neb., July 10, 1909.
I promise, God helping me, to abstain from the use of all intoxicating liquor as a beverage.   W. J. BRYAN.

Mr. Bryan is anxious to do his part, and to have the support of Endeavorers in doing it, in making this a dry country.

Miss Frost was the speaker from New Hampshire, voicing the purpose of her State as the desire to make good. "We propose to be more spiritual, to do more work for the Builders' Union, and to do more for the motto on the badge of the Woman's Temperance Union, which said, 'New Hampshire is going dry.' "

New Jersey, the State that will welcome the next Convention, was represented by Mr. Sproull, State president. He said: "New Jersey will endeavor to have a part in the bringing in of the Kingdom, by emphasizing the Quiet Hour and Tenth Legion, and by having its share in the realization of the grand ideal of our beloved president, Dr. Clark, during the next two years, by gaining ten thousand new societies and one million new members."

New Mexico was represented by Laura W. Collings. "We intend to be admitted into the Union with a prohibition plank in our programme."

Miss Mary Morall spoke for New York. "We will stand this year for better consecration, for better service, and for an increase in membership. 'Not by might, . . . but by my Spirit.'"

The North Dakota delegation was led by State President Rich. He said that North Dakota had sent four delegates to Seattle; but to St. Paul she had sent more than one hundred. This is the rate of increase for which the Endeavorers are working. The motto, "Without Him we can do nothing."

State Secretary Poling was at the head of the Ohio Endeavorers. "Ohio accepts the vision of our leader," he said, "and aims at five hundred new societies, more Junior societies, and a purer civic life—all by the grace of God, and for Christ and the church."

Oklahoma, the youngest of the States, was represented by State President Wheeler. He said: "We will do our part to attain the object Dr. Clark has mentioned, and we will try to make Christ king in Oklahoma."

Oregon, led by State President Hurd, said: "We are doing some things that we think are worth while. We shall go back and ask our friends to help us organize one hundred new societies. We will work for efficiency, betterment, and Bible-study."

Pennsylvania voiced her purpose through State President Bannen. "We are here to pledge ourselves to the new increase and add to our four thousand societies one thousand more." The beautiful sentiment expressed was, "The kingdom of God cometh not with observation. The kingdom of God is within you."

From Rhode Island came J. K. Ralph, who said. "We will furnish our part in the increase campaign for 1911."

Rev. J. P. Anderson, South Dakota, referred to some undesirable things, like easy divorce, for which the State had been famed; but Christian Endeavor had helped to remove this stigma. "We are going to try to get South Dakota back into the list of prohibition States, where she once stood, and win our State for Christ Jesus."

President Dean was present from Tennessee. "I pledge Tennessee," he said, "to back the slogan for the Atlantic City Convention, 1911."

From Texas came State President Beeman. "We go back

to the Lone-Star State with the burden of work upon us.
We have set our mark at one hundred per cent increase all
round."

Utah was represented by State President Horn. "We covenant with you that we will increase our societies fifty per
cent in membership. Before January 1 we shall have every
society on the honor roll of the Builders' Union. And after
we have paid at the rate of twenty-five cents a member, we
will take off our coats and do it some more."

Washington was led by Claude H. Eckhart. He said:
"When the apportionment of a certain number of shares in
·the Builders' Union was made to our State, we said, 'It is
yours.' When you ask our share in the increase campaign,
we say again, 'It is yours.'"

Dr. W. T. Johnson and his wife, representing the negro
race, pledged the hearty support of his people both for the
increase campaign and for the building fund.

Secretary Shaw read the message from President W. W.
Smith, of West Virginia, as follows: "We want to see a
church on every hilltop, a schoolhouse in every valley, and
a Christian Endeavor society in both, and to see every society
contributing its quota to the Christian Endeavor headquarters
building as an everlasting monument to Dr. Clark and an
endowment for all time to link together the churches and the
nations of the world with the Christian Endeavor chain."

President Ganfield headed three hundred and fifty Wisconsin Endeavorers, whose waving banners made a brave showing in the hall, as in a few well-chosen words he pledged his
State to the Christian Endeavor increase campaign.

Wyoming, too, expressed the same sentiment through two
young lady Endeavorers, who promised that their State would
advance in step with the others.

The march of the States around the hall, the delegates
carrying their multicolored banners, was a sight never to be
forgotten. It was the church militant, an exhibition of youth
consecrated to the Master.

Credit was given to the St. Paul and Minneapolis joint
committee for the great labor expended on the Convention,
and then Dr. Clark delivered his closing message. He thanked
God for the Convention because of its promise of future work.
It means a larger fellowship, greater courage, and renewed
hope. "Take the inspiration home with you," he said. "You
have a special mission to perform. Take the Convention to
your homes, your societies, your unions. Have echo meetings. Tell the people about the enlarging fellowship; tell
them that our friends are coming with us from the different
denominations."

With bowed heads the first sentence of the pledge was solemnly repeated, a brief prayer was offered, and the twenty-fourth International Convention of Christian Endeavor was declared adjourned.

CHAPTER XXXIII.

GREETINGS FROM OTHER LANDS TO THE TWENTY-FOURTH INTERNATIONAL CHRISTIAN ENDEAVOR CONVENTION.

Greeting from Burma.

We are a united band of enthusiastic workers talking many languages,—Burmese, Karen, Shon, Chin, Kachin, Tamil, Telugu, English,—and in our own societies there are representatives of many other peoples. We hope to welcome you to our World's Convention at Agra, India, next November. Burma is to be there in force.

(PROF.) A. C. RICE, Rangoon.

Greeting from Germany.

I might send as the one word that has become so important for us, Rom. 6:6, *"We are crucified with Christ."* May it be so in the future with all our members, that we all have God-created fruit through the consecration meetings, and not endeavor in vain to lose by our own works our old life of sin and selfishness, seeing Christ has already prepared all. Then we shall fulfil and live out the principles of our dear, blessed movement. May the above-mentioned chapter, Romans 6, become the dearest chapter to many of the delegates and members. United with you in spirit, love, and service.

(REV.) F. BLECHER, Friedrichshagen bei Berlin.

Greeting from France.

> " 'Worthy of all adoration
> Is the Lamb that once was slain!'
> Cry in raptured exultation
> His redeemed from every nation."
> —*F. R. Havergal.*

"Wait on the Lord; be of good courage, and he shall strengthen thine heart: wait, I say, on the Lord." (Ps. 27:14.) Our watchword in France in Christian Endeavor is, EVANGELIZE! We hope that American Endeavorers will remember in prayer our country and our present duty. (REV.) V. VAN DER BEKEN, Paris.

Greeting from Hungary.

Hungarian Christian Endeavorers send you enthusiastic greetings. We had success already, but we have now a great undertaking on our hearts and purses. We have bought a large deaconess hospital. This will bring honor to Christian Endeavorers, love to many poor, sick people. Allow not Dr. Clark to overwork. Send him to Europe. The grace of our Saviour with us all. DR. A. SZABO, Budapest.

Greeting from Italy.

To know that you are gathered together from every part of the field in which the Christian Endeavor Society extends its roots for praise, prayer, and fraternal exultation, is a delightful thought for us who work under the same banner in Italy.

Though far from you in body, we are near you in spirit; our prayers ascend with yours to the "King eternal, immortal, invisible," and our enthusiasm mingles with yours in the cry, "JESUS REIGNS!" Italy is a field white unto the harvest; pray the Lord to send us good laborers.

Our prayers for this convention are comprised in the words of the apostle Paul: *"Now our Lord Jesus Christ himself, and God our Father which loved us and gave us eternal comfort and good hope through grace, comfort your hearts and establish them in every good work and word."* (2 Thess. 2: 16, 17.)   (Rev.) GIUSEPPE CERVI, Milan.

Greeting from Iceland.

From the old famous island, which keeps a guard alone far from other countries against the polar current, comes a greeting to brethren and sisters in the warmer countries. Our island thanks the mild weather which the Gulf Stream brings from the coast of America hither. Could you not also send us with it prayers, prayers for a revival and more love for the old, old story, that we all may be one from the cold valleys of Iceland and the sunlit plains of India?

With sorrowful longing I sometimes think about your great work and great conventions. But the way to the white throne is of the same length also here, and the Lord understands also as well Icelandic as other languages.

May we all grow in grace, and in the knowledge of our Lord and Saviour Jesus Christ. To him be glory both now and for ever.
                              S. A. GISLASON, Reykjavik, Iceland.

Greeting from Macedonia.

From Thessalonica, the chief city of Macedonia, whose Christians in the time of Paul were beloved by the great apostle, we, who are privileged to tread in his footsteps, send greeting to the great army of Christian Endeavorers gathered at the twenty-fourth International Convention at St. Paul, the city which bears the apostle's name.

We greet you in the name of the Bulgarians, Servians, Albanians, and Wallachians, who form our fourteen societies.

The recent stirring events in Turkey, which have made our city, under its modern name, Salonica, well known the world over, show the rising importance of the city, and it is our hope that by God's blessing the Christian Endeavor societies, which centre around this city, may grow in numbers and spiritual power and take a commanding place in the evangelization of the many nationalities of these regions. Remember this work in your prayers. (REV.) JOHN HENRY HOUSE, Salonica.

Greeting from Costa Rica.

We rejoice in the steady growth of.Christian Endeavor, and view with considerable pleasure the wholesome influence it is exerting among the nations of the earth. It is our earnest desire and fervent prayer that the power of the Holy Spirit may be manifest in your midst during all the sessions of the Convention, and that from it may go forth an influence which shall in larger measure even than heretofore spread among the nations that righteousness which exalteth.
                              (REV.) E. A. PITT, Costa Rica.

Greeting from Demerara, British Guiana.

The Demerara Christian Endeavor Union begs hereby to greet and to render its heartiest congratulations to the fellow Endeavorers, officers, and delegates gathered together at St. Paul, Min., for the twenty-fourth International Convention, and pray that a rich blessing may rest upon their meetings for praise, prayer, and deliberation; and that the results therefrom may redound to the glory of our common Master in the ingathering of many souls and the edifying of the body of Christ.

JOHN DINGWALL, Georgetown, Demerara.

Greeting from Samoa.

"Our Father,—thy kingdom come" "Lo matou Tamae—Ia oo mai lou malo."   (REV.) J. E. NEWELL, Samoa.

Greeting from Cuba.

We send the heartfelt greetings of our National Association of Young People and Sunday Schools of Cuba, and assure you of our sympathy and prayers that God's richest blessings may rest upon your deliberations.   (REV.) H. B. SOMEILLAN, Guanabacoa.

Greeting from the Philippine Islands.

The Endeavorers of the Philippines send you hearty greetings, and wish for you one of the greatest of all your conventions.

We hope some of you are going to the Fourth World's Convention in India, and will visit us on your way home. We will make you heartily welcome.   (REV.) GEORGE WILLIAM WRIGHT, Manila, P. I.

Greeting from Australia.

"Sow to yourselves in righteousness, reap according to mercy; break up your fallow ground: for it is time to seek the Lord, till he come and rain righteousness upon you." (Hosea 10:12.)

The unanimous desire from Australasia is, I am confident, that St. Paul's may prove to be an apostolic convention, in the deep spiritual character of its gatherings, and the joy-note struck.

HENRY BUSH, Lindfield, N. S. W.

Greeting from our Brothers in Bonds.

As much as we would like to share with you in the blessings of the great International Convention at St. Paul, the stern dictate of the law sets up a barrier, over which, in person, we may not pass.

The Michigan State Prison Society of Christian Endeavor grew out of an organization, formed in 1886, called the Prison Mission Band. The Christian Endeavor society has been in existence for the past twenty years.

We are sorry to be compelled to report that our Christian Endeavor society has had no meeting since the last week in December, 1906.

The men under whose authority we have been compelled to live and struggle were like one of old, who "cared for none of those things."

But, while having no organized body, there are yet some who will not bow the knee to Baal, whose prayers will go out for the spiritual victory of the great Convention.

We trust we may have a place in your devotions, that God may grant

unto us all the fulness of his grace, that we may with you be partakers
of the inheritance of those which are sanctified in the kingdom of his
glory.

We expect a new warden within a few weeks, and trust that his
heart will be "big" enough to allow us to resume our Christian Endeavor meetings.

Wishing you every success in the Master's work, I am,

Sincerely yours,

Michigan State Prison. J. M. Miller, Jackson, Mich.

Greeting from the British Embassy.

My dear Sir:—Greatly to my regret I cannot come to Minnesota
to address your Convention on July 7, as I am then engaged to represent Great Britain at the Champlain celebration in New York and Ver-
mont. I am the more sorry to be unable to be present because I know
how wide-spread the Christian Endeavor movement is in Great Britain
and the British colonies, and how much good it has effected there; and
I would gladly have expressed my sense of its value to all the branches
of our race.

The movement seems to me to be one of the most hopeful signs
of our times. It is a sign that nothing better can be done for the progress of mankind than to set the example of a serious and sustained
effort to apply the principles of the gospel to daily life, carrying those
principles into all the relations of life, family relations, business relations, public affairs, international affairs. In and for these the gospel
teachings are as full of force and truth as they were when first delivered. If all who call themselves Christians were to follow them out in
practice, the evils that afflict the modern world would be swiftly and
mightily reduced.

Believe me to be, with best wishes for the success of your gathering, Faithfully yours, James Bryce.

Greeting from Spain.

Fifteen hundred of Spanish Endeavorers in fifty-five societies send
their heartiest Christian greetings to the Endeavor hosts assembling
at St. Paul.

Last year we could realize the encouraging power of our Christian
Endeavor brotherhood, when we enjoyed the privilege of having amongst
us our honored leader, Dr. Clark, who brought the loving greetings of
our brothers and sisters across the seas, at our last national convention
in Barcelona. Since then three new societies have been formed in our
country, and others have received a new impulse.

We need the prayers and sympathy of all our comrades in our efforts
to win for Christ many of Spain's young people. We rejoice in your
triumphs and success. "We will rejoice in thy salvation, and in the name
of our God we will set up our banners: the Lord fulfil all thy peti-
tions." Psalm 20:5.

William H. Gulick, President, Madrid.
Carlos Araujo, Jr., Secretary of the Spanish Union.

Greeting from South Africa.

We, your fellow Endeavorers in South Africa, send you greetings.
Our annual convention in assembly at Grahamstown during Easter last
resolved to send you a response. Our three ambitions:

(1) 1 Thess. 4:11. Our Quiet Hour, the secret of all effort.

(2) 2 Cor. 5 ;9. Our pledge, that we may be well pleasing to Him.
(3) Romans 15 :20. Our aim, to make Christ known.
Praying God's richest blessing on your assembly, we are,
Yours in C. E.
S. J. THOMAS, Honorary Secretary.
ALFRED LAW PALMER, President.
Johannesburg, S. A.

Greeting from Japan.

"Wagga Nippon kiristokyo kyoeikwaiwa St. Paul ni hirakaretarn
Taikwai ga Shito Paul no dendoteki diaseishinga shushi ikkan shite
kamini taishitewa tatashiki to kyodai no taishitewe aito kokka no aidan-
iwa heiwa arankotowo kibo su."
Freely translated, the message in English renders itself:
"Japan to St. Paul, greeting.
"City of Noble Name and Honorable History:
"May the missionary spirit of the great apostle to the Gentiles take
full possession of your convention; and may we all, Endeavorers from
North America and Eastern Asia alike, give ourselves upreservedly
to the grandly glorious endeavor of practising the presence of God in
our own lives, and of winning the world to the loyal allegiance to the
threefold cause of righteousness-towards God, love of our brethren, and
peace among the nations."

THE CONVENTION CHORUS.

"THE MESSAGE OF THE NATIONS" IN THE JUNIOR RALLY.

CHAPTER XXXIV.

RESOLUTIONS.

Adopted at the Twenty-Fourth International Convention.

Resolved, That we commend to the attention of good-citizenship committees in all our city and State unions the practical accomplishment of the Denver and other Endeavorers in their successful warfare against evil men and measures, and that we further urge Christian Endeavorers everywhere to take advantage of the present moral awakening in political and business circles to press the claim and right of Jesus Christ to dominate every sphere of life.

Resolved, That we join forces with the Endeavorers of our national capital in their effort to prohibit the sale of liquors in the nation's city, and urge all our representatives in Congress to use their influence and their votes to accomplish this result at an early date.

Resolved, That we call upon our national Congress to pass such legislation as will forbid the sale and transportation of intoxicating liquors into prohibition territories, and urge Endeavorers throughout the country to petition their representatives to that effect.

Resolved, That we reaffirm our belief in total abstinence as one of the most potent means for driving out the liquor traffic, and urge all Christian Endeavor temperance workers to take advantage of the present most auspicious day to urge upon the rising generation of young people the duty and privilege of pledging themselves to a life of total abstinence. Years have gone by since this country has had a temperance pledge-signing campaign. We believe the time is ripe for a new movement in this direction. At the same time, let there be no cessation of effort to restrict and eliminate the liquor business by process of law.

Resolved, That as followers of the Prince of peace we ally ourselves with every effort that is being made for the suppression of war. The immense and ever-increasing tax which war and preparations for war levy on peaceful industries, and the frightful horrors of war itself, demand that every lover of God and humanity should unite for its suppression.

Resolved, That in view of the splendid possibilities of influence and service open to a federated army of young people, enlisted in a common cause under a common Master and bearing a common name, in view of the world's need of such united service, in view of the fact that the young people's societies of the United Brethren have by denominational action recently become United Brethren Societies of Christian Endeavor, and in view of the action taken at this Convention by the Baptist Christian Endeavor societies looking toward unity of Baptist young people's work, under the name of the Baptist Young People's Union of Christian Endeavor, overtures be made once more to the Epworth Leagues of the Methodist Episcopal Church to join in this great federation of

193

194   TWENTY - FOURTH INTERNATIONAL CONVENTION

young people, and by becoming affiliated as Epworth Leagues of Christian Endeavor make possible an all-inclusive young people's federation of the world.

Resolved, That the sincere and hearty thanks of the Convention be extended to the St. Paul committee of arrangements for their splendid preparations for this meeting, and to the Minneapolis committee for their helpful co-operation; to the pastors and churches of the city who have opened their buildings for the uses of the Convention; to the public press for their excellent reports; to the city officials for their cordial welcome; to the business men and citizens for generous financial support; to the leader and chorus who have rendered helpful service in song; to the speakers, and to all who have helped make this Convention memorable through its delightful fellowship, its intellectual stimulus, and its spiritual uplift.

S. H. Woodrow,
G. B. Stewart,
J. P. Rice,
Committee on Resolutions.

CHAPTER XXXV.

SIDE - LIGHTS.

Noted During the Convention.

The Exposition chorus of forty Minneapolis singers in the costume of different nations proved an interesting feature of the Convention.

Wisconsin had perhaps the most enthusiastic and largest delegation in line in the parade to the capitol.

Rev. Frank E. Higgins, the "sky pilot" to the lumbermen of northern Minnesota, and who was portrayed so vividly in the leading article in the July *Harper's*, was one of the interesting characters at the Convention.

One of the most enjoyable features of the Convention to the Minneapolis delegation and others who camped with them on Capitol Hill were the camp-fire meetings held from eleven to twelve o'clock at night.

The State capitol was open each evening during the Convention for the inspection of visitors in the city. The interior and exterior were illuminated and guides were on hand to explain the paintings and wonders of the building.

Some of the ladies who wore their official badge on their belts were nearly excluded from the Convention hall because the doorkeepers couldn't see the badges.

Said *The St. Paul Dispatch:* "One of the fine sayings of the Christian Endeavorers refers to Dr. Francis E. Clark, the president of the U. S. C. E, 'To look at him is a benediction.' Once in a while it does fall out that way, a man gets so much in the habit of loving his fellow men and saying his prayers that it is pictured in his face."

Percy S. Foster, one of the musical directors of the Convention, has been a member of the Christian Endeavor society for twenty-seven years. Mr. Foster has been at all the Conventions except two for the past seventeen years.

"No piano here," said the musical director. "That's nothing for a Christian Endeavorer. It means more work, and that's what we are all here for."

And the singing went with a swing as usual.

Three of the original seven directors of the Christian Endeavor movement in St. Paul were President Francis E. Clark, Howard B. Grose, editorial secretary of the American Baptist Home Mission Society; and James L. Hill, D. D., Boston.

"I remember well," said Dr. Grose, "the first meeting at Old Orchard Beach, Me. There were only two of us delegates from outside of New England and it was considered a wonder that any one should come so far. The two were George B. Graff, St. Louis, now business manager, and myself, from New York."

195

Seventy-five delegates from Texas arrived in St. Paul an entire day late, as a result of the floods in Kansas. "We feel that we are lucky to get through at all," said one of the Texans, "for there certainly is a lot of water running loose in that prohibition State," which may speak well for the new State government.

"Are your hens sitting or setting, auntie?" a little girl asked her aunt.

"When my hens cackle, honey, I ain't concerned whether they are sitting or setting. What I want to know is whether they are laying or lying."

Rev. W. F. Richardson, Kansas City, Mo., made use of this illustration to show the importance of co-operation and fellowship, not in word only, but in fact.

Perhaps the best thing Mr. Bryan said in any of his speeches is that "you can answer a speech, you can answer a book, but you cannot answer a life." Which also is the best testimony that can be offered of Mr. Bryan. The man has lived a life of service, and he defined "greatness as the greatest degree of service."

Prof. E. O. Excell, one of the musical directors at the Auditorium, who had charge of the singing at the big building, is certainly one who excels in his work. The professor can get a response from the crowd simply by raising his big voice in praise, where many another would not be able to do it short of a Gatling gun or a brace of forty-fours.

"Can you tell me where the Esperanto Convention meets?" inquired a *Dispatch* man at the counter of the Ryan Hotel. The kind clerk had never met Esperanto. Did he carry a game-cock under his arm and wear slashes on his trousers? Then a stranger spoke up:

"Find Prof. Wells, and he will tell you all about it."

Prof. Wells, of Boston, was up-stairs.

"Go to that man right over there,—Mr. Anderson," he said. "He is the whole Esperanto thing," and he smiled that nice measured Boston smile.

And Rev. Mr. Anderson, of Boston, did come near to being the whole Esperanto thing. He knows Esperanto so well that he can dream in that universal language.

On the opening day of the Convention lemonade and ice-cream stands made their appearance in vacant lots and private yards in the vicinity of the Auditorium and the Armory. They were freely patronized by the thirsty delegates.

Never had the trustees listened to such bursts of eloquence as came from the leaders of the contesting delegations for the next Convention.

Listen to this: "From the home of the greatest of American poets, from the home of two of our greatest American novelists, from the home of one of our most beloved presidents, from the home of two of our most gifted ex-vice-presidents, I, and seventy-four more enthusiastic Hoosiers, come here, gentlemen, to present the claims of that greatest of all American cities, that centre of the universe, Indianapolis, Ind."

And to this: "We will take you out seven hundred feet over the bosom of the broad Atlantic, and there on the mightiest structure that has ever been erected over the mightiest of waters, amid the brine-scented winds that will cool your brows and the tender cadence of the

surf that will furnish sweet music for your words, we will help you
to make the Atlantic City Convention of 1911 the greatest religious
gathering since the dawn of man."
And this: "To that mart of industry and strenuous endeavor that
in fifty short years has grown to be the greatest railroad centre in America, to that wonderful city, which in ninety days erected the great hall
that housed the Democratic national convention of 1904, to the mistress
of the Southwest, to the city whose boundaries are so great that they
extend into two sovereign States, to Kansas City, the brightest star
that sheds its lustre over the Mississippi valley, I bid you come."

All of the delegation that were after the Convention for 1911 had
their own special songs. Here is one that was sung lustily by the hust-
ling Kansas City delegates:

(*Tune: "Tramp, tramp, tramp, the boys are marching."*)

Kansas City is the town; it has surely won renown,
For its greatness and its hospitality;
We are striving to be good; you could help us if you would
Send to us the great Convention of C. E.

Chorus.

Tramp, tramp, tramp, we hear you marching,
In nineteen eleven we bid you come;
And we'll hand you out the key to the town of old K. C.
And we'll "show you" if you'll only come and see.

In our great convention hall we can seat you one and all;
Our hotel accommodations can't be beat.
If you put us to the test, we will surely do our best,
And we'll "show you" if you'll only come and see.

Chorus.

The exhibits at the Armory attracted much attention from the Christian Endeavorers. One corner was devoted to medical exhibits, another
to temperance work, a third to the various illustrations of life among
the people among whom foreign-mission work is being done, and the
fourth to trophies and insignia from former Conventions.

The Dallas, Texas, delegation was delayed by floods and was nearly
a day late in reaching the Convention. It was headed by Mayor Hay
of Dallas, who also made an eloquent plea for the next Convention to
be held in the Lone-Star State. He displayed an immense map on the
wall, and showed the location of Dallas and the size of the surrounding
country from which the Endeavorers could expect to get aid and support.
"Texas needs no material aid," he said, "from any part of the country: and that is why, when I was invited to go to Philadelphia to try
for the next Credit Men's Association convention, I did not do so. But
instead I have come here, because what Texas needs is spiritual aid,
and this we can secure by having this Convention come to our city."

During the time when the trustees of the city were voting on the
selection for the next Convention (and the meeting lasted until 12.30
A. M.) the Indianapolis delegates, who had headquarters on the same
floor, invited the Kansas City and Dallas Endeavorers to call on them.
They sang songs, talked, and told stories, and then a unique contest

along the lines of the "glories of Duluth" was indulged in. One of the very modest claims made by a Kansas City gentleman was that, "if the hogs killed in Kansas City were made into one great hog, he could stand with his hind feet on the island of Cuba, put his front feet on Central America, and with one great root of his enormous snout he could build the Panama Canal."

The mayor of Dallas then had a few words to say for Dallas, and he assured the Missourian that this same hog could be fitted into a small county in Texas, and there would still be room for several hundred more of the same type. This jibing and jesting was good-humoredly kept up for some time. When the news of the result came, Texas and Missouri and Indiana agreed with each other that the Atlantic Ocean, the great friend of Atlantic City, could easily accommodate both States, and then have room for a few besides.

A beautiful Christian Endeavor banner was flung to the breeze from the flagstaff of the court-house and city hall, on order of the municipal-building commission, and signifies the welcome of Minneapolis to the visitors in the Twin Cities.

The adornment was the idea of Miss Elsie Williams, a member of Lyndale Church, who works in the office of the county auditor at busy times. One day she asked a member of the commission whether his commission would not decorate for the visitors with banners. Mr. Scott said he could not; but, if the young woman would provide a banner, he would fly it from the flagstaff.

Miss Williams at once took the matter up with the young people of the church, and the next Mr. Scott knew of it, he was reminded by the arrival of a banner, the gift of the young people of the Lyndale Church.

At a little luncheon in Field's tea-rooms Mr. Bryan was reminded by Dr. Swearingen of the House of Hope Church that he was the first president of the first Christian Endeavor society in Lincoln, Neb.

"Yes," he replied, with a twinkle, "and it is the only thing that I have ever been president of."

As he descended the steps of the platform in front of the capitol, an old woman grasped Mr. Bryan's hands and said: "Now, I don't want you to get discouraged!"

"Never you mind, mother, there is no danger of my ever getting discouraged."

This brought a roar from those about.

When it was announced that his duties kept Hon. George P. Nicholls, member of Parliament, away from a meeting, Mr. Bryan laughingly remarked, "I have never been able to offer any such excuse for not attending a meeting."

"I am not an evangelist."

"This was the flat declaration of Mr. Bryan at the Convention. But some thought that statement was only a patent proof of the utter inability of a man to gauge himself. For Mr. Bryan is an evangelist, or he is nothing. I am not of those who think he is nothing; he should not think he is not an evangelist.

"For, by fashion of face, depth of nature, riches of heart, Mr. Bryan is an evangelist. Farther, he is the evangelist. Everything he has done, everything he has said, has been of a piece with evangelism. His sermon in the Opera-House, his speech before the Chicago convention in 1896—there is no difference in kind of these. They preach the gospel, whether it be that of free silver or free grace."

Said "The Lookout" in *The Pioneer Press*:

The Convention is the modern crusade. Perhaps future history will never look upon these pilgrimages of Christians, men and women coming from the four corners of the country, and from the islands of the sea, quite as history looks upon those Crusades of the Middle Ages, when men, and sometimes children, massed themselves together in one grand army, and traversed the infidel seas and the more infidel lands, to reach the shrine of Christendom. These modern crusaderers are still seeking the shrine. But they have captured the great lesson of modern religious search, that the shrine is not at Jerusalem, nor at Mecca; it may be in St. Paul.

Every convention is a crusade, the political meets no less than the religious. For, after all, the objects of one are the objects of the other, the promotion of the feeling of brotherhood, co-operation between people mutually interested, and the help that comes from association. These are the objects of democracy. When government is of and by and for the people, it is small wonder that politics and religion equally become affairs of generous and general association.

The Christian Endeavor Society is the largest religious society not recognizable as a denomination. It is the common meeting-ground of Protestant denominations, of the young people of these denominations, who are sufficiently democratic to believe that the essential things are things which may be held in common, that the things which divide may be neglected.

Twenty-eight years ago the first small chapter of this society was organized, without a thought that it should grow into a mighty thing. Later on a central society was organized in Boston to combine the work, to place the local societies in a communion. From those dates up to 1909 is a short time, shorter than the period intervening between the old crusades at times. But in that time more than four million young people the world over have found in this association a something which delimited denomination could not give, a communal something which answers to the community spirit pervading not only American life, but all vital living everywhere to-day.

It is impossible to overestimate the possibilities of a world-circling organization. The strength of the Catholic Church is in its catholicity, its universality. In such a society as the Christian Endeavor there is an instinct for the same things, the common things of the spirit, which makes the society really existent in a place almost before it is formally organized

Without this order church unity would be farther off. With this society, church unity appears like a possible thing.

Friday evening of the Convention, Christian Endeavor took possession of St. Paul in no uncertain or hesitating way, when just an hour before midnight several thousand members of that great religious democracy marched through the down-town streets singing the songs of the gospel as they moved along, and brought up at the Ryan Hotel with what is probably the greatest open-air religious demonstration that the city has ever beheld.

The parade started at the Auditorium just after the meeting there. Half a dozen policemen in charge of Sergeant Andy Call headed the parade. The marchers sang first "We are marching to Zion, beautiful Zion." Half a score of paraders started it, and bit by bit it was taken up by the whole procession, until its volume had increased to a mighty chorus.

Pedestrians stopped and watched the marchers go by; many joined in the parade; and the scoffer stopped to have his joke. But these were earnest people, and they heeded not, nor did they see.

As the parade progressed down Sixth Street, its enthusiasm increased, and when somebody started "That will be glory," every throat in the line opened wide, and poured out such a volume of song that it reached way down the side streets half a dozen squares away. On every corner groups of people awaited the marchers when they were still some distance away.

In the march were old and young, clergy anl laity. The venerable Bishop Fallows marched, and not far behind was Bishop Weekley of Kansas City. A square or two back came the four Hawaiians, walking briskly, singing, open-mouthed and full-throated. Mr. Makino, brown man from the land of the Rising Sun, hurried his short steps and sang the songs of Christ with his Christian brothers.

At the Ryan the head of the parade stopped and waited for the others to come up. While they waited, they sang one hymn after another. Windows in the hotel snapped open, and both men and women stuck their heads out and remained there listening. The loungers about the corners gathered around, and the men idling about the lobby of the hotel came out on the street and looked on.

Many of them joined in the singing. Several interruptions by obstreperous eighteen-year-old would-be sports were quickly squelched by people, many of them not affiliated with the organization that was conducting the demonstration.

By the time the crowd had all reached the hotel, Dr. Clark and other officials of the society appeared on the Sixth Street balcony. With them was Prof. Foster. In his garb of white he led the singing. Standing on the very edge of the balcony and waving his hands high, he made a figure striking and picturesque. One after another several hymns were sung, and sung lustily.

Finally William Phillips Hall, New York millionaire safe-manufacturer and evangelist of no mean ability, stepped to the front of the balcony. He called on the crowd to bow their heads as he prayed. Christian Endeavorer and looker-on alike bowed, and the businessman evangelist raised his voice on high, and in tones that might be heard many blocks away called down blessings on the people of St. Paul for their kind reception of the Endeavorers, on the governor of the State for the courtesy he had shown, on the mayor for his aid and support, on the press of the Twin Cities, and on the police department for the way in which it had maintained order. Deep-throated "Amens" came from every direction as he finished.

Prof. Foster then called for another hymn, after which he asked the crowd to proceed in orderly fashion to their homes. The hymn was sung; and, as the first words began, the crowd started to disperse, singing as it went. It scattered in every direction towards the car lines, and the volume of sound spread out in diminishing power, but continued until Selby-Lake, Como-Harriet, interurban, and all the care hove into sight. And not even then, for many sang as they boarded the cars, and continued singing after they were whisked on their way homeward.

Next to a trip around the world, a good long chat with Merritt B. Holley, whose Christian Endeavor Muesum was one of the features at the Armory, is the best-known tonic for chronic stay-at-homes.

The best collection of flags in the world, and the largest, with the exception of that of John Wanamaker, is the way Mr. Holley describes his assemblage of 137 banners of different nations, to say nothing of the flags of States which he is now collecting.

The flag of Burma, the only genuine one in the United States, according to the collector, was one of those curiosities that were years in the getting. It is a peacock made out of flat brass beads, sewn on peculiar red cloth. The spread tail of the peacock made the work long and difficult.

The only complete collection of Christian Endeavor International Convention badges, complete since the year 1900, in the country, is at the Armory in Mr. Holley's exhibit. He has also one thousand Christian Endeavor badges from minor meetings of the Society held in the different States.

Among the queer things that primitive people bow down to, the Holley collection contains some fine specimens. The Genesa or elephant-headed idol from Tiramangalam, India, is a perfect accident-policy.

The smallest idol in the collection is the monkey idol made out of the precious jade stone, and only two inches in height.

A whiskey-flask, containing a cross hung with the Christian Endeavor emblem and the scales of justice inside it, makes Mr. Holley feel very happy. It was done by a life convict in Iowa State penitentiary in acknowledgment of the work of the Society on his behalf.

Side by side he the hat of an Indian pariah or peasant and the rich turban of a high-caste Brahmin. When the high-caste Brahmin passes by the pariah, the hat of the latter, made out of splints of palm-leaves, has to touch the ground, and the pariah has almost to back off the earth in humility.

Not the least interesting objects in the collection of curios are the samples of Chinese women's footwear. One wet-weather shoe with a block for a heel to keep the foot out of the water is five and a half inches in length, while the fashionable house-shoe is only four inches long. These compressed foot-packages have been discarded by the Chinese women as a result of the efforts of missionaries.

One of the most striking scenes of the Convention occurred at the Armory Friday afternoon.

Rev. T. Makino was presented with a beautiful silk-embroidered banner by Dr. Milton D. Neff, from the Sunrise Christian Endeavor Union of Cleveland, O.

It was the occasion of an annual exchange of greetings between the Japanese and Cleveland Endeavorers.

The support of Rev. T. Sawaya as field secretary of the Sunrise Kingdom is pledged by the Sunrise Union of Cleveland, named in honor of Japan.

Banners of previous exchanges were displayed on the platform.

On presenting the gift the speaker held the new banner in his hand rolled up; at the moment of handing it over, with the statement that Christian Endeavor might join the two nations closely together, Dr. Neff unfurled it, showing the flags of both nations embroidered on a crimson field, linked together with the emblem of Christian Endeavor.

The large audience was moved to prolonged applause, so significant was the scene of Christian Endeavor fellowship as an agency of international peace.

INDEX.

203

www.ingramcontent.com/pod-product-compliance
Lightning Source LLC
Chambersburg PA
CBHW032116040426

42449CB00005B/162